Teaching Mathematics in the Elementary School

SECOND EDITION

LOLA JUNE MAY

THE FREE PRESS
A Division of Macmillan Publishing Co., Inc.
New York
Collier Macmillan Publishers
London

The Free Press
A Division of Macmillan Publishing Co., Inc.
866 Third Avenue, New York, N.Y.   10022

Collier Macmillan Canada Ltd.

Library of Congress Catalog Card Number: 73–11694

Printed in the United States of America

printing number
7 8 9 10

Library of Congress Cataloging in Publication Data

May, Lola June.
    Teaching mathematics in the elementary school.

    Includes bibliographies.
    1. Mathematics--Study and teaching (Elementary)
I. Title.
QA135.5.M45 1974   372.7'3'044   73-11694
ISBN 0-02-920370-8

To
Margaret
The limit of her concern
is infinity.

Contents

Preface to the Second Edition

When the time came to prepare the second edition, I added a most important chapter to this methods book—a chapter on the role of the teacher. Individualized instruction in mathematics is a key objective of most schools, and the role of the teacher in this situation should be clarified. The chapter explains what is needed in techniques and in materials for any system of individualized instruction.

Just a few years ago, when the original edition was written, the emphasis was not on the metric system of measurement in the elementary school. This situation has changed, and metric measurement is now going to be required. The chapter on the metric method tries to clarify the system for the teacher and gives suggestions on how to teach it to the students.

An alternate method of teaching addition and subtraction of fractional numbers has been added to help teachers when they have students who do not understand the usual way. The method of teaching bases has been changed to the method that has been successful with children of all ages. More games have been included to help teachers with variety for drill and practice.

The basic plan of the book is just the same. The whole theme is how to teach mathematics more meaningfully to all students. The more I teach children the more sure I am that if you can make the teaching techniques simple, students will understand and will be successful.

L. J. M.

Preface to the First Edition

This book was written to answer the need for materials which emphasized methods of presenting mathematical content to elementary school youngsters. In writing this text I have been concerned with the balance between discussion of content and pedagogy. Many fine books have been written on the content of mathematics, but only a few have been directed to the problems of how to present that content. This book is an attempt to fill that gap. I believe that all teachers of mathematics should know mathematics. Therefore, I recommend that elementary teachers study some of the fine texts available that stress content, even though elementary teachers need not prepare themselves as thoroughly or extensively as high school teachers.

It used to be that mathematics was taught in high school and minimum computational skills in arithmetic in the elementary grades. Such is no longer the case. Computational skills should not be separated from mathematical activity. Learning results from the planned activities of the teacher. All children must be involved. All must respond. The learner must take part in selecting, creating, and operating of the procedures involved in generating algorithms. Learning to make decisions and putting together pieces is an important part of mathematical thinking. This means teachers must teach so the learner feels that he is the creator and not the sponge. This book is written to advance this viewpoint and to furnish insights into more imaginative teaching.

The concrete suggestions in this book are presented in enough detail so that the teacher can read them and employ them immediately in the classroom. Before making a specific suggestion to her class, however, a teacher should read a complete chapter because the ideas are presented in developmental sequences. A teacher should determine where in the sequence her students stand before taking up a particular suggestion. The learning sequence for each topic generally follows this sequence: (1) Use concrete materials to illustrate an idea. (2) Give a concrete representation to illustrate the mathematical description. (3) Give a mathematical description to illustrate a concrete representation. (4) Work with the mathematical statement alone. (5) Commit to memory the mathematical facts. (6) Study the properties of the mathematical ideas.

I dedicate this book to elegant teaching of mathematics. Be enthusiastic and instill in your students the desire to learn this lively subject. To all who read these pages I offer my best wishes for the most successful venture you have ever had in teaching mathematics.

Deep appreciation is due to Julia Berlet for assistance in the preparation of the manuscript. Without her dedication this manuscript would never have been completed. To her I extend my heartfelt thanks.

L. J. M.

Editor's Introduction

Most text and reference books do not merit revision and publication as second editions. Only books that prove to be successful in the marketplace and in the academic community are published in second editions. *Teaching Mathematics in the Elementary School*, by Lola June May, is such a book. The first edition, published in 1970, met the rigorous requirements of (a) sound scholarship, (b) useful and meaningful content presented in lucid language, and (c) imaginative and practical teaching techniques that teachers can actually use and adapt in classrooms. The success of the first edition of Dr. May's book—as measured by adoptions as a textbook in colleges and universities throughout the country, its use by teachers in numerous in-service education programs, and its enthusiastic endorsement by students in teacher preparation programs—attests to its excellence and usefulness.

Through continued scholarship and close contact with teachers and classrooms, Dr. May has revised, updated, and added significant new material in this second edition. Included is new content on individualized instruction, the metric system, techniques for teaching bases, and additional material useful for student drill and practice.

Characteristic of books in the *Introduction to Teaching* series, *Teaching Mathematics in the Elementary School* bridges the gap between theory and practice. Neither mathematics content nor teaching methodology can be taught or learned effectively as discrete subjects. Good books that contain mathematical content needed by teachers in elementary schools are available. Typical methods books on the market, however, are abstract and theoretical and remote from the experience of teachers and prospective teachers. What is needed is a book that presents both appropriate subject matter and empirically tested techniques for teaching.

The response to the first edition of *Teaching Mathematics in the Elementary School* convincingly demonstrated the need for materials presenting in succinct and straightforward language teaching methods and mathematics content that involve students and teachers in meaningful learning. Throughout the book emphasis is on how students and subject matter can be related in meaningful ways by skilled, interested, and enthusiastic teachers.

Several features of this book commend it to both prospective and experienced teachers as well as to teacher educators. *Teaching Mathematics in the Elementary School* abounds with fresh ideas for presenting significant mathematics topics. Concrete and specific suggestions are presented with sufficient detail and clarity so that a teacher or student teacher can make use of them immediately in the classroom. A developmental learning sequence is suggested.

Another unusual and outstanding characteristic of this book is the author's emphasis on student involvement in the learning process. She emphasizes that interests of students must be engaged. Children need manipulative materials to work with. Adequate developmental work is a must for student understanding. A variety of models should be presented so that the teacher can communicate with more children. Meaning and understanding should precede practice and memorization. The key concept as expressed by the author is that "Teachers must teach so the learner feels he is the creator and not the sponge." This fundamental concept is exemplified by excellent teachers in all fields.

Professor May is noted as an excellent teacher. For several years she has held a joint appointment with the Winnetka, Illinois, Public Schools and Northwestern University. She has taught mathematics to elementary school children from the economically favored suburb and from the inner city, and with equal success. As a member of the faculty of the School of Education at Northwestern she plays a key role in the preparation of prospective teachers. Her professorial effectiveness has recently been attested to by undergraduates throughout the University, who honored her as one of the six outstanding teachers at Northwestern. On the national scene she is in great demand as a speaker, consultant, and author—and in each role she is ever the teacher.

B. J. Chandler, Dean
School of Education
Northwestern University

Teaching Mathematics
in the
Elementary School

SECOND EDITION

The Role of the Teacher

INTRODUCTION

The success of teaching mathematics will depend not on the materials that are available but on the skill of the teacher in using the materials. The best textbooks and the best concrete or supplementary materials, if not used properly, will not produce successful learners of mathematics. The issue is not new mathematics versus traditional mathematics. The real issue is how teachers teach mathematics. Teachers who have liked mathematics and understood the meaning of mathematics have always been successful, regardless of the label that was attached to the content. Research has proven time and time again that those who possess the real art of teaching can use any materials.

All teachers can improve their methods of teaching mathematics by learning more about various teaching strategies. Creative teachers are not all born creative; some become creative by learning from the teacher next door. Teachers should learn from each other; they should also learn by trial and error. Anyone can be a textbook wired for sound. The question is, "What more do you do?" Being ordinary is no longer adequate. There is a need to improve techniques, for the art of good teaching is providing good models. All learners of mathematics, regardless of age, need to be provided with models that will help to build bridges to the abstraction of mathematics.

SEQUENCE OF MATHEMATICS

Mathematics has a sequence, and each school system needs to have a scope and sequence for its teachers. This usually is provided by the textbook company or by the curriculum department of the school system. No teacher or small group of teachers should be required to provide their own sequence.

The sequence of mathematics is a suggested road map that covers the required content of material. Teachers have freedom to adapt the section of the sequence that pertains to their group of students. Most scope-and-sequence charts for the primary grades state that the subtraction facts are learned before the multiplication facts. Primary teachers know that each year there are children who have difficulty with the subtraction facts. For these children the decision can be made to go on to the multiplication facts because, if the children can add and know how to count by tens, fives, and twos, they can learn the beginning multiplication facts. Once the children have had success in multiplication they return to working on the subtraction facts. Geometry in the primary grades can be learned at any time. If some children are bogged down with numbers the teacher can turn to geometry for a change of pace. The same is true of measurement and fractional numbers in the primary grades. The sequence should be adapted to the best interest of the children.

The role of a teacher is one of a guide. A good guide uses judgment about when to take a detour and how to return to the main road after the detour. Knowledge of which skills have certain prerequisites is required on the part of the teacher. You cannot learn long division without knowing place value, multiplication, and subtraction. You can delay long division and detour to geometry, fractional numbers, or measurement. Great teachers make decisions, and those who can make decisions will find students becoming more successful in learning mathematics.

CORE OF MATERIALS

Teachers should be provided with a core of materials to teach mathematics to a group of children. This core of materials is some system or textbook adopted by a school system. Teachers should not be required to provide their own core of materials. The talent of the teachers should be employed in implementing a system. Research has proven that the material that has the greatest effect on how children learn mathematics is the basic core material. Other materials usually only supplement the teaching that comes from the textbook or core materials.

What type of core materials are needed for individualizing mathematics? This question is asked constantly. Carlton Washburne, when faced with this question in the early twenties in Winnetka, Illinois, stated that the materials should be organized in units and not in a spiral approach. He decided to write his own mathematics materials because all the major textbooks at that time were written in a spiral approach. A unit is written around a few basic objectives, and an effort is made to teach only these objectives. Pretests that test the objectives of the unit should be provided. The teacher and student can then evaluate the pretest to determine which of the objectives are already mastered and which objectives need to be learned. The development for teaching the objectives should be written into the student's materials in a manner that a child can understand. The language and development should not be so pure that only a mathematican could understand what is being expressed. The students who have great capacity for self-learning can then use the development for self-instruction. Some of the exercises should have answers so the learner can tell whether progress is being made without constantly having to check with the teacher. There should be a posttest that checks only the objectives of the unit so both the student and the teacher can evaluate the progress.

To teach students how to learn means in mathematics that teachers will help students learn to read mathematics. Mathematics is a language, and the learner of mathematics has to know the vocabulary and the symbols that make up the language. In grouping students, those who have learned to read mathematics are able to work part of the time independently. Those who need most of their instruction from a teacher should be taught slowly how to read mathematics and to pay constant attention to what is read. Without this attention, students will remain as dependent upon the teacher for instruction as they were the year before and will never learn how to become independent.

SUPPLEMENTARY MATERIALS

Concrete materials are needed to provide models before students can understand the diagrams in a textbook. No diagram is meaningful for subtraction if children have not had experiences with taking away objects from a given set. The diagrams for multiplication and division of fractional numbers are confusing unless they are preceded by experiences of using materials. The key is that teachers have to learn more about using materials. Activities must be planned to create the models that will be meaningful. Piaget said, "In order to understand, children have to invent—that is, reinvent—because they can't start from the beginning again. But I should say that anything is only understood to the extent that it is reinvented." This means materials must be used by children to help them reinvent.

There is no one best materials for all children. Some children find that rods built on the concept of ratio are meaningful materials to help solve simple equations, operations with fractional numbers, and other skills. Other children find the rods confusing and will build models using just ordinary counters. Numbers lines are helpful for some in solving problems. For others this geometric representation of number is far too abstract. This means that the teacher has to be flexible and willing to use mny types of materials and allow the children the freedom to choose the ones that are the most meaningful for them.

Lessons on teaching machines or tapes can be used for reteaching when instruction beyond that which is available in the regular core of materials is needed. Answers can be provided so that the student receives immediate reinforcement. If an error is made, only the student and the machine know, and the machine will never tell. If the software for the machines has all the steps needed to learn a skill, a teacher can feel secure that learning will take place. This is another pair of hands in a classroom.

Mathematics laboratory materials can be used for group or individual activities. This is where materials are provided to extend or strengthen learning. Horizontal enrichment is learning more about mathematics not in the main stream, as long as the skills needed for the enrichment have already been acquired. Games that require game strategy are excellent for building up skills in problem-solving. Geometric constructions are excellent for observing properties of geometric shapes. There is a great variety of materials that can be used and will benefit all students.

EVALUATION FOR GROUPING

The mathematical ability of students should be diagnosed before any type of grouping takes place. The skill of computation can be diagnosed with paper-and-pencil tests. Also, the teacher should diagnose how a student perceives mathematics. One can be very accurate in computation and not be a talented mathematics student. To tell if a student is mathematically inclined or not, a teacher needs to diagnose what students say and what they do as they solve a problem. This means teachers have to learn to evaluate what they hear and what they see. For example, an eight-year-old was asked, "What is the product of 7×9?" The child responded, "$9 \times 9 \doteq 81$ and $2 \times 9 = 18$. Then 81 take away 18, whatever that is." This response told a teacher that was listening that the child had a mathematical mind, for only one who sees patterns would understand at such a young age that the sevens can be found by using the doubles and the twos in multiplication. Another example is when six-year-olds are given twelve index cards and asked to make sets of four with the cards. After all the children have three sets of four the teacher asks them to now make sets of three. Most of the children will scatter the cards and start all over by counting by threes. A few of the children will take a card off the top of the three original piles and make the fourth set. These children are seeing some patterns in mathematics and should be watched to see if they have special talents in mathematics.

In the middle grades students were given some papers that had six congruent squares drawn on them. The students were asked to use a ruler and divide each square in two congruent parts. They should find as many different ways as possible to divide the squares into two congruent parts. Most of the students found only four ways to divide the squares, but a few students divided all the squares into congruent parts using different ways. When one of the students was asked how he found so many ways he answered, "Oh, there are many more. All

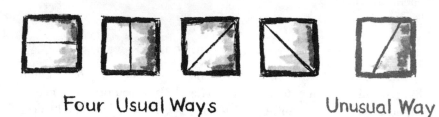

Four Usual Ways   Unusual Way

you need to do is be sure your line goes through the middle of the square, and you have two congruent parts." Students who respond like this have a special mathematics ability and will be noticed by a teacher who is willing to learn all about the ability of a student.

The content of mathematics can only be varied if the teacher has diagnosed how a child learns mathematics. Children who have mathematical ability can do more abstract work than those who are not mathematically inclined. Some students should be required to work out the generalization of adding all odd numbers and all even numbers after having many experiences with adding specific examples of odd numbers and even numbers. Other students should only do the specific examples with the odd numbers and even numbers. For some students the study of number theory is meaningful because they have a talent for numbers. Others need to spend most of their time on learning how to compute. One way of individualing is learning to vary the content of mathematics according to the ability of the students.

DIAGNOSTIC TESTS

Teachers can learn to write small diagnostic tests of mathematics skills to help in grouping. The tests are constructed using the major objectives of a given skill. To write a diagnostic test for addition, the objectives are as follows: (1) the basic facts through the sum of 10; (2) the basic facts with sums less than 20; (3) renaming or carrying once from ones to tens; (4) renaming or carrying more than once; (5) adding more than three numbers in column addition. All that is needed are a few problems for each of the objectives. The test should be short so it can be administered in no more than twenty minutes. Once you have the information you can start to group according to the skill in addition. Those who missed problems with sums through 10 are in one group. Those who have no difficulty with facts in sums up to 10 but have difficulty with the harder facts are in another group. Those who know the facts but have difficulty with renaming or carrying are in another group. Then, those who do not have any difficulties with addition are ready to go on to another skill or can do some horizontal enrichment that requires addition as a prerequisite. The small test provides information immediately, so grouping can take place without the great delay of having testing going on for days.

Teachers can make out small diagnostic tests for all the operations of whole numbers, fractional numbers, and decimals. If because of the shortness of the test not enough information is provided and some error is therefore made in the grouping, children can be shifted to another group to remedy the situation. Groups should be flexible and adjustments made according to the needs of the students.

Commercial tests are available to help with diagnosing objectives in terms of a year's work or in terms of a span of years. These are excellent tests to use at the beginning of the school year. They give an indication of the range of knowledge that exists in a particular group of students. To write these tests the authors have to know the sequence of mathematics from kindergarten through eighth grade. They also have to know what the main objectives are at various age or grade levels. Once the objectives have been established, they find test items that check only those objectives. The results of the tests are usually given in a profile so the teacher can see at a glance where the student stands in relation to the objectives. If these tests are available, teachers should use them to get all the information they can about the ability of their students.

To diagnose in mathematics a teacher needs to find out as much as possible about the ability of the learner. The more that is known about the learner, the more skillful the teacher can be in guiding the progress of learning. The key to individualized mathematics is knowing the ability of the student. The main difficulty is that most teachers have never been trained to diagnose. All the skill required to do so must be learned by doing. The effort on the part of the teacher to learn to diagnose is all worthwhile, for it means that fewer students will have to spend time on material they already know, and this eliminates being bored. Also, it means students will not have to try to be successful with material they are not ready for, and this eliminates failure. Yes, we can have schools without failure if teachers will learn more about diagnosing the skills of mathematics.

HOW TO PRESCRIBE

Prescription in mathematics is the area where the teacher uses the strategies of teaching mathematics. Children learn in various ways and, therefore, the method of learning must vary according to the needs of the learner. A skillful teacher needs to learn many ways of presenting an activity that leads to a skill and, also, many ways of solving the trouble spots of mathematics.

The first stage in learning something new in mathematics should be an activity. The activity should allow the learner to see how the operation or skill really works in either a life situation or in a concrete model.

If a group of primary children is to learn division facts, the activity should start with some life situation where the group needs to use division to solve the life situation. One activity could be a teacher placing a set of 27 jelly beans in front of 3 children and asking them, "How would you share these jelly beans evenly?" The children may go about the task in various ways. One way is by each child taking in turn one jelly bean. They keep this up until each of the 3 children has 9 jelly beans. After the children have found a way the question can be asked, "Is there another way? Let us see." This time the teacher can start to make 3 rows of jelly beans, using only 9 of the jelly beans. One of the children could be called on to finish placing the rest of the jelly beans in the 3 rows. The children then can see that there are 9 jelly beans in each of the 3 rows. Next, the question could be asked, "What multiplication fact does the array of jelly beans remind you of?" The children should respond, "$3 \times 9 = 27$," because arrays were used as a model for the multiplication facts. Another question is, "How does the multiplication fact help you solve the problem of sharing 27 jelly beans with 3 people?" Once the children see that the division facts come from the multiplication facts with a missing factor, they the ready to work on the content in a textbook that relates the division facts to the missing factor of multiplication. The final stage should be when the children are faced with some kind of transfer of learning. This means that after the children have finished the content part of the learning and have practiced the division facts, they use the facts. Transfer in this example could be having the children write a story after they are given a division fact so that the given fact is used to solve the problem in the story. If a child can write a story, then the teacher is fairly sure the child can use the knowledge of division facts in a life situation.

While the child is involved in the content part of learning the division facts the teacher needs to be involved in further prescription. Some children will have to leave the text and work on tapes that help with learning the facts. Others will have to play some games to help them to memorize the facts. Prescription means the teacher is constantly aware of the needs of the child and then finds a way of solving the need.

If it is not always possible to find a life situation to use for an activity, then a model must be created with materials to show the meaning of the skill. A group of students is going to learn how to multiply a fractional number times a fractional number. The activity can be accomplished by creating a model that uses two pieces of notebook paper that are the same size and shape. The problem for the model is $2/3 \times 1/4 = ?$

$$2/3 \times 1/4 = ?$$

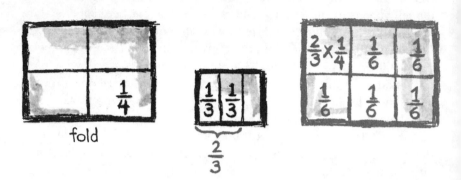

The one piece of paper is folded into fourths. The students state that each part of the whole is now one-fourth. Then one of the fourths is cut off from the whole piece of paper. This fourth is then folded into thirds. The students see that the fourth is now divided into thirds, and each part is one-third of the fourth. Then, two-thirds of the fourth is cut off. This piece of paper is a model of $2/3 \times 1/4$. This model or piece of paper is now placed on the second whole piece of notebook paper. The question is asked, "How many times will the piece of paper fit on the whole piece of paper?" The students will respond, "Six times." Then, the model or piece of paper is what part of the whole? The answer is one-sixth. Now the students can see that $2/3 \times 1/4$ does equal $1/6$. Using the papers to create the activity shows the students that the answer to the multiplication problem is in terms of the whole. Once the model has been built, the students are ready to go to the content in the textbook, where they are shown how to multiply fractional numbers. They will learn to multiply numerators times numerators and denominators times denominators. The transfer of the skill can be in applying the skill to a life situation where there is a need for multiplying fractional numbers.

While the students are involved in learning the content the teacher is involved in prescription. Materials provided by industry need to be used at the proper time. A lesson on tape is a tutor for a child. Films or film loops done with animation provide additional models for understanding. Concrete materials may be needed to understand the concept of number or the properties of geometric shapes. Decisions have to be made; the right materials at the right time can make the difference between success or failure. Great teachers are not afraid to make decisions and to learn from the results of the decisions. No one knows all the right answers, but those who are flexible can prescribe many alternatives.

·EVALUATION ON PROGRESS

There are no standards of the marketplace that pertain to all students. There is no written or unwritten rule that says a child needs to know his basic facts at a given age. These are all mythical standards. If we had such standards there would be an average ten-year-old child in a glass case in Washington, D.C. Everyone could come to see if all other ten-year-old children measured up to the average.

Evaluation should be in terms of progress. This means that the teacher and the student need to know where the student starts in the steps to learn a given skill and where he has progressed in the sequence of steps. Pre- and posttests on the objectives of the skill can give part of that information. The other part of the evaluation is the ability of the student. If a student is mathematically inclined, more should be expected in terms of progress and in terms of content. If a student is not mathematically inclined, less should be expected. This type of judgment can be made only if the teacher knows the ability of the students. If you do not know the students, you have to have common standards and just grade according to the standards. There is nothing so unfair as treating students as if they all had equal mathematical ability.

One part of evaluation in mathematics is in the area of computation. Evaluation can be made on whether a child does or does not compute with whole numbers, fractional numbers, or decimals accurately. This is the easiest area to evaluate.

Another part of evaluation in mathematics is on problem-solving. This is where a teacher needs to report on observations of how a student goes about solving problems. Does the student use educated guessing? Is the student secure enough to use trial and error and to learn from the mistakes? What kinds of questions does the student ask? Can the student judge whether the answer is a logical one? Does the student look for patterns to help him find shortcuts in doing a problem? Answers to questions like the ones just stated are important in the evaluation of a student. These answers will tell you how the student perceives mathematics and how he operates with the elements of mathematics. Progress can be made in problem-solving if a teacher guides the learner and helps him become secure enough to try many approaches. The role of the teacher should be like the role of a coach or a guide. The teacher observes the movements being made and then gives suggestions that could improve the movements.

An evaluation program should describe the evolving cognitive abilities in mathematics. The evaluation should provide direct feedback for the teacher and the learner. The feedback is then used as a basis for the necessary future planning. The emphasis is on the learning activities of an individual. The only purpose of any type of evaluation is to provide information useful in the planning of future activities and progress. This is quite different from the evaluation that is concentrated on the comparison of groups to determine whether a group has attained a predetermined standard or whether one group has done as well or better than another. If one really is concerned with the individual, the evaluation should be in terms of what is known about the individual and his abilities.

ATTITUDE OF THE TEACHER

Motivation is important in any aspect of teaching. The teacher sets the tone of a class. A teacher excited about mathematics creates an atmosphere that makes others excited. Can you imagine the atmosphere that is created when a teacher says, "If you don't behave yourselves we will have arithmetic."

As one is learning there is a need to be stroked. The stroking is any kind of positive vocabulary that is used by the teacher. Students have a need to be seen. This means teachers must talk to students. The sentences may vary: "See, you can do it." "My, you sure are using your head today." "Did you do all that by yourself?" "You have improved a hundred percent." In the past few years computers have shown there is no substitute for the human touch. Some of the computer programs in elementary mathematics have responses such as "Good work," "You did it," "Finally made it," "Good for you." Students do not respond to the words on a screen. In fact, when students were asked about the words they said that they wished they were not there. This shows that words by themselves are not what is important. What is important is that a human being is talking. Dialogue is an act of love. Each child wants the teacher to spend a few minutes alone with him.

Teachers can improve their teaching of mathematics a great deal with one simple act. The simple act is changing the words "You're wrong," to "Show me." When you tell someone he is wrong and then give an explanation, you turn the person off and he seldom hears the explanation. When you say "Show me," the person gets involved in doing something and then, with some guidance, comes out with the right answer. The student learns when he is involved in reconstructing the problem. Teachers are not judges. They have no right to go around and say "You're right," "You're wrong," etc. Teachers are like medical doctors; their role is to heal, not to open, wounds.

One needs to learn to remain positive. No child knows nothing. It is important to give the student the feeling that he does know something. You then build from that point. It is true that many students in the middle grades do not know all the basic multiplication facts. It is also true that they need the facts before they can go on to learn compound multiplication and long division. Yet, it is not true that any student knows none of the basic facts. Students should be told, for example, they do know most of the facts, but they are still having trouble with the six difficult facts. Then they should be given the choice of memorizing the six difficult facts or looking up the product in a table. If a student is told he knows none of the facts and should go home and memorize them, he will usually do nothing. The instruction is negative and vague. This does not mean a teacher should not be honest. All this means is that you tell them what they do know and what they do not know. Then you give suggestions on how the unknown can be learned.

The only sin committed in school is the failure to communicate.

We have to learn to talk to students. Students need to be told what they have to do to accomplish a certain task. They need to feel the teacher knows what is best. Questions that are asked should be answered. There are no silly questions. If the question is important to the learner it should be important to the teacher. Once a student knows the teacher is really concerned about him, the two can start to work together. Success is only in the eyes of someone else. We have to talk to students and tell them what progress they have made so they can see and feel the progress. A teacher is a mature person. All mature persons have one trait in common: they are more concerned about others then they are about themselves.

SUMMARY

The success of a mathematics program is determined by the teacher. All teachers can learn more about teaching strategies. There is no one right way for all learners. The teacher has to be flexible and must present many ways. If one is willing to bend down, then one is willing to continue to learn more about how to teach mathematics.

There is only one way to individualize mathematics: to first learn all about the abilities of the student. After one has diagnosed the abilities, then one can prescribe. Prescription can involve total group work, small group work, and individual work. Materials will be varied and depend on the needs of the learner.

Evaluation will be in terms of the progress of an individual. From the evaluation will come feedback that will determine what is needed for the next step in the sequence in learning.

The attitude of the teacher is the ingredient that will either make mathematics a pleasant subject to be learned or something to be endured. The teacher must be positive and find time to become involved with the student. No child fails; only teachers fail in reaching the child. All students want to succeed. The challenge is to find ways to make this desire come true.

EXERCISES

1. What is needed in the core of materials for individualized mathematics?
2. How does an individual teacher use the scope-and-sequence chart in mathematics?
3. What does it mean to evaluate the progress of a student in mathematics?
4. What is involved in diagnosing the abilities of a student?
5. What words should replace the words "You are wrong"?

SELECTED READINGS

BIGGS, E., *Learning Mathematics: A Critical Appraisal of the Developments of the Past Twelve Years*, John Wiley and Sons, New York, 1970.

FURTH, H., *Piaget for Teachers*, Prentice-Hall, Inc., Englewood Cliffs, N.J., 1970.

WASHBURNE, C., *Winnetka: The History and Significance of an Educational Experiment*, Prentice-Hall Inc., Englewood Cliffs, N.J., 1963.

The Relationship of Sets to Number Concepts

INTRODUCTION

Mathematics is a universal language that has special words and symbols for communication of concepts and relationships of number. The language and symbols of sets are part of the universal language. The term *set* is another way of expressing the idea of collections or groups. Pupils learn about the abstract idea of number through the use of sets of objects. After pupils understand that some sets have a common property called number they can learn the phrase *equivalent sets*. To teach set language in isolation just to be modern would be a waste of time. The language of sets needs to be integrated with the teaching of number to help with communication.

USE OF SETS IN THE PRIMARY GRADES

One of the first goals of the kindergarten and first-grade teacher is to acquaint pupils with the idea of *number*. Number is an abstraction built on the concept of quantity, and acquaintanceship with it comes through the planned activities of the teacher. All activities should involve all pupils, for learning occurs only when the learner is actively involved, not when he is merely a spectator at a "Show and Tell" performance. All pupils should have objects at their desks to use in forming sets. These objects can be plastic discs, cardboard discs, buttons, or even stones.

One of the teacher's first activities is to help his pupils learn to form a given set at their desks by matching the set model that has been illustrated on the chalkboard, flannelboard, or on a table. The pupils are asked to show that they have as many objects as are contained in the teacher's set. Most pupils will resort to one-to-one correspondence, matching each member of their sets to each member of the teacher's set. Then the pupils count the number of members and find that their sets and the teacher's set have, say, five members. This tells them that the common property of the sets is the number property. Sets that have the same number property are called equivalent sets. Children need a great deal of practice in learning to form equivalent sets and then to establish their number property by counting. After they have established their proficiency in this area, they are ready to move on to the next phase.

EQUIVALENT SETS

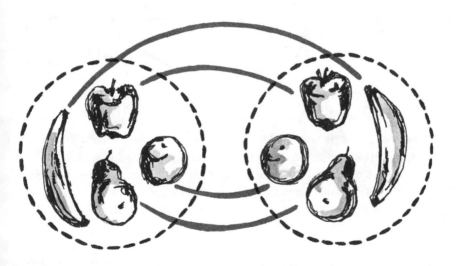

The next step in one-to-one correspondence is to confront pupils with sets whose members do not always match—i.e., one of the sets will have more members than another. These sets are called non-equivalent and do not have the same number property. Pupils can be asked to make the sets equivalent either by adding some objects to the smaller set or by removing some objects from the larger set.

NON-EQUIVALENT SETS

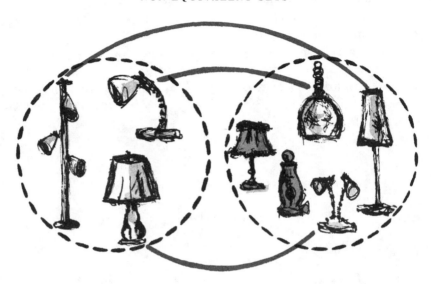

At first, only sets with 1, 2, 3, 4, or 5 members should be used. Vary the activities so that sometimes you are using a large set with 5 members, then a smaller set with 1 or 2 members. Before moving on to larger sets with 6, 7, 8, and 9 members, make sure your pupils can form sets with 5, 4, 3, 2, and 1 members when you direct them to do so.

Pupils should be given small cards with the numerals 1, 2, 3, 4, and 5 written on them. These cards are used by pupils to respond to the questions directed by the teacher. Children should learn to match the numeral card to the set that shows that many objects. The teacher produces a set of five members and then asks the pupils how many members it contains. All pupils who know the answer will hold up numeral card 5. In this way all pupils are responding individually to each question.

The larger sets should be built upon what pupils have learned about the smaller sets. Form a set of 5 and ask the children to make an equivalent set with their counters. Then have them add one more counter. Tell them this is a set of 6. Six is one more than five. Then give them a card with the numeral 6 on it. Continue the process of matching numerals to sets and keep referring to equivalent and non-equivalent sets. It is not necessary for pupils to use the words "equivalent" and "non-equivalent" but after they hear the teacher use them repeatedly, most of them will pick up the words and use them too. Continue building the set of 7 as one more than the set of 6. Then give the pupils cards with numeral 7 on it. After a few days you can introduce the set of 8, which is one more than a set of 7. Continue in this way until you reach a set of 9.

Some pupils will not be ready to move on to sets of 6, 7, 8, and 9 as soon as some others. It is difficult to group for mathematics in the first grade but the effort should be made. The slower pupils should stay with the sets up to 5 until they understand them and not be forced to move ahead until they do. Children should move along at their own pace so that they will neither become bored nor experience unnecessary failure. Have the brighter youngsters draws sets of 6, 7, 8, and 9 and match their numeral cards to the sets. While they are working, the other children can be forming sets up to 5 and matching numerals to them. Children vary in their mathematical ability at the first grade and should start off at their own level.

After pupils have established the idea of numbers from 1 through 9 by matching members of sets and matching numeral cards to sets, they are ready for a standard model of each set. There are many standard models but the one suggested here adapts itself to many patterns. The following is the model for each set.

Ideally, each pupil should be given a card with the set pattern on one side and the corresponding numeral on the other. Then when the pupil holds up the card to show the set, he can read the numeral on the back. And when he is showing the numeral, he can see the set pattern on the back. The cards can be used to show how subsets can be joined to make a larger set. Subsets are sets made up of all the members or some of the members of a given set. "Show me two sets that make five." Here the teacher simply is saying that she wants to see two subsets that when joined will form the larger set with five members. The pupils can display cards 4 and 1, 3 and 2, 2 and 3, or 1 and 4. This procedure readies the children for addition. Many activities should be planned in which pupils name all the subsets that make up a given set. Once again, because all the children have cards, they are all involved in the activity.

The next stage is to ask the pupils to display the numeral cards that make 6. When you ask them to prove that 4 and 2 is the same as 6, they should show the sets of 4 and 2 and count the objects to see that there are 6. The activity should be varied, using a large set like 8, then a small set such as 3.

It is worthwhile having pupils draw sets on a piece of paper. Ask them to draw two sets which, when joined, make a set of 7. Drawing the sets gives them a better image of each set.

Another activity involves having pupils show subsets of a given set by shading some of the objects. Draw the set that shows 4. Now shade some of the objects to show other names for 4. The following shows some of the ways the pupils can show subsets of the set with four objects.

3 and 1   2 and 2   1 and 3

Pupils like to draw objects and they enjoy shading. Moreover, this activity is further preparation for addition.

ZERO

Zero is an important number and needs to be introduced as the number property of the empty set, a set with no members. Games can be played in which pupils think up sets that do not have any members Then the numeral 0 should be introduced to stand for the number property of set. Teachers should not permit their pupils to refer to *zero* as "nothing." This creates the impression that the number 0 does not count. In the study of mathematics zero is a very important number. In fact, some primary teachers call him *Mr. Zero* to lend him prestige.

After zero has been introduced and the children are given cards bearing a 0, they can use 0 as one of the subsets when supplying many names for a number. For example, in naming two subsets of five, one of the answers can be 5 and 0.

RATIONAL COUNTING

The order of numbers must be established so pupils can perform rational counting. Using the standard model of sets, pupils should respond correctly to the question: Which set comes before a given set and which set comes after a given set? The next stage involves responding to which numeral comes before a given numeral and which numeral comes after a given numeral. Draw the sets that come before and after a given set. When pupils can carry out operations like the ones just described, they have a clear idea of the order of numbers from 0 through 9.

Classrooms with magnetic boards are very convenient for primary teachers. Magnetic discs can be used to form sets on the board and magnetic numerals can be attached to match given sets. If a magnetic board is not available, a flannel board can be used.

Some teachers use Cuisenaire Rods, which are of different lengths and colors. The smallest rod is white. If it represents *1*, then the red rod can represent *2* (twice as long), and so on to the orange rod, which represents 10. Children can use the rods as counters, thus imparting meaning to the numbers 1 through 10. Some children find it difficult to associate the length of a rod with a given number; others find it easy and a very handy way to solve problems.

Catherine Stern materials also provide a way of imparting to children the idea of numbers from 0 through 10. A group of 10 students can work with the material at one time. The materials are made up of wooden rods of various length that represent numbers. The rods fit into frames in which there are grooves whose lengths correspond to rods that represent numbers. For example, the rods that represent 2 and 5 can be fitted into a groove on the frame that represents the number 7. Pupils can name a number in many ways by fitting the rods in the grooves. It is a concrete approach to establishing the idea of number.

Any of this equipment can be used very successfully by a trained teacher. Each provides pupils with concrete materials; the type of material is not important, however, so long as the teacher has the pupils actively involved in using the equipment and has planned goals clearly in mind.

More will be said in later chapters about how sets can be used in the primary grades for teaching numeration, addition, and subtraction. Sets should be used primarily to establish the idea of number. This concept should not be hurried. Teachers should not be overly anxious about having their pupils write numerals or equations. The first step is to make sure that they know the numbers 0 through 9.

USE OF SETS IN THE MIDDLE GRADES

Students learn that the set of counting numbers is 1, 2, 3, 4, . . . and the set of whole numbers is 0, 1, 2, 3, 4, 5, . . . Both these sets are infinite sets because all the members cannot be enumerated. The three dots following the last numeral indicate that the set continues indefinitely. Most students learn early that there is no largest whole number. The sets written in set notation look like the following:

$$C = \{1,\ 2,\ 3,\ 4,\ 5,\ .\ .\ .\}$$
$$W = \{0,\ 1,\ 2,\ 3,\ 4,\ .\ .\ .\}$$

A capital letter is used to stand for the set and the members or elements of the set are enclosed by braces. The members or elements of a set are separated by commas. Students learn set notation by being told about it; then they simply follow the rules set up. The only difference between the set of whole numbers and the set of counting numbers is that 0 is a member of the set of whole numbers and not a member of the set of counting numbers. The set of counting numbers is also sometimes called the set of natural numbers.

Sets in which all the members are enumerated are called finite sets. The members of a class are a finite set; you can enumerate all the members. An example of a finite set is the odd numbers between 12 and 20. If students know what odd numbers are, they can name the members of the set. A capital letter can be assigned to the set and the members can be written in set notation.

$$N = \{13, \ 15, \ 17, \ 19\}$$

Set N is the odd numbers between 12 and 20, or the odd numbers that start with 13 and end with 19. Finite sets are sometimes used as replacement sets for finding the variable of a number sentence. The replacement set is often called the universal set or the domain. Only the numbers in the universal set or domain can be used as numbers to replace a variable in a number sentence. Finite sets are sometimes used in the seventh and eighth grades to determine whether the number properties such as associative and commutative are still true. Both these uses of finite sets will be explained in more detail in following chapters.

SUBSETS

If two sets A and B are related in such a way that every member belonging to A is also a member of B, then A is defined as a subset of B. Every set is a subset of itself and the empty set is a subset of every set. Many of the important subsets of the set of whole numbers are infinite sets. The sets of odd and even numbers are important subsets of the set of whole numbers, and both are infinite sets.

The idea of subset is very important because it gives the learner a feeling for the way sets of numbers are related. In the beginning stages of mathematics, pupils confine their operations to the set of whole numbers. Later on they are introduced to the set of fractional numbers and learn to operate with this set. Pupils discover that by definition the set of whole numbers is a subset of the set of fractional numbers. When the set of integers is introduced, students learn that the set of integers is made up of three disjoint subsets: the set of positive integers, the set of negative integers, and the set with the number zero. All this is simply to give the reader an idea of how subsets show a relationship between sets of numbers.

OPERATION OF SETS

The mathematical system of sets involves operations. One of the best ways to introduce two of the four operations is to draw a picture of two streets with automobiles on them. The numerals on the drawings of the automobiles distinguish one automobile from another. Set *E* is

the numerals naming the automobiles on Elm Street and set G is the numerals naming the automobiles on Glendale.

$$E = \{1, 2, 3, 4, 5, 6\}$$
$$G = \{7, 8, 3, 4, 9, 10\}$$

The first operation is the operation of union. The symbol for this operation is $\cup$, called *cup*. The union of sets E and G includes all the numerals naming the automobiles on both streets.

$$E \cup G = \{1, 2, 3, 4, 5, 6, 7, 8, 9, 10\}$$

Note that the numerals 3 and 4 were not repeated when the members of the two sets were joined because there is only one automobile with the numeral 3 and one automobile with the numeral 4. When you form a new set by the union of two sets you never repeat members. The order of the members of the set does not make any difference. $E \cup G$ means set E union set G and you start with all the members of set E, then join the members of set G, but do not repeat members. $G \cup E$ means set G union set E. Start with all the members of set G, then join all the members of set E, but do not repeat members. $E \cup G$ is the same as $G \cup E$. Let students discover this for themselves. Then they will see that the operation of union in sets is commutative. This is the same property they have observed in the operations of addition and multiplication in the set of whole numbers.

The next operation is called intersection. The symbol for operation is $\cap$ and is called *cap*. The intersection of sets E and G is the automobiles that are on both streets or in the intersection of the street.

$$E \cap G = \{3, 4\}$$

The only members common to E and G are the numerals 3 and 4. The intersection of two sets creates a new set formed from the members the two sets have in common. $G \cap E$ means set G intersects set E and the new set is the members 3 and 4. Intersection also is commutative. Pupils should discover this fact as they work with set intersection.

The union of disjoint sets is used as a model of the operation of addition in the set of whole numbers. Disjoint sets are sets that have no members in common. We will go into them in more detail in the chapter on addition and subtraction, Chapter 3.

The empty set should be used as one of the sets in the operations of union and intersection. Choose set A, which can stand for anything you wish. Then form the union of set A and the empty set. The symbols of the empty set are $\{\ \}$ or $\emptyset$.

$$A \cup \emptyset = A$$

If you join the empty set with any set, the union will be the other set. For example, think of set A as the first five counting numbers. Join set A with the empty set and you still have the first five counting numbers, which was set A. The intersection of set A and the empty set is the empty set. To understand this operation, notice that set A and the

$$A \cap \emptyset = \emptyset$$

empty set have no common members; therefore their intersection has no members. If you substituted the symbol $+$ for $\cup$ and the number 0 for the empty set, you would have $A + 0 = A$. Now you can see that there is a relation between the operation of union in sets and the operation of addition in the set of whole numbers. You can also see that the empty set in sets plays a role similar to 0 in the set of whole numbers in addition. It is this connection between the operation of sets and the operation of whole numbers that must be clearly understood by middle graders.

The operations of union and intersection will be used in the study of non-metric geometry. Knowing the operations will make it easier to show relationships between intersections and unions of lines, line segments, rays, and angles. Another application of the two operations will be simplifying fractions in a set of fractional numbers by finding the greatest common factor and the least common denominator. Both of these applications will be explained in chapters 6 and 7.

Learning the operations of sets and then not applying the knowledge to our number system would be a waste of time in the elementary grades. Knowing the operations of sets will help pupils understand some mathematics that they otherwise could not master.

The third operation of sets is the Cartesian product. The Cartesian product is the set of ordered pairs made by matching every member in a first set with every member in a second set.

$$A = \{1, 2, 3\}$$
$$B = \{4, 5\}$$
$$A \times B = \{(1,4), (1,5), (2,4), (2,5), (3,4), (3,5)\}$$

There are 3 members in set A and 2 members in set B. In the Cartesian product $A \times B$ there are 6 members. You can see that there is a relationship between the Cartesian product in sets and the operation of multiplication in the set of whole numbers. In the example given, the first member of each ordered pair is a member of set A and the second member of each ordered pair is a member of set B. This follows because the Cartesian product was written $A \times B$. If the Cartesian product had been written $B \times A$, then the first member of each ordered pair would be a member of set B and the second member of each ordered pair would be a member of set A.

$$B \times A = \{(4,1), (4,2), (4,3), (5,1), (5,2), (5,3)\}$$

As you can see, there are still 6 members in the product of $B \times A$. From the Cartesian product the model of multiplication called the rectangular array is derived. A rectangular array is an arrangement of objects in which the same number of objects occupy each row. We will discuss the rectangular array in the chapter on multiplication, Chapter 4.

VENN DIAGRAMS

Venn diagrams are named after an English mathematician, John Venn, who first devised them. The diagrams are circles or other shapes and their interiors represent sets. Drawing Venn diagrams to represent sets illustrates the relationship between sets.

One circle and its interior represent set A and the other circle and its interior represent set B. The members of set A are 1, 2, and 3. The members of set B are 3, 4, 5, and 6. The intersection of the two sets is the member 3. The union of the two sets is 1, 2, 3, 4, 5, and 6.

If two sets have no members in common, they are represented by Venn diagrams that do not intersect.

The members, 1, 2, 3, and 4 comprise set A, and 6, 7, and 8 comprise set B. The intersection of the sets is the empty set and the union of the sets is 1, 2, 3, 4, 6, 7, and 8.

Three sets can be illustrated by Venn diagrams. Set A includes members 1, 2, 3, 4, 5, 6, and 7; set B, the members 3, 4, 5, 9, 10, 12, and 13; and set C, the members 6, 7, 5, 8, 9, 10, and 11.

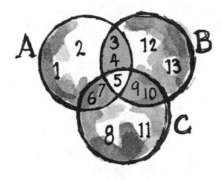

$A = \{1, 2, 3, 4, 5, 6, 7\}$
$B = \{3, 4, 5, 9, 10, 12, 13\}$
$C = \{5, 6, 7, 8, 9, 10, 11\}$

$A \cap B = \{3, 4, 5\}$ $A \cap C = \{6, 7, 5\}$
$B \cap C = \{5, 9, 10\}$ $A \cap B \cap C = \{5\}$

Set A intersect set B is the members 3, 4, and 5. Set A intersect set C is 6, 7, and 5. Set B intersect set C is 5, 9, 10. Set A intersect set B intersect set C is the member 5. The diagram makes this all clear by the manner in which the circles intersect.

Venn diagrams can be used for drill in the elementary grades. In the picture below, one set is made up of odd numbers and the other set is made up of numbers greater than 20. Students should take the numerals in the set below the diagram and place them in the diagram according to how they apply to the sets. A numeral can be written only once.

ODD   **NUMBERS**
NUMBERS   **GREATER THAN 20**

$\{11, 33, 24, 27, 9, 48\}$

Number 11 is odd but not greater than 20 so it is written within the part of the circle that represents odd numbers. Number 33 is odd and greater than 20 so it is written in the region that overlaps the circles. Number 24 is not odd but is greater than 20 so it is written within the circle representing numbers greater than 20. Number 27 is odd and greater than 20 so it is written in the region that overlaps both circles. Number 9 is odd but not greater than 20 so it is written in the area of the circle representing odd numbers. Last, the number 48 is not odd but is greater than 20 so it is written within the part of the circle that represents numbers greater than 20. Which numbers are odd and greater than 20? The answer is 33 and 27. The numbers 33 and 27 lie in the intersection of the two sets. Which numbers are odd or greater than 20? The answer is 9, 11, 33, 27, 24, and 48. These numbers are in the union of the two sets. The word "and" in mathematics implies the intersection of two sets and the word "or" in mathematics implies the union of the two sets. The inclusive use of "or" in mathematics means one or the other, or both. The exclusive use of the word "or" in the English language means one or the other, but not both.

Another way Venn diagrams can be used for drill in the upper grades is to establish two sets like the ones pictured here.

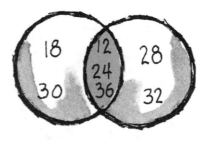

{18, 12, 28, 24, 30, 32, 36}

The one set is the set of multiples of 6. This means that all products that have 6 as one factor are in the set. The other set is the set of multiples of 4. The numerals in the set below the Venn diagram are written in the diagram according to how they apply to the sets. Again, a numeral can be written only once. Number 18 is a multiple of 6 but not a multiple of 4 so it is written in the part of the circle that represents the multiples of 6. Number 12 is a multiple of 6 and a multiple of 4 so it is written in the region that overlaps both circles. Number 28 is a multiple of 4 but not a multiple of 6 so it is written in the area of the circle representing the multiples of 4. Number 24 is a multiple of 6 and a multiple of 4 so it is written in the region that overlaps both circles. Number 30 is a multiple of 6 but not of 4, so it is written in the area representing the multiples of 6. Number 32 is a multiple of 4 but not of 6 so it is written in the space representing the multiples of 4. Last we have the number 36, which is a multiple of 6 and 4 and so is written in the region that represents both circular regions. Which numbers are multiples of 6 and 4? The answer is 12, 24, and 36. Would the number 48 be in this set? Students should now see that the intersection of the two sets is the multiples of 12. Which numbers are the multiples of 6 or the multiples of 4? The answer is 18, 12, 28, 24, 30, 32, and 36. Once again, the word "and" implies the intersection of two sets and the word "or" implies the union of the two sets.

The operations of union, intersection, and Cartesian product are all *binary* operations. This means you need two sets to perform the operation. There is an operation in sets that is unary, which means you need only one set to perform it. This operation is called complementation.

To understand the operation of complementation one must understand the role of the universal set. When we discuss any given set in mathematics, it is understood that the given set always exists in relationship to some reference set called the universal set. In reality, every set under consideration exists as a subject of some universal set. If we speak of the set of vowels of our alphabet, it is understood that the members of the set were selected from the universal set of all letters of our alphabet.

Given $\cup = \{1, 2, 3, 4, 5\}$ means that the universal set is limited to the five members. $B = \{1, 2\}$ is a subset of $\cup$. The set consisting of all the members of $\cup$ that are not members of B is called the complement of B. One symbol for complementation is $\sim$. Then $\sim B = \{3, 4, 5\}$ means that the complement of B is $\{3, 4, 5\}$. Another symbol for complementation is ^{1} and B^1 means the complement of B. $B \cup B^1 = \{1, 2, 3, 4, 5\}$ or the universal set. Also $B \cap B^1 = \emptyset$ because the set and the complement of the set have no members in common. The detailed study of complementation is reserved for the upper grades.

The set concepts and terminology introduced in this chapter will be used throughout the rest of the book. These ideas are models and bridges that will improve pupils' understanding of number and geometric concepts. For example, a pupil who understands that equivalent sets are sets that have the same number property has a bridge that leads to the idea that equivalent equations mean equations that have the same truth set.

EXERCISES

1. List the sets that match (are equivalent) among the following:
   $A = \{a, t\}$ $B = \{a, 4, 6\}$ $C = \{c, a, t\}$ $D = \{0, 1\}$ $E = \{c, 0, a, t\}$

2. Use the sets listed in problem 1 to perform the following operations:
   a. $A \cup C$ b. $C \cap E$ c. $B \cap D$ d. $B \cup E$ e. $B \cup D$

3. Give the cardinal number of each set listed in problem 1. (How many members?)

4. Draw Venn Diagrams to show how the following sets are related:
   a. A and E b. B and D c. B and C

5. If E is any set, then what is $E \cup \emptyset$?

6. If F is any set, then what is $F \cap \emptyset$?

7. Why are sets B and D in Exercise 1 called disjoint sets?

8. $W = \{0, 1, 2, 3, 4, \ldots\}$ $N = \{1, 2, 3, 4, 5, 6\}$
   a. Which set is finite?   b. Which set is infinite?

9. What number is in the set of whole numbers but is not in the set of counting numbers?
10. Name a subset of every set.

SELECTED READINGS

BIGGS, E. E., and J. R. MACLEAN, *Freedom to Learn, An Active Learning Approach to Mathematics*, Addison Wesley (Canada), Ltd., Don Miles, Ontario, 1969.

COPELAND, R. W., *How Children Learn Mathematics: Teaching Implications of Piaget's Research*, The Macmillan Company, New York, 1970.

CROUCH, R., G. BALDWIN, and R. WISNER, *Preparatory Mathematics for Elementary Teachers*, Chapter 2, John Wiley and Sons, Inc., New York, 1965.

FEHR, H., and T. J. HILL, *Contemporary Mathematics*, Chapter 1, D. C. Heath and Company, Boston, 1966.

McFARLAND, D., and E. M. LEWIS, *Introduction to Modern Mathematics for Elementary Teachers*, Chapter 5, D. C. Heath and Company, Boston, 1966.

Sets, Booklet No. 1 of Topics of Mathematics for Elementary School Teachers, National Council of Teachers of Mathematics, Washington, D.C., 1964.

VAUGH, H. E., "What Sets Are Not," *Arithmetic Teacher*, 17:55–60, 1970.

Numeration Systems

INTRODUCTION

Numeration systems are ways of writing numbers. Man in the past has used many systems of numeration, all different in some ways and similar in others. The one similarity of all systems is that each of them had a symbol for the number 1. The other symbols in each of the systems stood for various groupings of the basic unit 1. Our system is known as the Hindu-Arabic numerals because it was invented by Hindus, and Arab scholars spread its usage to other countries. Because of its "ten" grouping idea, it is called a decimal system. Deci means ten.

Certain features of the decimal system make it superior to other numeration systems. Most of the ancient systems did not employ the idea of place value. Without place value calculations are very difficult. Many systems had no symbol for zero and, strange as it may seem, zero was the last symbol to be included in the Hindu-Arabic system. The decimal system has ten symbols—0, 1, 2, 3, 4, 5, 6, 7, 8, and 9—which are called digits. These ten symbols and the idea of place value make it easy to express very large numbers and very small numbers.

To really understand all the operations in our number system, a student must first fully understand place value. This understanding begins in the first grade and continues to grow in each succeeding grade.

PLACE VALUE IN THE PRIMARY GRADES

After pupils have learned the meaning of the numbers 0 through 9 they are introduced to a set with one more object than a set of nine.

The symbol to represent this set is 10 and is read "one-zero." The symbol is called ten only in base ten. Ten is the smallest number represented by a two-digit numeral. The digit 1 stands for a set of ten and the digit 0 stands for *no ones*. Pupils have difficulty with this symbol for several reasons. First, a teacher often bundles together a set of ten objects such as tongue depressors and holds it up and says, "This is one set of ten." The children see ten ones and wonder why it is called one set of ten. The numeral 10 has two meanings. Learning that one meaning is *1 set of ten and no ones* and the other meaning is *ten ones* is difficult and requires careful teaching. The other difficulty pupils encounter is understanding why in a written numeral the larger unit is to the left of the smaller unit. In reading and writing, children are taught always to go from left to right; then in mathematics they are required to write numerals from right to left.

Teach them to read the symbol 10 as "one-zero," which means one set of ten and no ones. Pupils should use plastic discs of different colors, or money. Using discs, the white ones could represent ones and a stack of ten ones could be traded for a red disc, which represents a ten. Now one red disc can stand for the symbol 10. The digit 1 stands for the unit ten and the digit 0 stands for no ones. Pupils should learn to represent two-digit numerals with the discs. The teacher might write the numeral 34 on the chalkboard, but it is not necessary at this stage for pupils to learn to record or call the numeral 34. The teacher asks them to show her what this numeral means. Each child should lay out on his desk 3 red discs and 4 white discs depicting the 3 tens and 4 ones. The same idea can be illustrated with pennies and dimes. The pennies represent the ones and ten of them could be traded for a dime. The dime represents the unit ten. Very often money is more meaningful to children than any other kind of aid. Teachers who use Cuisenaire rods let the white rods represent ones and the orange rods represent tens. Pupils discover that the orange rod is the same length as 10 white rods.

TWO-DIGIT NUMERALS

After pupils have represented several two-digit numerals with discs, money, or rods, they need to learn the other meaning of the symbols.

How many ones is 24? Now the pupils must trade their red discs for sets of white discs. They should show that for each red disc they receive a set of 10 white discs. By using two sets of 10 white discs and 4 single discs they will see that 24 means twenty-four ones. Activities should be planned so that pupils are sometimes asked to show the number of tens and the number of ones when they see a two-digit numeral. Sometimes they should be asked to show the total number of ones.

Pupils should use their numeral cards when asked to show a two-digit numeral. The teacher may display 2 tens and 4 ones using discs, money, or rods, then ask the pupils to tell the numeral that stands for the sets by holding up the correct cards. It is important that they hold digit 2 to the left of digit 4. Explain to them the difference between numerals 24 and 42, that 24 means 2 tens and 4 ones and that 42 means 4 tens and 2 ones.

After the pupils have been taught to write numerals, they can write their responses. Writing numerals is merely a memory function and should not be required before the pupils thoroughly understand the numerals. When responding to an exercise, pupils often reverse digits, not because they do not know the correct answer but because they have difficulty in remembering how to form the digits and how to write them. Writing or recording often interferes with learning mathematics in the early grades.

The names of the two-digit numerals have to be learned by association. The symbol 11 (one-one) is called eleven in base ten. Pupils must learn first that 11 means 1 ten and 1 one; next, that it has a special name called eleven. The same is true of the name *twelve* for the numeral 12. Thus the teen numbers have more meaning because thirteen relates to a ten and 3 ones, as the other teen numbers relate to their names—fourteen, fifteen, sixteen, and so on.

The names for sets of tens are also learned by association. The name for 2 tens is twenty. When a pupil sees the symbol 20 it at first should mean 2 tens; later he learns that there is a special name for 2 tens called *twenty*. Then, the special name for 3 tens is *thirty*, and so on to ninety. When pupils know the names of the sets of tens they can learn the names for the other two-digit numbers greater than twenty. The symbol 21 means 2 tens and 1 one and is called *twenty-one*. They will soon see that they use the special name for the 2 tens, then add the name for the ones to it. Therefore, the name for 28 is *twenty-eight* because the numeral stands for 2 tens and 8 ones. Help them to relate the names to the symbols after they understand the symbol. Remember that pupils should learn the meaning of the two-digit numerals before they learn their names and begin writing them.

Too often first-grade teachers spend too much time teaching the two-digit numbers between 10 and 20 when in their reading class the same pupils are being asked to turn to page thirty-four. How can a pupil recognize the symbol 34 as *thirty-four* when in mathematics class he is only up to eleven or twelve? Teach all the two-digit numerals in activities as explained above, then go back and teach the special names. Once you have introduced the symbol *ten,* go directly to several other two-digit numerals up to ninety-nine.

Using concrete objects such as discs, money, or rods is one stage in teaching the two-digit numerals. The next stage is semi-concrete wherein children make standard drawings to represent numerals. There are standard models for the numerals 1 through 9 as described in Chapter 1. The model for ten was also given there but another model can be used that is quicker to draw. This is a line with ten discs on it.

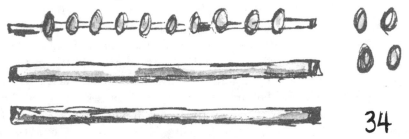

The drawing represents the number 34. Ten discs are drawn on the first line to represent ten ones and the other tens are simply represented by lines without discs to save time in drawing. The standard model for 4 is drawn to the right. In some of their activities pupils should be given two-digit numerals and instructed to make the drawings that represent the numbers. Or the drawings can be prepared for the pupils and they can be directed to write the numeral that goes with the drawing. These same drawings will be used in the first stages of learning to add and subtract. The old requirement that children keep copy books is still good training. They learn to draw a picture of the number, which gives them a good mental picture of it, and they do less work mechanically. Pupils should understand the numbers from 0 through 99 before they start to operate with numbers.

EXPANDED NOTATION

The next stage of place value in the primary grades is more abstract and should not be started until a child is able to make drawings of all the two-digit numerals. This stage is the beginning of expanded notation.

$$26 = \underline{\quad} \text{ tens } 6 \text{ ones}$$
$$48 = 4 \text{ tens } \underline{\quad} \text{ ones}$$
$$59 = \underline{\quad} \text{ tens } \underline{\quad} \text{ ones}$$
$$\underline{\quad} = 8 \text{ tens } 3 \text{ ones}$$
$$60 = \underline{\quad} \text{ tens } \underline{\quad} \text{ ones}$$

Exercises should be designed so that pupils respond in various ways. In some of the exercises above, the child fills in the number of ones, in others the number of tens, in others, both the tens and ones. They should also write a two-digit numeral when they are told the number of tens and the number of ones. Some of the pupils should first make a drawing of the numeral before they fill in the blanks so they will be more sure of their answer. The equal sign should be taught as a symbol that means "is the same as." Tell the children that whatever is written on the left must be the same value as the number indicated on the right. These are simply different names for the same number. When a pupil can fill in numerals in various positions correctly, you can be fairly sure that he understands place value in two-digit numerals.

INEQUALITY

Besides understanding the meaning of two-digit numerals, pupils must understand the order of the numbers. Children think in terms of inequality far more frequently than they think in terms of equality. It is a rare child who says, "I have exactly the same as someone else." More often they are saying his is bigger than mine, he has more than I have, I have fewer than he, mine is smaller than his. For this reason pupils can understand that numbers can be compared—one is larger than the other, or one is smaller than the other.

Two drawings should be presented. The first question to ask is, "What numbers do each of the drawings stand for?" When the pupils respond 37 and 43 by showing their response cards or by writing the

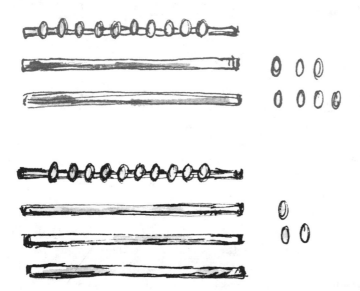

numerals, the next question should be, "Which is larger?" Some children may say that 37 is larger because 7 is larger than any of the other digits, but most pupils will say that 43 is larger. Ask "Which number has the most tens?" "Which number has the most ones?" These questions are important because they bring out the idea of looking first at the ten's place to tell which two-digit number is larger. Even if there are more ones in the one's place in 37 it is still smaller than 43 because 43 has more tens.

The next exercise should involve two drawings that have the same number of tens but a different number of ones.

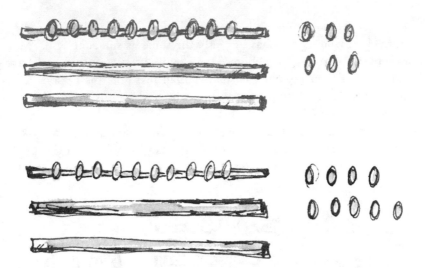

Ask, "Which is larger, 36 or 39?" "Which number has the most tens?" "Which number has the most ones?" This time when they look at the ten's place they see that they are the same so the difference must be in the one's place. With some of the drawings the question should be "Which number is the smallest?" Scattered throughout the activities should be some drawing exercises in which the two numbers represented are the same or equal.

The next step is to give the pupils two numerals such as 57 and 49. Have them make drawings for each numeral, then circle the numeral that is largest. Sometimes they should circle the numeral that is smallest. If the teacher sees that some of the children are having difficulty, she should give them special help, beginning by asking questions similar to the ones she asked when the activity first started. The other children can work independently.

In the more advanced stage, give them sets of numerals such as the groupings below and ask them to draw a circle around the largest number of each pair. Some of the numbers should be much higher than others; others should be very close. It is easier to see that 73 is greater than 46 than that 25 is greater than 24. Next, have the pupils circle the

46   and   73   60   and   58   24   and   25   75   and   76

numbers that are smaller. In this set, a pair such as 34 and 43 should be included. Check constantly to be sure pupils realize that the position of the numeral does make a difference. All the pupils will not reach this stage at the same time. Some will require considerable practice with pictures before they can decide about order; others will simply look at the numerals and make a decision quickly.

Another type of activity is to tell which number comes directly before the one indicated—or after the one indicated. Use one-digit numerals the pupils are more familiar with so that they will have more chance of succeeding. Draw a model of the number that comes before the number indicated; then draw the model of the number. This ac-

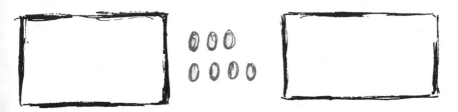

tivity can be varied by asking pupils to hold up the response card that corresponds to the models so they do not always have to draw each numeral. After they are working successfully with the order of numbers 0 through 9, extend the activity to the two-digit numerals.

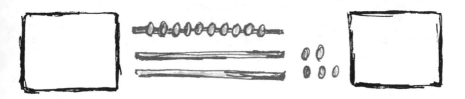

Draw a model of the number that comes before the number indicated and draw the model of the number that comes after the number. Some pupils will need help to see that they need change only the number of ones. The other point to stress in this activity is that each number succeeding another one is *one more* than the preceding number. In other words, 24 is one more than 23. Also, by the same token, 24 is one less than 25. This idea will come alive as children make drawings of the numbers before and after. They will find themselves drawing one less dot on one side and one more dot on the other side. The experience they gain from this exercise is far better than having the teacher tell them about it, for they may not be sure of the meaning of the words the teacher uses in her explanation.

When a child is successful in making drawings, take up the more abstract stage of writing the numerals that come before and after a given numeral. These exercises should be made up of small and large numbers, all the way to number 99.

— 14 —   — 47 —   — 79 —

This is a difficult assignment for some children and the teacher should help by asking, "What does fourteen mean?" When the child says, "One ten and four ones," ask, "What number is one less than 1 ten and 4 ones?" "What number is one more than 1 ten and 4 ones?"

SEQUENCE COUNTING

Counting in sequence is another activity in place value for the primary grades. A floor counting frame with 100 beads can be used to start the counting by 5s. The frame has 10 wires and 10 large beads on each wire. Pupils can slide five beads at a time and count: 5, 10, 15, 20, 25, 30, etc. The same bead frame can be used to count by 10s to 100. After the children have practiced counting by 5s and 10s using a bead frame, have them try to fill in blanks where the sequence is started for them.

5, 10, 15, ___, ___, 30
45, 50, 55, ___, ___, 70, ___, ___
10, 20, 30, 40, ___, ___, 70, ___
50, 60, 70, ___, ___, 100

Counting forward and filling in the blanks with the numerals to complete the sequence is not too difficult. Some difficulty occurs in learning to count backwards in sequence. This requires a lot of practice and at first pupils are not too successful at it and will require help. Going backwards is always difficult for youngsters.

75, 70, 65, 60, ___, ___, 45, ___

80, 70, 60, ___, ___, 30, ___, ___

If some pupils are having difficulty, let them look at a number line from 0 to 100 so that they can see the sequence while they use it. The

0 5 10 15 20 25 30 35 40 45 50   95 100

number line is a geometric representation of numbers. Pupils must learn to count the line segments, not the dots.

Counting by 2s, 5s, and 10s should be encouraged. The counting frame as well as the number line can be used as an aid. At first the exercise should be planned to begin with even numbers, going forward, for this is the easiest type of sequence. Counting backwards by 2s is

2, 4, 6, 8, ___, ___, 14, ___

20, 22, 24, ___, ___, 30, ___

44, 46, 48, ___, ___, 54, ___

difficult. Having a number line to look at often helps pupils who are not too sure of themselves.

0 2 4 6 8 10 12 14 16 18 20 22 24 26 28 30 32 34 36 38

12, 10, ___, ___, 4, ___

36, 34, 32, ___, ___, 26, ___

58, 56, 54, ___, ___, 48, ___

Counting forward, beginning on an odd number, is more difficult than beginning on an even number. Again, the number line can be used as an aid, or looking at the hundred chart often helps.

1	2	3	4	5	6	7	8	9	10
11	12	13	14	15	16	17	18	19	20
21	22	23	24	25	26	27	28	29	30
31	32	33	34	35	36	37	38	39	40
41	42	43	44	45	46	47	48	49	50
51	52	53	54	55	56	57	58	59	60
61	62	63	64	65	66	67	68	69	70
71	72	73	74	75	76	77	78	79	80
81	82	83	84	85	86	87	88	89	90
91	92	93	94	95	96	97	98	99	100

Using the hundred chart the pupils can begin on 1 and count by 2s, by touching 3, 5, 7, 9, and so on. The hundred chart also is a good visual aid for 5s and 10s. The exercises should be planned so that pupils can fill in the blanks by looking at the chart or the number line. When the pupils are successful counting forward by 2s, starting on odd numbers,

1, 3, 5, ___, ___, 11, ___
23, 25, 27, ___, ___, 33, ___
77, 79, ___, ___, 85, ___

they should count backward starting on an odd number.

11, 9, ___, ___, 3, ___
25, 23, 21, ___, ___, 15, ___
63, 61, 59, ___, ___, 53, ___

In the first grade, after pupils understand the numbers through 99, they can start to learn the operations of addition and subtraction and use the numbers. Later in the year, and in second grade, they are introduced to the second level of numeration.

INTRODUCING   HUNDREDS

The second level of numeration involves learning about the new unit called a *hundred*. A hundred is made up of 10 sets of ten. Again, pupils should learn this unit by using concrete materials. If plastic discs are used, the white discs represent ones and red discs represent ten. A set of 10 red discs can be traded for a blue disc. The blue disc represents the unit, *a hundred*. If money is used for the concrete objects 10 dimes are traded for a dollar. The dollar represents the unit called *a hundred*. If cardboard objects are used, a small square represents ones, and a strip made of 10 ones represents ten. A flat made up of 10 strips represent a hundred. The objects are needed to convey to pupils

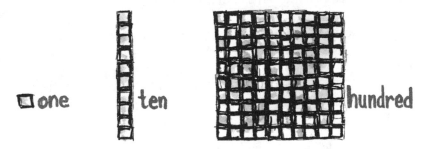

one   ten   hundred

the meaning of three-digit numerals. The teacher might produce 3 flats, 4 strips, and 5 squares and ask the pupils how many hundreds, how many tens, and how many ones are represented. Then as they

3   4   5

respond, "3 hundreds, 4 tens, and 5 ones," the teacher can write numeral 345 on the chalkboard. Remind the pupils that the hundreds are being recorded to the left of the tens.

An activity to reinforce the meaning of three-digit numerals is using numeral cards and pupils. Ten cards can be made up with the digits 0 through 9, each written on one card. Ten pupils are each given a card. Then someone calls out three digits, such as 3, 8, and, 1. The pupils with these cards come forward. Commands are given, such as, "Make the largest number possible," "Make the smallest number possible," or "Make as many different numbers as you can with the three digits." Questions like the following can be asked: "What is the total worth of each digit?" "How could you increase the number by 200?" The teacher should be sure someone calls out a three-digit number that includes zero, such as 402. Questions that pertain to the zero should be asked. What would happen if 0 and 2 changed places? What would happen if 0 and 4 changed places?

EXPANDED NOTATION WITH HUNDREDS

After pupils can represent a three-digit numeral with objects and are able to write a numeral when it is represented by objects, they are ready for the more abstract stage of expanded notation. Exercises should be designed to allow for various responses.

$$467 = \underline{\hspace{1cm}} \text{ hundreds 6 tens 7 ones}$$
$$573 = 5 \text{ hundreds } \underline{\hspace{1cm}} \text{ tens 3 ones}$$
$$602 = 6 \text{ hundreds 0 tens } \underline{\hspace{1cm}} \text{ ones}$$
$$784 = \underline{\hspace{1cm}} \text{ hundreds } \underline{\hspace{1cm}} \text{ tens } \underline{\hspace{1cm}} \text{ ones}$$
$$\underline{\hspace{1cm}} = 8 \text{ hundreds 5 tens 3 ones}$$

By filling in the blanks in various positions, pupils are demonstrating that they know in which place the digits belong and that they can write a three-digit numeral when they know the number of hundreds, tens, and ones it contains.

The next stage in expanded notation is to get pupils to see that our numeration system has an additive principle. The number of hundreds is added to the number of tens and this amount is added to the number of ones to give the total value of the three-digit number. Exercises again are designed so that pupils can write their responses in various ways.

$$569 = 500 + \underline{} + 9$$
$$807 = \underline{} + 0 + 7$$
$$937 = 900 + 30 + \underline{}$$
$$538 = \underline{} + \underline{} + \underline{}$$
$$\underline{} = 700 + 50 + 2$$

In this type of expanded notation the pupils are showing they know that the digit 5 in 568 means 500, the digit 6 means 60, and the digit 8 means 8 ones.

SYMBOLS FOR INEQUALITY

Activities similar to the ones used with two-digit numbers should be planned for three-digit numbers. Ask, "What number comes before 546 and what number comes after 546?" "Which is larger, 574 or 498?" Now, in discussing order, the symbols for "greater than" and "less than" can be introduced. The symbol > means "greater than" and the symbol < means "less than." This is really one symbol, but because we always read left to right, the symbol has to be turned to indicate the order. For example, 4 < 7 means 4 is less than 7. If we wish to state that 7 is greater than 4, we must rewrite the sentence as 7 > 4 because we cannot read the sentence from right to left. The symbol points to the smaller number, or opens toward the larger number. This symbol should be taught by the primary teachers.

The inequality symbol is difficult for primary pupils. To help them make the symbol correctly, encourage the pupils to make two dots by the larger number and one dot by the smaller number and then connect the dots. By making the dots the pupils are first looking to see

$$6 \overset{.}{\underset{.}{>}} \cdot 3 \qquad 34 \cdot \overset{.}{\underset{.}{<}} 40$$
$$5 \cdot \overset{.}{\underset{.}{<}} 8 \qquad 417 \overset{.}{\underset{.}{>}} \cdot 223$$

which number is greater and which number is less than. Then connecting the dots completes the symbol. Pupils think in inequality as well as equality; they should therefore be taught the symbols that go with both concepts.

To fill in the correct symbol, pupils must know the order of numbers through 999. The symbols for order will be used later for drill in the middle grades as well as to show the order of larger numbers.

When a pupil states that 4 is less than 7 he has decided first, that 4 does not equal 7. The symbol for "not equal" is $\neq$. Pupils should know that in mathematics they always use a slanting line to indicate the term "not."

OTHER NUMERATION SYSTEMS IN THE PRIMARY GRADES

To really appreciate our numeration system pupils should compare it with other numeration systems used in the past. Roman numerals are taught in the upper primary grades to afford this comparison and to teach pupils another system of numeration that is still used today.

The Romans used seven basic symbols to write numbers. The table below shows the symbols and their corresponding value in our system.

Roman system	I	V	X	L	C	D	M
Our system	1	5	10	50	100	500	1,000

Originally the Romans repeated symbols to indicate large numbers. Later they developed some new techniques. One was subtractive. A symbol representing a smaller number was to be subtracted if written immediately to the left of a symbol representing a larger number.

1. Instead of writing 4 as IIII it could be written as IV, which is: V — I, which equals IIII
2. Rather than writing 9 as VIIII it could be written as IX, which is: X — I, which equals VIIII

The following restrictions were used by the Romans:

1. I before only a V or X
2. X before only an L or C

3. C before only a D or M
4. V, L, and D never appear before a symbol representing a larger
   number

In the beginning pupils are given only the symbols I, V, X, L, and
C. They learn that the symbol XXXIV in Roman numerals is the same
as 34 in our system. In translating from Roman numerals to our system
they discover that the Romans used an additive principle as well as a
subtractive one.

$$XXXIV \text{ means } 10 + 10 + 10 + 4 \text{ or } 34$$

Also, pupils will notice that the Romans could repeat symbols in the
numeral. They had to repeat symbols because they did not use place
value. This means the X always stands for 10 no matter where it is
written in the numeral. When pupils learn that IV means 4, IX means
9, XL means 40, and XC means 90, they can translate all numbers
through 499.

Roman numerals are used as chapter headings in some books, for
dates on films, and for dates on tombstones and cornerstones of buildings. Pupils can be assigned to find buildings, books, or other examples
of ways in which Roman numerals are still used today.

Point out to the pupils that the Romans did not have a symbol for
zero. This is one of the reasons why they could not use the place value
idea in writing their numerals. Teaching Roman numerals gives a
teacher the opportunity to point out the positive features of our system
in the process of comparing it with the Roman system. We have zero,
"the hero," and place value.

In the middle grades the Roman symbols D and M can be introduced. Now students can translate numerals that stand for larger numbers. They also will learn that the Romans used a bar above a symbol
to indicate 1000 times its normal value. Instead of writing MMMMM
to stand for 5,000, they could write $\overline{V}$, which means 5×1000. This is
the multiplication idea used by the Romans much like the additive and
subtractive ideas mentioned earlier.

Pupils in the primary grades enjoy making up their own numeration systems. Let them invent symbols to stand for certain numbers, then use these symbols to write other numbers. For example, a child might invent a system in which I stands for 1, L stands for 2, △ stands for 3, and ☐ stands for 4. Then 5 could be written ☐ I, 8 could be written ☐ ☐, and 20 could be written ☐ ☐ ☐ ☐ ☐. Children are code-minded and enjoy inventing ways to decode numbers as well as words. They will enjoy trying to decode one another's numeration systems. Inventing a numeration system helps pupils understand that they must make up symbols and indicate what the symbol stands for. Then they must decide how they are to use the symbols to write other numbers. This is what early man did when he invented numeration systems.

PLACE VALUE IN THE MIDDLE GRADES

In the third level of numeration students are introduced to the place value chart in base ten to learn the meaning of numbers through thousands. A thousand is the unit made up of ten sets of hundreds. Students should be asked to add $100 + 100 + 100 + 100 + 100 + 100 + 100 + 100 + 100 + 100$ to see that the sum is 1,000. This symbol, 1,000, stands for the number we call one thousand in base ten. Then ten thousand is the next larger unit made up of ten sets of thousand. The last unit in the thousand period is hundred thousand, made up of ten sets of ten thousand. The place value chart shows this relationship clearly. It shows that one is the starting place from which all the other numbers generate.

PLACE VALUE CHART IN BASE TEN

HUNDRED THOUSAND	TEN THOUSAND	ONE THOUSAND	HUNDRED	TEN	ONE
100,000	10,000	1,000	100	10	1
$10 \times 10,000$	$10 \times 1,000$	10×100	10×10	10	1
3	5	6	7	1	8

VALUES OF EACH DIGIT

Each digit in a numeral such as 356,718 has three different values. The first value is a *face value*. The face value answers the question, "How many?" The face value of digit 7 in the numeral 356,718 is seven. The face value of digit 3 in 356,718 is three. The face value of a digit is the same, regardless of what position the digit occupies in the numeral. The next value is *place value*. The place value answers the question, "How many what?" The place value of digit 5 in 356,718 is ten thousand. The place value of digit 7 in 356,718 is hundred. The third value of each digit is the *total value*. The total value is the product of the face value times the place value. The total value of digit 6 in 356,718 is $6 \times 1,000$ or 6,000. The total value of digit 3 in 356,718 is $3 \times 100,000$ or 300,000. The sum of the total values of each digit gives the value of the whole number. The total value of 356,718 is $300,000 + 50,000 + 6,000 + 700 + 10 + 8$. When the number is written as the sum of the total values of each digit, the numeral is expressed in expanded notation. Once again students can see that our numeration system has an additive principle because the value of the number is the sum of the values of each digit.

Exercises should be designed for students to find the face value, place value, and total value of the digits in a numeral. Then the exercises should be designed so that they can write the numerals in expanded notation.

EXPONENTS

It is also important for students to see that each place value is made up of powers of 10. Hundred's place is 10×10. Thousand's place is $10 \times 10 \times 10$, and ten thousand's place is $10 \times 10 \times 10 \times 10$. The number of zeros in the numerals for the name of each place value bears a relationship to the number of times 10 is used as a factor. For example, in 1,000 there are three zeros and one thousand is $10 \times 10 \times 10$. The number 10 is used three times as a factor. A table will show this relationship best.

One	1	1	10^0
Ten	10	10	10^1
Hundred	10×10	100	10^2
Thousand	$10 \times 10 \times 10$	1,000	10^3
Ten thousand	$10 \times 10 \times 10 \times 10$	10,000	10^4
Hundred thousand	$10 \times 10 \times 10 \times 10 \times 10$	100,000	10^5

The last column shows the numeral 10, called the *base*, written with *exponents*, the raised number to the right. Exponents usually are introduced at the fifth- or sixth-grade level. The exponent tells how many times the base is to be used as a factor. Therefore, 10^4 means 10 is used as a factor 4 times, or $10 \times 10 \times 10 \times 10$. From the table students can see the relationship of the zeros in each of the columns. For example, a hundred is 10×10, or 10^2 in exponential form. There are two zeros in the numeral for hundred; the exponent is 2. Once the children learn this principle, they can look at the numeral 1,000,000 and know the number can be written as $10 \times 10 \times 10 \times 10 \times 10 \times 10$ or 10^6 because it has 6 zeros in the numeral.

Exercises should be devised in which students write the numbers for place value as factors of 10 and as powers of 10. They should be able to translate from the exponential form to the number.

The exponential form that causes the most difficulty is 10^0, which stands for 1. At first, when this is introduced, the students are asked to accept the explanation that the exponents form a pattern of 0, 1, 2, 3, 4, 5, etc., and 10^0 is needed to complete the pattern. Mathematicians frequently used patterns in developing mathematics and the zero exponent is one of the patterns they used. From this pattern they established that any number to the zero exponent is another way of naming the number 1. The idea makes sense because if 10^2 means that 10 is used as a factor twice, then 10^0 means that 10 is not used as a factor at all. If 1 is a factor of every number then it is the only factor left and 10^0 means the same as 1.

At this point the teacher should explain briefly that any number divided by itself, with the exception of zero is 1. This means that $\frac{4}{4}$ or $\frac{8}{8}$ is another way of writing 1. In the set of fractional numbers this principle is called the *property of one*. Next, when operating with exponents students learn that when dividing identical bases they subtract the exponents. That is, $10^7 \div 10^4 = 10^3$. Let them prove the result by writing 10^7 as $10 \times 10 \times 10 \times 10 \times 10 \times 10 \times 10$ and 10^4 as $10 \times 10 \times 10 \times 10$ and see that four of the tens divide out and leave $10 \times 10 \times 10$ in the numerator, which is 10^3. Then $10^1 \div 10^1$ is another name for 1 because any number divided by itself is 1. Dividing exponents when the bases are alike, as in $10^1 \div 10^1$, is a subtraction process because $1 - 1 = 0$. Then 10^0 is another way of writing 1, for 10 divided by 10 is 1.

PERIODS

To learn to read and write large numbers, students must learn how periods function in our numeration system. In the place value chart

PLACE VALUE CHART IN BASE TEN

MILLIONS			THOUSANDS			UNITS		
Hundred	Ten	One	Hundred	Ten	One	Hundred	Ten	One
4	7	8	6	9	3	5	1	2

you see the words *millions, thousands,* and *units.* These are periods in our numeration system. In each period there are three places: hundreds, tens, and ones. All the periods with the exception of units are read when you read a number. The word "unit" for a period is seldom used, because we use small numbers more than large numbers. For example, we do not say that 456 is four hundred fifty-six units, we simply say four hundred fifty-six. The numeral shown in the chart is 478,693,512. It is read: four hundred seventy-eight million, six hundred ninety-three thousand, five hundred twelve. The three-digit numeral is read the same way in any period except that the name of the period must be stated. For example: 478 is read four hundred seventy-eight. Then, if it is in the millions period, attach the word "million" to it. If the three-digit numeral occurred in the thousand period, attach the word "thousand." The places, one, ten, and hundred, are like first names and the period names—thousand, million, billion, trillion—are like last names. A comma is used when writing the numerals to separate the periods. Start at the one's place in the numeral and count off three places and insert a comma. The word "and" is not used until the places to the right of the one's place are introduced. The word "and" indicates the position of the decimal point.

Students should practice writing the number in words when they are given its name with numerals and should then write the numeral when they are given the number in words. The difficult numerals are the ones with many zeros. These should be included in the exercises. For example, 4,000,107 is read 4 million one hundred seven. There are no thousands, so they are not mentioned in reading the numeral. The example given is easier than the reverse of writing the numeral for sixty-five million, three thousand, eighty-one. Now students should write 65,003,081 and be aware that they must write zeros for the hundred's, ten thousand's and the hundred thousand's place. The 3 is in the thousand's place, a zero is in the hundred's place, and 8 is in the ten's place, and a 1, occupies the one's place. To help students who have difficulty with this exercise, tell them to begin with the one's place and fill in the numeral from right to left. Start with eighty-one, then fill in 0 in the hundred's place. Write the 3 in the thousand's place, then fill in the zero for the ten's and hundred's of the thousand period; finally, write sixty-five in the million's place. This will be easier for some children than starting at the left.

Questions can be asked that require students to look at the place value chart. For example, the number 478,693,512, which is written in the place value chart. The following questions could be asked: "How would you change the digits to increase the number by 5,000?" (Change digit 3 to digit 8.) "How would you change the digits to decrease the number by 4,000,000?" (Change 8 to 4.)

RENAMING NUMERALS

Besides being able to read and write large numbers and gaining an understanding of place value in base 10, students need a more flexible way of looking at numbers when using division. This principle should be presented in the unit on numeration, then used in long division when it is taught. Ask, "How many tens altogether in 548?" To answer "54 tens" students must understand that the 5 in the hundred's place also means 50 tens, and that the 4 in the ten's place means 4 tens, making 54 tens altogether. Ask, "How many hundreds altogether in 2,348?" Again, to answer 23 hundreds, students must understand that 2,000 is also 20 hundreds and that 3 in the hundred's place is 3 hundreds, so the total number of hundreds is 23. Exercises must start by asking students to give the number of tens in hundreds and the number of hundreds in thousands.

$$100 = \underline{\quad} \text{ tens} \qquad\qquad 1{,}000 = \underline{\quad} \text{ hundreds}$$
$$300 = \underline{\quad} \text{ tens} \qquad\qquad 4{,}000 = \underline{\quad} \text{ hundreds}$$
$$540 = \underline{\quad} \text{ tens} \qquad\qquad 6{,}300 = \underline{\quad} \text{ hundreds}$$
$$679 = \underline{\quad} \text{ tens} \qquad\qquad 7{,}834 = \underline{\quad} \text{ hundreds}$$

After finishing several such exercises, asking total number of tens and total number of hundreds, some students will discover there is an easy way to find the answer. When you ask for total number of tens, place your hand over the one's place and read everything in front of it. When you ask the total number of hundreds, place your hand over the one's and ten's places and read everything in front of them. You are showing them that the places behind the number you are asking for do not count. Let them explain this short cut to you when they discover it. Do not explain it to them. In division, the dividend has to be thought of in total number of hundreds and total number of tens. This skill can be learned in the unit on numeration.

OTHER NUMERATION SYSTEMS IN THE MIDDLE GRADES

In the middle grades students should study other numeration systems. The Roman system, presented in the primary grades, should be reviewed and extended in the middle grades. Besides the Roman system, students should be introduced to a system such as the Egyptian numerals. Egyptian numerals date back to around 3200 B.C. The system has seven basic symbols. Each symbol is a picture of an object. These symbols are referred to as hieroglyphic or picture numerals. The chart shows the symbols and gives the value of each in our system.

OUR NUMERAL	EGYPTIAN NUMERAL	OBJECT PICTURED
1	|	vertical staff
10	∩	heel bone
100	୭	coiled rope
1,000	⸼	lotus flower
10,000	⸼	pointing finger
100,000	🐦	fish
1,000,000	👤	astonished man

The Egyptians used a combination of these symbols to represent numbers. They repeated a symbol as many times as necessary, the number represented being the sum of the repeated numerals. The numbers were usually written with the symbols representing larger numbers to the left and symbols representing smaller numbers to the right. For example, 4,000,325 was written as:

The idea of writing from larger to smaller was merely for reading purposes. The numerals actually could have been placed in any order; the value would still have been the same. For example:

$$| | | \cap \cap \; = \; 23$$
$$| \cap | | \cap \; = \; 23$$
$$| | \cap | \cap \; = \; 23$$
$$\cap \cap | | | \; = \; 23$$

Students should compare the Egyptian system with our own, in which the value of the number changes if the order of digits is changed. Thus, our system has a characteristic that the Egyptian system did not have— the idea of place value. Also, the Egyptians did not have a symbol for zero.

Students should translate from Egyptian numerals to numerals in our system, and from numerals in our system to Egyptian numerals. Then they should compare the two methods of adding and subtracting to see how much more difficult it is with Egyptian numerals than with our numeration system. They will discover that part of the difficulty with the Egyptian system is that it lacks the idea of place value.

Comparing our numeration system with others helps students fully appreciate all the advantages of our system. Also, it reinforces the idea of how a numeration system is built up. They learn that first of all, symbols stand for certain numbers. It happens that the Egyptians used the grouping in sets of ten as we do in our decimal system. If there is no place value in the system, symbols must be repeated to form other numbers. This repeating of symbols is what causes most other numeration systems to be very cumbersome. Some students may want to study other numeration systems, such as the Babylonian or the Mayan. As they study other numeration systems, students should be encouraged to make comparisons among them to see how they are alike and how they differ.

OTHER NUMBER BASES

Primary pupils as well as students in the middle grades can learn to translate the meaning of numbers written in other bases. Pupils can be told they are secret agents learning to crack codes. Then the teacher starts to make x's on the chalkboard. Each of the x's is called a schmoo. As the fifth x is made, the teacher makes a closed curve and says that this is a glob. Then four schmoos are made outside the glob. The children have to draw the picture on their paper. Then the

question is asked, "How many globs, and how many schmoos outside the glob?" As the response is given 1 glob and 4 schmoos outside the symbols are written below the picture. The word "five" is the secret

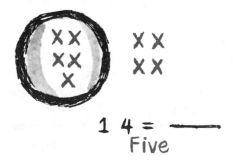

code word; it means there are five schmoos in a glob. The pupils need to write $14_{five} = $ _____ on their papers. Then the pupils are asked to crack the code "one-four base five." Most of them will say nine because they can see and count nine x's. Then 9 is written in the blank. It is important that 14_{five} is read "one-four base five" and not "fourteen." "Fourteen" is a word used only in base ten.

Another picture is made by the teacher on the board, with pupils making the same picture on their paper. It is important the pupils make the picture to help them create a model. The teacher can say schmoo, schmoo, schmoo, schmoo, schmoo, glob, etc., as the picture is being made. How many globs and how many schmoos outside? As

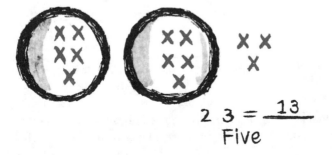

the pupils respond "2 globs and 3 schmoos outside the globs," the symbols are written below the picture. What is the secret code word? The response should be five, because there are five schmoos in each glob. Crack the code and tell what "two-three base five" means. Most of the pupils will say 13 because they can count the x's. Then 13 is written in the blank.

After a few more pictures are drawn using 3 globs, 2 schmoos, then 4 globs, 1 schmoo, the pupils are ready for the first brain-twister. This time the teacher writes $24_{\text{five}} =$ _?_ on the board and asks the pupils to copy the problem. They are now instructed to crack the code by either drawing a picture or not drawing the picture. Some pupils will write 14 in the blank without the picture; others will make 2 globs and 4 schmoos outside. Either method is fine. Give several such problems such as $43_{\text{five}} =$ _____ for the pupils to solve in their own way. Just remember, the only digits you can use are 0, 1, 2, 3, and 4.

Now is the time for the double brain-twister. The teacher writes a problem such as $23_{\text{four}} =$ _____ on the board, and the pupils copy the problem on their paper. The pupils need to be cautioned about the change in the secret code word from five to four. The problem can be solved by either making a picture or not making a picture. Most pupils will draw 2 globs with 4 schmoos inside of each and 3 schmoos outside. Then they will write 11 in the blank to crack the code. The teacher should have the pupils read the problem as "two-three base

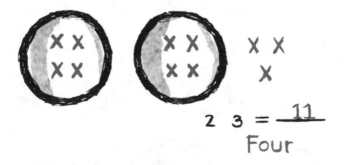

four equals eleven." Now other brain-twisters can be given. Crack the code for $21_{\text{three}} =$ _____. The pupils will draw the picture and crack the code by writing 7 in the blank.

The teacher has to know that in any base there are only as many digits as the number of the base, and zero is always one of the digits.

In base five the digits are 0, 1, 2, 3, and 4. It is incorrect to write 16 base five, for if there were 6 schmoos outside the glob in base five, another glob would be formed. The answer is 21 base five instead of 16 base five.

One way of testing the knowledge of the pupils is to give a problem such as "10 base nine equals what?" If most of the pupils shout out "nine" without drawing a picture, then the model for solving two-digit numerals in other bases has been established.

At first it may seem the words "schmoos" and "globs" are not necessary and even confusing. This is not true. The words with the pictures form a meaningful model.

GENERAL PLACE VALUE CHART

To work with numerals that have more than two digits in other bases the students need to understand the general place value chart. In all number bases the basic place value is the one's place. Ones are needed to group in sets to form the next place value. The place value to the left of the one's place is always the value of the base. The base

GENERAL PLACE VALUE CHART

Base × Base × Base	Base × Base	Base	One	
10 × 10 × 10	10 × 10	10	1	
1,000	100	10	1	All Bases
One hundred twenty-five	Twenty-five	Five	One	Base Five
Twenty-seven	Nine	Three	One	Base Three

is written with the symbol 10 (one-zero). The symbol 10 in base five means five because it is one set of five and no ones. The symbol 10 in base three means three because it is one set of three and no ones. The place value to the left of the base is always base times base. The symbol 100 (one-zero-zero) always stands for base times base in any base. The symbol 100 in base five means five times five, or twenty-five, no fives and no ones. The symbol 100 in base three means three times three, or nine, no threes and no ones. The place value to the left of base times base is base times base times base. This pattern of multiplying by a base for the next place value to the left continues on and on.

Once the students understand the place value chart they can decode a numeral in any base. They use the three values of each digit in

$$342_{six} = (3 \times 36) + (4 \times 6) + (2 \times 1)$$
$$= \quad 108 \quad + \quad 24 \quad + \quad 2$$
$$= \quad 134$$

a numeral. The face value is "how many," so the face value of each digit in the numeral 342 base six is 3, 4, and 2. The place value of each digit is "How many what?" The place value of digit 3 is base times base, or 36; the place value of digit 4 is the base, or 6; and the place value of digit 2 is 1. The total value of each digit is face value times place value. The total value of digit 3 is 3 × 36, or 108; the total value of digit 4 is 4 × 6, or 24; and the total value of digit 2 is 2 × 1, or 2. The sum of the total values of each digit is the value of the total number, which is 134. Once a student has worked through a problem like this he has the pattern for decoding a numeral in any base.

Base two is the base used by digital computers. The only digits used in base two are 0 and 1. Before a numeral such as 1011 base two

$$1011_{two} = (1 \times 8) + (0 \times 4) + (1 \times 2) + (1 \times 1)$$
$$= \quad 8 \quad + \quad 0 \quad + \quad 2 \quad + \quad 1$$
$$= \quad 11$$

can be decoded, the student has to know the place value of each digit. Start with the digit to the far right. The 1 there is in the one's place. The next 1 to the left is in the base, or two's, place. The next digit, 0, is in the base times base place, which is the four's place. The last 1, to the far left, is in the base times base times base place, which is the eight's place. The total value of each digit is 8, 0, 2, and 1, which comes to a sum of 11.

Practice is needed to really become an expert in decoding numerals. The time is not wasted because the students are thinking of place value, multiplying, and adding, and they are doing lots of good thinking.

Some students will be curious to know if you can use a base larger than ten. One fact is important: the number of symbols is the same as the number of the base. When dealing with bases larger than base ten the digits are not enough; letters are needed for the extra symbols. In base twelve the symbols are 0, 1, 2, 3, 4, 5, 6, 7, 8, 9, t, and e. The letter t stands for the set with 10 elements and the letter e stands for the set with eleven elements. The numeral $3t$ base twelve would mean 3 sets of twelve and eleven, or 47. The symbol 100 base twelve would mean base times base, which is 12×12, or 144. The system is the same, only letters are sometimes used as symbols along with the digits.

BASE TEN CHANGED TO ANOTHER BASE

The secret of changing from base ten to another base is thinking of place value. To change, for example, 41 base ten to a numeral in

$$41_{ten} = \underline{131}_{five}$$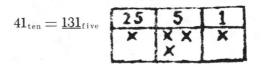

base five, you need the place value chart of base five. An x in the twenty-five's place shows you can make a set of twenty-five; then, 3 x's in the five's place shows you can make 3 sets of five; last, an x in the one's place shows there is 1 in the one's place. The numeral in base five is 131. As you punch out in the place value chart, the rule of the game is use as few punches as possible. To change from 91 in base ten to a numeral in base two you first need to make the place value chart in base two. Then you punch out 91 in the chart. You

$$91_{\text{ten}} = \underline{1011011}_{\text{two}}$$

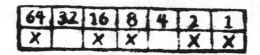

can make a set of 64 out of 91, but there is not enough left for a set of 32. There is enough left for a set of 16 and for a set of 8. There is not enough left for a set of 4, but there is enough left for a set of 2 and a set of 1. The numeral 1011011 base two is the same as 91 in base ten.

After students have made the place value charts and used punched out arithmetic to find the numerals in other bases, they find they can soon do the work in their head without the chart. When this happens they really have learned to think in other bases and can now transfer to any way of writing numbers.

SUMMARY

Teachers often make the mistake of thinking students will find the concept of number bases other than ten difficult because they, themselves, find it difficult. One must remember that adults have used base ten for so many years that it is hard for them to get out of their rut. It is difficult to think about various names for numbers when for years we have associated one name with each number. But young students are code-minded and can think in other number bases because to think thus is much like breaking a code. They learn to group in various sets, then write the numerals. There is nothing new about teaching number bases other than ten. In Illinois the examination for teachers in 1929 included problems involving the translation of numerals in other bases to base ten. Studying other number bases enhances our understanding of base ten.

Digital computers today use the language of base two. Many students in school today will be using computers later on in life and will have to be familiar with other number bases. We can help them by introducing other number bases to them in the middle grades. We do not know exactly what kind of mathematics our students will need when they become adults, but we do know that the more flexible they are in thinking about numbers, the more able they will be to adapt to any new future system. This is the challenge of teaching today. We do not teach for today but to communicate concepts that can be transferred to any system at any time. Therefore you and your students must learn to be flexible in thinking about numbers.

EXERCISES

1. What shortcomings in the Egyptian and Roman numeration systems did our numeration system overcome?
2. Use the following symbols for a system of numeration.

x	xx	xxx	$xxxx$
do	re	mi	fa

   a. How would you write the number of fingers on one hand?
   b. How would you write the number of fingers on two hands?
3. Find the decimal numeral that expresses the same number as:
   a. 342 base five   b. 26 base seven   c. 1011 base two
4. Write 54 and 609 in expanded notation.
5. What does the symbol "10" stand for in base twelve?
6. Name the face value, place value, and the total value of each digit in 3,789.
7. What digits are used in base six?
8. Change 41 base ten to base five.
9. Change 30 base ten to base two.
10. Change 100 base nine to base ten.

SELECTED READINGS

DWIGHT, L. A., *Modern Mathematics for the Elementary Teacher*, Holt, Rinehart and Winston, Inc., New York, 1966, pp. 189–243.
JOHNSON, D. A., and W. H. GLENN, *Understanding Numeration Systems*,

Webster Publishing Division, McGraw-Hill, Inc., St. Louis, 1960, 56 pp.

SWAIN, R. L., and E. D. NICHOLS, *Understanding Arithmetic*, Chapters 1 and 2, Holt, Rinehart and Winston, Inc., New York, 1965.

Topics in Mathematics, Twenty-Ninth Yearbook of the National Council of Teachers of Mathematics, The Council, Washington, D.C., 1964, pp. 1–47, 102–130.

WHEELER, R. E., *Modern Mathematics: An Elementary Approach*, Chapter 2, Wadsworth Publishing Company, Inc., Belmont, California, 1966.

Addition and Subtraction with Whole Numbers

INTRODUCTION

In the beginning man did all his computation by counting. So long as he had few possessions, he could keep track of them by counting. Today most problems in elementary mathematics involving whole numbers can still be solved by counting. In some cases, where the numbers involved are large, it would take a long time, but it could be done. Addition was invented as a short method of counting. Instead of taking the objects of two or more sets and joining them, then counting each object, the answer can be found by adding the number of members of each set. Learning the 100 basic addition facts in base ten and having a knowledge of place value allows one to add very large numbers with relative ease. Students should know that when all else fails, they can still resort to counting to find answers.

There is a difference in being able to add and in understanding addition. One can be a good technician and still not understand mathematics. It is important for students at some time to memorize the 100 basic addition facts; but besides this, they should understand the operation. They should know that addition is *part plus part equals whole.* Addition is a binary operation. This means only two numbers can be added at one time. Also, the properties of addition should be understood, for by knowing the properties you learn the meaning of the operation. The commutative property of addition states that the order of two addends can be changed but the sum will remain the same. The associative property states that when you have more than 2 addends you can group the addends in any manner and the sum will remain the same. Zero is an important number in addition. Zero is the identity element of addition because when you add zero to a number the sum becomes the same as the number. Man invented mathematics and mathematics is a game that has certain rules. To play the game with skill, you must know the rules.

Subtraction is the opposite of addition. In subtraction, the whole and one part is given; the unknown part is to be found. To understand subtraction, one must first understand addition. Inverse operations are always harder to learn than the primary operation—addition and multiplication.

ADDITION IN THE PRIMARY GRADES

Pupils are ready for addition when they begin to take sets of objects and join them to form a new and larger set. When pupils have learned the number property of sets of objects through 10, they are ready for the first stage of addition. The standard model for sets through 10 should be used in determining pupils' readiness for addition. These sets should be contained on individual cards with the number property of the set written on the other side of the card. To test which pupils are ready, use the standard model of sets through 10 on cards. Show the cards to the class and ask, "How many?" In this way you can tell which pupils still need more practice in learning the number property of some sets. Now test them with numerals from 1 through 10 written on cards. Ask the pupils to match a numeral to a given set. Try some of the smaller sets, then some of the larger sets. When pupils can match the numerals to the sets, they are ready to begin joining sets. This is a model for the operation of addition.

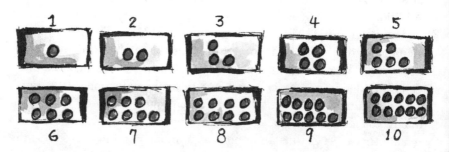

Pupils should be asked to lay out on their desks the set with 4 objects and 3 objects. Then they should be asked to find the set that is formed by joining these two sets. In the beginning some pupils will have to count the 4 dots on the one set and the 3 dots on the other set. They will find the set with 7 objects by first counting 4, then 3. Pupils should be allowed to count. Do not give them shortcuts; let them discover for themselves. Restrict the first activities to sets of objects, using no numerals. Some of the activities should involve small sets; some larger sets. The teacher might say, "Join a set of 5 with a set of 3," and then ask, "What is the total set?" In designing the activities, some of the exercises should involve joining a set of 3 with a set of 2. Then the next exercise should be joining a set of 2 with a set of 3. In this way you are planting a seed that later will grow into an understanding of the commutative property of addition. Watch your pupils as they work. Some will soon stop counting the number of objects in the first set and will use the number of that set to start counting the objects in the second set. For example, in joining a set of 4 and a set of 3, a pupil will count 4, 5, 6, 7. This is an advanced stage and when a pupil gets to it, it indicates that he is becoming ready to use numerals instead of sets.

The next stage is to ask pupils to draw the sets of objects instead of picking up the response cards. Draw a set of 2 and a set of 5. Now draw a set that shows the total of the two sets. By drawing the sets pupils are acquiring a better mental image than merely by picking out the cards that contain the sets. Some of the activities should include the empty set. An empty set is a set with no members. Ask your pupils to draw a set with no members, and a set of six members. Then ask them to draw the set that represents the total of these two sets. Some of them may smile while trying to draw the empty set, but they will see that the total set is the same as the set of six. The seed is now being planted for adding 0 to an addend at a later time.

Pupils should use numerals and sets in the next activity. Tell the pupils to lay out two sets such as 5 and 3 with the numerals to match the sets. Then ask them to show the total of the two sets and the numeral that matches the set. The diagram shows the pupils' response.

Pupils who are having difficulty determining the total sets should be given objects such as discs. Ask them to take five discs, then 3 discs, and actually join the sets, then count to find the number property of the total set. Slower pupils will need activities like this until they are able to pick out the response cards that correctly indicate the total set. Joining objects is usually confined to the kindergarten year; most first graders do not need it. For those who do, extra help will be necessary. Some first-grade teachers fail to discover which pupils need practice in joining objects and require it of all children. Those who already are skillful with the response cards should not be required to join objects. Teachers should be aware of the level of learning of all their pupils, in first grade as well as in the more advanced grades.

Next, ask the pupils to describe a number in a variety of ways. The teacher might, for example, write the numeral 5 on the chalkboard and ask his pupils to use sets and describe 5 in as many ways as they can. They can show a set of 1 and a set of 4; a set of 3 and a set of 2; a set of 5 and an empty set; a set of 2 and a set of 3; a set of 4 and a set of 1. Pupils should be encouraged to show as many different sets as they can, for by so doing they are beginning to learn the facts about 5. At first, the activity should be restricted to small numbers; later, graduate to larger numbers.

The symbols + and = should be introduced. Pupils should be told that the symbol + is called *plus* and the symbol = is called *equal*. Then show them a number sentence such as the following:

The sentence is read: 4 plus 3 equals what number? The frame or square stands for the missing number. Ask what number will make the sentence true? The pupils should be allowed to use the objects above the numerals to find the answer, 7.

Pupils should be told we *add* numbers and *put* together objects. Therefore, $4 + 3 = 7$ should never be read: 4 put together 3 is 7. It should always be read: 4 plus 3 is (or equals) 7. Many students reach junior high school mathematics still using the phrase "put together" for the word "plus." This is not good mathematics; it is akin to the level of baby talk. Teachers must be sure that they do not use the wrong terminology when they are working with number sentences.

The phrase "put together" is the language of concrete mathematics. In concrete mathematics we join objects or put them together. Adding numbers and using plus to indicate addition is the language of computational mathematics. Teachers must remember that there are three kinds of mathematics: concrete, computational, and generalization. Each type has its own language that should be used only when one is involved in that particular type of mathematics. All three types of mathematics are taught at each grade level.

Cards contain the symbol $+$ on one side and the symbol $-$ on the other and other cards with the symbols $=$ and $>$ on alternate sides may be distributed to pupils. With these cards and the other response cards they can make number sentences at their desks. To review symbols with pupils, ask them to hold up the plus symbol, then the equal symbol. The inequality symbol $<$ was introduced in the unit on numeration when they learned the order of numbers to 99.

FRAME ARITHMETIC

In beginning activities with frame arithmetic—number sentences with frames—the teacher should write a sentence on the board and ask the children to display the results with response cards of sets. For example, the teacher might write: $2 + 3 = \square$. Pupils should display the set of 2 and the set of 3; then the total set of 5. Next have the pupils make the number sentence at their desks using the numeral cards and the cards with symbols. They should be told that the 2 and 3 in the sentence, $2 + 3 = 5$, are the parts and that the numeral 5 is the whole. They can grasp this point by looking at the sets that represent the numerals. Addition can be defined as part plus part equals whole. Some of the exercises should illustrate that the parts can be changed while the sum remains the same, such as $3 + 4 = \square$; then the following: $4 + 3 = \square$.

In some exercises pupils should be given sentences in which they are to draw the sets of objects described by the numerals.

$$4 + 2 = \boxed{6} \qquad 3 + 5 = \boxed{8}$$

$$6 + 4 = \boxed{10}$$

When they finish drawing the sets of objects they should write the numeral in the frame to make the sentence true. In other exercises they may be given sets of objects and instructed to write the number sentence described by the sets.

$$6 + 1 = \boxed{7} \qquad 4 + 4 = \boxed{8}$$

$$5 + 4 = \boxed{9}$$

Pupils never have to rely on memory or guesswork because the sets of objects are always at hand for them to count and find the missing number. In planning some of the exercises, the frame representing the sum should be written at the left. If this variation is not introduced early, pupils will assume that the sum is always written to the right. There are many adults who think the unknown must always be written on one side of the equation because all the exercises they ever solved

$$\boxed{7} = 5 + 2 \qquad 6 + 3 = \boxed{9}$$

$$\boxed{10} = 3 + 7$$

were written in that manner. We mold pupils' minds, not by what we say, but by the way we plan activities and exercises. If the responses are varied, there is less chance of inflexible thinking. Now have the pupils draw the objects of the set above the numerals, then solve the number sentence.

Cuisenaire rods may be used to show the solution of addition exercises. Pupils can represent the sentence by showing the rods, then placing the rods end to end for addition. The diagram shows a green rod representing 3 and a yellow rod representing 5. Then the brown rod is laid next to the two rods to show that they are the same length. The brown rod represents 8.

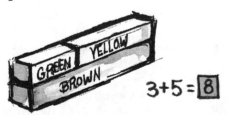

$$3 + 5 = \boxed{8}$$

Give pupils a piece of paper containing number sentences and have them find the missing number by using the rods.

At some time while working with number sentences pupils should be told that the parts in addition are called *addends* and the whole is called the *sum*. The teacher should use the words "addends" and "sum" so that his pupils learn to use the terms. Also, asking them to write the words *addend* and *sum* below the numerals in a sentence will help fix the words in their minds. The addends or parts always appear on both sides of the plus symbol.

All the facts through the sum of 10 can be practiced from the beginning so long as pupils are using sets of objects or rods. They can always find the sum by counting the objects or by showing the rod that is the same length. It is not necessary to limit the facts to the sum of 6. Often, this will simply bore children.

NUMBER LINE

The number line is another model for helping pupils solve number sentences. The frequent error in using the number line is pupils count dots instead of line segments. To help eliminate this error pupils should make a number line. Each pupil is given a piece of cardboard or index card about one inch long and a piece of paper with a line drawn on the paper. On the line there should be a point labeled 0. The pupils put one end of the cardboard on the dot labeled 0 and make a mark at the other end of the card. Then they put the cardboard at the mark they made and make another mark on the line. They continue this until they have marked off five line segments on the line. Then they should write 1, 2, 3, 4, and 5 above the line by the marks they make on the line. Now the pupils can point to the mark

that shows 3 steps from zero, 4 steps from zero, 2 steps from zero, etc. Now they are ready to use a number line to 10 that is made for them. It is important in the primary grades that the numerals are written above the line. As pupils put their fingers on the line they should not cover up the numerals they are looking at.

The arrowheads on the number line indicate that numbers go on and on in both directions. Many pupils will know that ten is not the largest number and some will know that there are numbers less than zero. Zero is the important number on the number line because zero is the starting point.

Pupils have to be taught how to use the number line in solving their problems. Before the sentence $4 + 5 = \square$ is solved the pupils

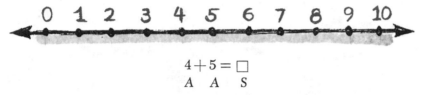

$$4+5 = \square$$
$$A \quad A \quad S$$

should write the letter A below the addends and the letter S below the sum. Addends are the numbers you add; they are always on both sides of the plus symbol. Pupils should be encouraged to analyze a sentence before they start to solve it. In solving the sentence $4 + 5 = \square$ a finger from the left hand is placed on the first addend, 4, and

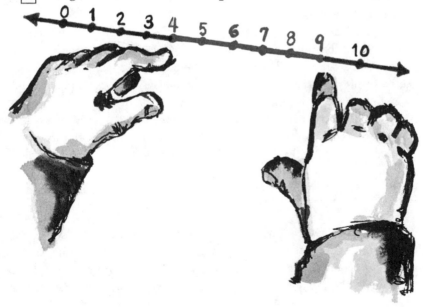

a finger from the right hand counts 5 steps to the right from 4. The finger lands on 9, which is the sum. The diagram shows how the fingers are used to solve the sentence. You can see it is important that the numerals are written above the line so the pupils can read the numerals while they have their fingers on the line.

Using fingers instead of drawing arcs or vectors on the number line is easier for most pupils. If arcs are drawn the pupils should draw an arc to each number as they are counting, instead of one long arc, which is shown in some workbooks. The arc from 0 to 4 shows the first

addend; the 5 small arcs are drawn to show the second addend. The last small arc lands on 9, which is the sum.

Pupils should use the number line, counters, or rods to check their work. If an error is made, such as $6 + 3 = 8$, the teacher should say "Show me," instead of "you are wrong." When the pupil shows 6 plus 3 he will see, with some aid, that the answer is 9. The best way of learning is to correct your own errors; in the process of correcting his own errors the student is involved.

After a teacher is sure a pupil knows the meaning of the facts—in other words, the pupil can show 4 and can show 3 and then can show the sum is 7—the pupil is ready to memorize the facts. To memorize facts the pupil must write them, say them, play games using the facts, even take speed tests on the facts. Flash cards, rolling dice, and regular playing cards can all be used for games to help with memorizing the facts. Sometimes just memorizing one fact a day is the most productive way. Vary the method, but the objective should be to learn the facts.

INTRODUCING SUBTRACTION

After you have a good running start with addition, subtraction should be introduced. At first, the pupils are told to lay out a set of objects on their desks and then to take away a certain number. The question is, then, How many objects are left? Taking away objects from a given set is the standard model for illustrating the operation of subtraction. Pupils need to understand that the large set they start with represents the sum. The objects they take away represent a subset, or one of the addends. The objects that are left is the other subset and represents the other addend. In subtraction, the whole and one part is given. The other part is to be found. When a pupil is using objects and taking away objects, he is operating in the realm of concrete mathematics and can use the phrase "take away."

After activities using objects, ask the pupils to take out their response cards with sets. Have them find 8 by using sets of 5 and 3. What addition fact does this represent? The pupils also may use their response cards with numerals and symbols and show the equation $5 + 3 = 8$ at their desks. The teacher should say, "You now have a set of 8 when the cards are joined. Take away the set of 5 and what set is left?" Record the work on the chalkboard by writing $8 - 5 = 3$. The symbol $-$ is called *minus* and the sentence is read: Eight minus 5 is (or equals) 3. It is permissible to say "take away" when using sets but when a number sentence is written, "minus" must be used.

Now write subtraction sentences on the board such as $9 - 3 = 6$ and ask the pupils to show with the set cards what this means. They must pick out the cards with 6 objects and 3 objects. They first join the sets to form the 9, then take away the set with 3, leaving the set of 6. At this stage, pupils are not recording. They are merely representing the sentence with sets. Joining the cards teaches them that they must first start with the whole set. They can then take away one subset to show the other subset.

Next, draw or hold up some sets of objects such as 5 and 4. Ask the children to use their response cards with numerals to show the addition sentence represented by the sets. They should show $5 + 4 = 9$. Now hold the cards together or put a circle around the sets on the board to show one set being taken away, such as the set of 4. Now ask the pupils to show the subtraction sentence represented by this step. They should show $9 - 4 = 5$. During this activity, continually ask how many in the total set, and how many in the subsets? Pupils must understand that in addition, part plus part equals whole; in subtraction, whole minus part equals part.

The Cuisenaire rods also can be used to illustrate subtraction. Start with the rod that represents the sum. Now place the rod representing one part on top of the rod representing the sum. Then ask the pupils to find the rod that fits the empty space. In the sentence $8 - 3 = \square$, pupils will start with the brown rod representing 8. Place the green rod which represents 3 on top. Now they are to find the yellow rod that represents 5. They then can take away the 3 rod, leaving the 5 rod. This exercise is illustrated in the following diagram.

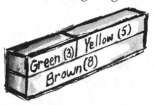

Using rods points up the necessity to start with the number that represents the sum. Then use the number that represents the part to be taken away to find the other part. This procedure again illustrates that in subtraction the whole and part are given and the missing part is to be found.

The number line, too, can be used as an aid to solve subtraction problems.

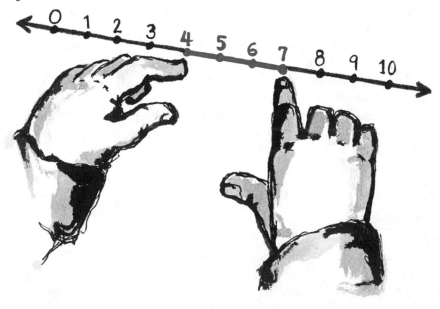

In the sentence $7 - 4 = \square$, the pupil puts a finger of his right hand on the 7 and a finger of his left hand on the 4. The right hand is always used to show the sum and the left hand is used to show the part. Now the pupil can take the finger of his left hand and count the line segments up to 7, or he can take the finger of his right hand and count the spaces down to 4. If arcs are used on the number line, the arc is drawn to the left, starting at 7 and ending on 3. The pupils count back (to the left) 4 units.

In subtraction as in addition, the terms *addend* and *sum* are used. In the sentence $8 - 3 = 5$, the 8 is the sum and the 3 and 5 are the addends. In subtraction the sum and one addend are always on opposite sides of the minus symbol; the other addend is on the right side of the equation. In some exercises the pupils should use A for addend and S for sum below the numerals and the frames. They need not solve for the unknown. This type of exercise helps them to learn to analyze a sentence before they solve it. Too many students solve before they look, so that, in the upper grades, they often add when they should subtract.

$$4 + 5 = \square \qquad 10 - 6 = \square \qquad 6 + \square = 10$$
$$A \quad A \quad S \qquad\quad S \quad A \quad A \qquad\quad A \quad A \quad S$$

Exercises like these are meaningful exercises and not merely computational. Pupils need both types of exercises, beginning in the first grade. But pupils should be taught to analyze before they compute.

In subtraction, as in addition, pupils should be allowed to use aids to find answers until they are ready to work without them. The important thing is to have a method or aid that works for each individual.

MISSING ADDENDS

Missing addend problems, in which the variable or unknown is one of the addends in an addition sentence, is really subtraction. This type of sentence should not be introduced until a pupil understands subtraction. To be successful pupils must analyze the problem.

$$6 + \square = 10$$
$$A \quad A \quad S$$

Put a sentence like the one above on the board and ask questions such as: Which number represents the sum? What does 6 represent, an addend or the sum? What are we finding, the sum or an addend? What number makes the sentence true? Once the pupils respond by saying that 10 is the sum and 6 is the addend, they are finding the missing addend and should realize that this is a subtraction problem. They should show 10 objects; then take away 6 objects. They see that 4 objects are left. Those who use the number line would put a finger of their right hand on the 10 because it is the sum, and a finger of their left hand on the 6 because it is an addend. Then they would move to the right or left to find the missing addend by bounding the line segments between their two fingers. Another way of knowing that this is a missing addend problem is that addends are always on each side of the *plus* symbol. This is additive subtraction.

The variable in the first position does not cause too much difficulty if pupils look at the addition sentence and analyze it first. Ask,

$$\square + 3 = 9$$

"What are you looking for, an addend or a sum?" "If you are looking for an addend, do you subtract or add? Then what number makes the sentence true?" Sentences with missing addends really test whether pupils understand the meaning of addition and subtraction, or if they can only compute. Teachers who say missing addends are too hard for most first graders are really confessing that they have not taught their pupils the meaning of the operations; they have merely taught them to memorize the facts.

So far, we have confined ourselves to the horizontal form of addition and subtraction. Pupils also should be taught the vertical form. These are different skills. In the vertical form of addition the addends are given and the sum is to be found. Pupils soon learn that they may start with either addend to find the sum. In the vertical form of subtraction, the top number is the sum, the bottom number is the addend, and the missing addend is to be found.

DIFFICULT ADDITION FACTS

Addition involving sums between 10 and 20 is more difficult. There are several ways of teaching it. One way is to use the doubles. For some reason unknown to educators, doubles such as $4 + 4 = 8$, $5 + 5 = 10$, $6 + 6 = 12$, $7 + 7 = 14$, and so on, are relatively easy for most pupils. Hence, the doubles may be used to communicate some of the harder facts. If $8 + 8 = 16$, then what is $9 + 8$? Point out that the one addend is now 1 more than the original addend. Therefore, the sum is 1 more than 16, or 17. If $7 + 7 = 14$, what is $6 + 7$? In this case, one addend is 1 less than the original addend. Therefore, the sum is 1 less than 14, or 13. Some pupils quickly learn this method after a teacher points out the increase or decrease of one addend. To other students the entire procedure will be confusing. They should be taught another method.

An alternate method is called "make a ten." The facts pertaining to numbers up to ten are usually easy for most pupils and should be thoroughly mastered before they go on to the numbers between 10 and 20. To play "make a ten" the child needs a piece of paper or cardboard containing two rows of numerals from 1 to 10 and some discs in two different colors. For the problem $8 + 7 = \square$, pupils lay out 8 discs of one color on the top row and 7 discs of another color on the bottom row. In order to make a ten, the pupils take 2 discs from the bottom

row and make a ten on the top row. Now they can see 10 on top and 5 on the bottom, which shows them that $10 + 5$ is 15. It is important that the pupil actually move the discs to see that 8 and 2 are 10. The 2 used to make the ten comes from the addend 7. Seven minus 2 is 5. The game should be played with $9 + 6$, $7 + 6$, $8 + 7$, $7 + 9$, and so on. Each time the pupil solves a problem he is asking, What makes the ten and what is left? This seems like a difficult method to some teachers but it fits in with the problems found in commercial workbooks in which pupils are asked to find what makes a ten and what is left. Also, this is the exact method used by finger counters. In working with $8 + 7$, the finger counters start with 8, flash out two more, and then 5. The "make a ten" provides a mental image for the pupil to use in place of the finger counting.

When using rods for the numbers between 10 and 20, the orange rod represents 10 for the "make a ten." In dealing with $8 + 7$, the pupil lays out the brown rod representing 8 and the black rod representing 7, end to end. Now place an orange rod next to the rods and ask the pupil to find another rod that when added to the orange rod will be the same length as the brown rod and the black rod. The yellow rod fits and the yellow rod represents 5. So the orange and yellow rod, end to end, represent 15, the sum, as the diagram here indicates. The pupil knows

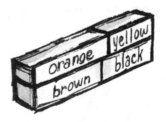

that $8 + 7$ is more than 10 so he needs the orange rod and one more. Finding the other rod provides the amount over 10 needed.

After sufficient practice pupils will begin to memorize many of the facts involved. Now the teacher should provide individual exercises to permit students to work on the facts they have not yet learned. The facts should be presented in both horizontal and vertical form.

DIFFICULT SUBTRACTION FACTS

Subtraction facts whose sums are between 10 and 20 should be based on pupils' knowledge of addition. Consider the exercise $12 - 5 = \square$. What do you add to 5 to get 12? This type of question should be asked so that the child learns to ask it of himself. Additive substraction is a good method for finding out about the facts of subtraction. Once again, practice will help pupils learn the facts. At all times they should be able to use any aid they wish.

ADDITION CHART

One of the aids to use in the second and third grades to help pupils with their facts is to fill in the addition chart; then use the chart (as illustrated below) to find answers to problems. The numbers in the top row and the first column are the addends. The numbers in the squares are the sums.

+	0	1	2	3	4	5	6	7	8	9
0	0	1	2	3	4	5	6	7	8	9
1	1	2	3	4	5	6	7	8	9	10
2	2	3	4	5	6	7	8	9	10	11
3	3	4	5	6	7	8	9	10	11	12
4	4	5	6	7	8	9	10	11	12	13
5	5	6	7	8	9	10	11	12	13	14
6	6	7	8	9	10	11	12	13	14	15
7	7	8	9	10	11	12	13	14	15	16
8	8	9	10	11	12	13	14	15	16	17
9	9	10	11	12	13	14	15	16	17	18

To find the sums pupils look for the first addend in the column and find the second addend in the row. The sum is found in the square where the two columns meet. To solve a subtraction problem, find the addend given in the vertical column, then go to the right in that column to the sum. Look up to the top of the row to find the missing addend. For example, $12 - 5 = \square$. Find 5 in the column, go across to the right to 12 (the sum), then look up to 7, the addend at the top of the row. Pupils should be taught to use the chart and then to use it every time they are not sure of a fact. It is better that they always give a correct response. Also, each time they look up the fact they are practicing as well as memorizing the fact. Even students in the upper grades should use the addition chart if they have difficulty with the facts of addition or subtraction.

From the chart, pupils see that adding 0 to the sum is the same as the other addend. They also can see that facts such as $4 + 2$ and $2 + 4$ are the same. This illustrates the commutative property of addition. The name of this property may be learned later, but the idea of it is planted now in the child's mind as he looks for patterns in the chart.

ADDITION AND SUBTRACTION
WITH TWO-DIGIT NUMERALS

Adding and subtracting two-digit numbers should be started as soon as pupils have a command of the facts to a sum of 10. This is addition and subtraction without renaming. Pupils derive confidence from using larger numbers. Adding and subtracting two-digit numbers is a welcome change of pace from working on the harder addition and subtraction facts between 10 and 20. In addition and subtraction, only like units can be added or subtracted in our number system. This means ones are added to ones, tens to tens, hundreds to hundreds, and so on. Usually, ones are added first, then tens. Pupils may add the tens first, then the ones, but when they are required to rename, the task becomes more difficult. Problems should be given first in vertical form because it is easier with the ones and tens lined up. The pupils must think of 74 as 7 tens and 4 ones, then add 2 tens and 5 ones. The ones add up to

$$74 \qquad 89 \qquad 42 \qquad 79$$
$$+25 \qquad -35 \qquad +37 \qquad -46$$

9; the tens add up to 9. So the sum is 99. The same is true in subtraction. Subtracting 5 ones from 9 ones leaves 4 ones. Subtracting 3 tens from 8 tens leaves 5 tens. The answer is 54. Pupils should be asked to check the subtraction problem by adding the addends to see if the sum is the same as the one they started with in the problem. In the exercises shown, students need know only the facts to the sum of 10.

Some pupils will be able to do the exercises with two-digit numerals in horizontal form, such as $45 + 32 = \square$. They will add the ones, then the tens, and write 77 in the frame. This skill needs practice but pupils derive great satisfaction from it when they are successful.

Too often teachers in the primary grades worry about mastery of the facts. Mastery of the facts is not required earlier than the third grade. The important thing is that pupils learn a way to find the answers. It is also important that they understand what they are doing.

VARIOUS WAYS TO DRILL

Practice will ensure retention. Practice should be varied. Games can be played and exercises should vary. One way of practicing that many pupils enjoy involves using cross-number problems. The numerals outside the squares are sums; the numerals inside the squares are ad-

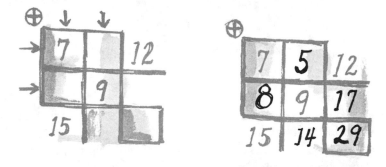

dends. Ask, What number added to 7 makes 12? Then write a 5 in the square. Then ask, What number added to 7 makes 15? Then write an 8 in the square. Now ask, What is the sum of 8 and 9? Write 17 below the 12. Next ask, What is the sum of 5 and 9? Write 14 next to the 15. That accomplished, ask, What is the sum of 12 and 17? The sum, 29, is written in the small square. Finally, what is the sum of 15 and 14? The sum, 29, is the same as the grand sum in the box and is a check. Pupils like filling in the squares with sums, and in doing so they are adding and subtracting. Any numbers may be used for the two addends and the two sums. They must be placed where the x's are located in the following diagram.

Another drill involves having pupils work with letters in an equation. They look at the squares and substitute numbers for the letters. So

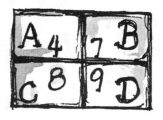

$A + B = \square$ means that pupils substitute 4 for A and 7 for B and find the sum, 11. In $D - A = \square$ they substitute 9 for D and 4 for A to find the remainder, 5. Looking for the number that goes with the letter adds a little spice to the drill. It also teaches children to follow directions by cracking the code.

"Follow the rule" is another type of activity for drill. The pupils look at the rule at the top and then add or subtract that number to the other numbers in the column. Using numbers in a table means

+8	
4	
7	
9	
6	

−4	
10	
12	
14	
17	

+9	
8	
4	
7	
6	

the pupils are doing many problems and they are not aware of the number of facts they have practiced.

Writing answers in the squares and $>$, $<$, or $=$ in the ring to make sentences true also provides lots of drill on the facts. For each

$$\boxed{11} \;\; \bigcirc\!\!>\;\; \boxed{9}$$
$$4+7 \qquad\quad 13-4$$

problem the pupil is doing the work of three problems. He has to find two answers and then make a judgment on the order of the answers. Many pupils enjoy this challenge.

COLUMN ADDITION

Column addition can be taught after pupils have mastered the addition facts through the sum of 20. In adding $4+6+7$ they must add two numbers to get the sum, then add the third number to the sum. They must decide whether to add 4 and 6 to get 10, then add the 7 to get the sum of 17 or whether to add 6 and 7 to get the sum of 13, then add 4 to get the sum of 17. This is a hard skill for some pupils to master because they must add an unseen number to a seen number. The first sum is not seen. Pupils must keep this sum in their heads while adding the third addend. In the beginning pupils can be encouraged to write the first sum on paper, then add the third addend. More than two addends can be in horizontal or vertical form and both forms should be practiced. Students see that the way they group the first two addends will not make any difference in the result.

Another way to practice column addition is to have pupils supply the addends when they are given the sum. The sentence below says that

$$\square + \triangle + \text{☁} = 12$$

$\square$	$\triangle$	☁
10	1	1
9	3	0
4	4	4
1	1	10

square plus triangle plus cloud equals 12. Pupils should have learned at this point that when frames are different in a sentence, different numbers or the same number can be used to replace the variables or unknowns. Some pupil may say $10 + 1 + 1$ and the teacher will fill in these numerals in the table. Another may say $9 + 3 + 0$. These numerals then would be recorded in the table by the teacher. Another answer could be $4 + 4 + 4$ and these would be the numerals recorded. When a pupil says $1 + 1 + 10$ the other students recognize that numbers can be scrambled but the sum will remain the same. Pupils will find many different answers to the problem and learn that a sentence can have more than one answer.

In the following sentence, square plus square equals 8, there is only one answer because the frames are alike in the sentence and the same number must be used to replace both frames.

$$\square + \square = 8$$
$$4 + 4 = 8$$

In the sentence square plus triangle equals 8, there are nine answers if the solution is limited to whole numbers. Pupils should give all the answers to the equation.

$$\square + \triangle = 8$$

$\square$	$\triangle$
1	7
7	1
5	3
3	5
6	2
2	6
4	4
0	8
8	0

More than one operation can be used in a sentence. The sentence square plus 4 minus triangle equals 10 requires pupils to think to find

$$\square + 4 - \triangle = 10$$

$\square$	$\triangle$
7	1
8	2
6	0
9	3

etc.

some correct solutions. If they choose 7 for the square, they must say to themselves $7 + 4 = 11$. What do I subtract from 11 to get 10? They write a 1 in the triangle. Some pupils will see that the number to replace the square cannot be smaller than 6 or the problem will be impossible to solve with whole numbers. Let them try many solutions and each time add and subtract to get the correct solution.

Frame arithmetic permits a teacher to devise many problems that will test his pupils' knowledge of addition and subtraction. The problems are fun because they utilize frames and each exercise is different.

Another way to test knowledge of addition and subtraction is to ask pupils for many names for the same number, say 14. As the pupils reply $10 + 4$, $12 + 2$, $15 - 1$, $20 - 6$, $2 + 2 + 10$, and so on, the teacher writes

$$14 + 0$$
$$2 + 2 + 10 \qquad \boxed{14} \qquad 12 + 2$$
$$10 + 4 \qquad 15 - 1 \qquad 20 - 6$$
$$7 + 7$$

the answers on the board. Everyone at first will be surprised to see how many different names there are for one number. This gives pupils a flexible feeling for numbers, which is essential. Also, they are using their knowledge of addition and subtraction.

Number sentences do not need to be limited to equations. Pupils can solve inequalities as well. Given the set of numbers: $\{0, 1, 2, 3, 4, 5, 6, 7, 8, 9, 10\}$, use a sentence such as: $\square + 4 < 12$. Which are the numbers in the set when transferred to the square, will make the sentence true? The sentence asks what number plus 4 is less than 12? Some pupil will say 7, because $4 + 7$ is 11 and 11 is less than 12. Another will say 6, because $6 + 4$ is 10 and 10 is less than 12. This will continue until they have named the set $\{0, 1, 2, 3, 4, 5, 6, 7\}$. This set is the *truth set*. In doing this type of exercise pupils must add each time, and they must make a judgment on order. Use "greater than" in some sentences, and in some, use subtraction as well as addition.

In the primary grades the students must learn the one hundred basic addition and subtraction facts. They must also learn what the operations mean. Practice and drill must be varied. Frame arithmetic can be used to provide the drill. Mathematics can be fun for all students if the teacher knows her goals and can reach them through interesting games and exercises.

ADDITION AND SUBTRACTION
IN THE MIDDLE GRADES

Students entering the middle grades who do not know the basic addition and subtraction facts should begin there. Teachers will have to help them use a number line or the addition chart so that they can find correct answers. They should be told to look up the facts they are not sure of, or to find the answers on the number line. The more they respond correctly, the closer they are to knowing the facts without an aid.

RENAMING IN ADDITION

Renaming must be taught when some of the numerals have two or more digits. When adding $8 + 7$ in the one's place, the sum is 15 ones. This sum must be renamed as 1 ten and 5 ones. Therefore, exercises on renaming for addition precede the addition exercises. These exercises are similar to expanded notation in the unit on numeration. The exercises should be designed so that student responses will vary.

35 ones = ___ tens 5 ones   47 tens = ___ hundreds 7 tens
___ hundreds = 3 thousand 7 hundred
___ ones = 8 tens 7 ones

In some exercises students are asked to provide the number of ones and in others they are asked to write the two-digit numeral which is the same as the number of tens and ones. In others, they should supply the number of hundreds. For most students in the middle grades this task is not too difficult because they know place value well enough to think of 47 tens as 4 hundreds and 7 tens. Nevertheless, it should be reviewed to get them in the frame of mind to use it.

In column addition of numerals with more than two digits, students should solve the problems first the long way to find the partial sums.

Long Form	Short Form
4 5 6	4 5 6
8 7	8 7
+ 3 6 9	+ 3 6 9
2 2 ....ones	9 1 2
1 9 0 ....tens	
7 0 0 ....hundreds	
9 1 2	

In the long form ones are added to find the sum, 22 ones. Then the tens are added and the sum is 19. Last, the hundreds are added and we find there are 7. This drill emphasizes that ones are added to ones, tens to tens, and hundreds to hundreds. When any place has a number larger than 9 it is overloaded and must be renamed. Adding 2 tens and 9 tens makes 11 in the tens place. The 11 tens must be renamed as 1 hundred and 1 ten. The short form shows how the task is performed mentally. Adding the ones, we get 22 ones, which is renamed immediately as 2 tens and 2 ones. The 2 ones is recorded. Now the tens are added. The sum is 21 tens, renamed as 2 hundreds and 1 ten. Last, the hundreds are added. The term "carrying" may be used so long as the students and the teacher understand what renaming the number really means. Sometimes students and teachers balk at using the long form. There is some value in doing a few problems this way to show what happens behind the scenes in the short method. To help emphasize place value in addition, some problems can be done in a table.

HUNDRED	TEN	ONE	
3	5	8	
2	0	7	+
	6	4	
	1	9	...ones
1	1	0	...tens
5	0	0	...hundreds
6	2	9	

Using the table with the place values labeled, students can readily see that 19 ones is 1 ten and 9 ones and that 11 tens is 1 hundred and 1 ten.

The size of the numbers being added does not increase the difficulty of the problem. When adding $8 + 7$, the sum is 15 whether it be hundreds, millions, or ones. So most of the difficulty in addition arises from not knowing the facts. The next difficulty is learning to add unseen numbers to seen numbers. When adding more than two addends, always have the sum of the first two addends as the unseen number to add to the next addend. This will reveal to the teacher that some students need practice on supplementary facts. For example, $(8 + 3) + 9$ is a supplementary fact. First add 8 and 3; then add 9. This exercise should be practiced separately from the addition problems involving large numbers in column addition.

PROPERTIES OF ADDITION

Students should be aware of the properties of addition and know their names. First of all, addition is a binary operation. This means the operation can be performed only if there are two numbers. Every teacher should begin a class by saying, "Let us add." Then she should say "four"—nothing else. The students will sit, not responding. When asked what is the matter, someone will say, "We are waiting for the next number." Then the teacher can say, "That tells us something about addition. You can't add if you are given only one number. You need two numbers." Ask your students to think of another operation that always requires two numbers. Some will say multiplication, others subtraction, and some division. Ask if they can think of any operation that requires only one number to perform. If some students know about squaring or finding the square root, they will mention these "unary" operations. For example, the square of 4 is 16. It is possible to perform the operation with one number given. If asked the square root of 25, the answer would be 5 and again, the operation is performed with one number. But we have shown that addition is a binary operation.

Ask the class if the sum of $6 + 5$ is the same as the sum of $5 + 6$. The answer will be "yes." Ask if it is always possible to change the order of the two addends and arrive at the same sum. Their adding experiences earlier has shown them that this is true. This is called the *commutative property of addition*. It means that in addition, the order of the addends may be changed but the sum remains the same. Some teachers in the primary grades call this the "buddy property." Who is the buddy of $8 + 7$? The children respond $7 + 8$. In the middle grades they should use the correct name for the property.

Is $(4 + 6) + 7$ the same as $4 + (6 + 7)$? The answer is "yes". Did any of the addends change place? No, it was 4, 6, 7 in the first exercise and 4, 6, 7 in the second exercise. What did change in the two exercises? The answer—the grouping of the addends changed. In the first exercise the addend 6 is associated with the addend 4. In the second exercise, the addend 6 is associated with the addend 7. This is known as the *associative property of addition*, which means that the grouping of the addends may change but the sum will remain the same. Some teachers call this the "gossip property." In the first exercise the parentheses point out that 6 is going around with 4; in the second exercise the parentheses point out that 6 is going around with 7. In other words, 6 is fickle and the writer of the problem is a gossip. This method is used only to get students to concentrate on grouping the addends.

The properties are used in short-cuts. All students like short-cuts because they make their work easier and it is smart to use them. In the example shown below, the reasons for each step are given.

$25 + 37 + 75$	original problem
$25 + 75 + 37$	commutative property of addition
$(25 + 75) + 37$	associative property of addition
$100 \quad + 37$	binary operation of addition
137	binary operation of addition

Ask students to add $25 + 37 + 75$ and they will answer 137 very quickly. Then ask them how they arrived at the answer. They will tell you that they added 25 and 75, then added 37. Then ask them what gives them the right to change the problem. They have every right to change the order of the addends for there is a property or rule that allows them to do so. In adding $25 + 75 + 37$ they may add only two numbers at one time so they must decide which two to add. Since $25 + 75 = 100$, the intelligent decision is to add $25 + 75$, thus utilizing the associative property and the binary operation of addition. They use the binary operation again when adding 100 and 37. After going through this procedure with a fifth- or sixth-grade class, some students will ask if all that routine is necessary to get the answer. The answer is, "no." Use the short-cut by grouping to get the answer quickly. Impress upon them that they should know the short-cut works, not because of black magic or because someone says it does, but because the properties of mathematics allow it.

The number *zero* is a very important number in the operation of addition. When zero is one of two addends, the sum is always the same as the other addend. Zero is the only number that does not change the sum when used as an addend. Zero is known as the *identity element of addition*, another property of addition.

There are 100 basic addition facts, which are the single-digit addition facts through the sum of 18. Nineteen of these facts have zero as one or more of the addends, and there are 9 facts which are the doubles, in which the addend is used twice, such as $1 + 1, 2 + 2$, and so on. After you subtract these 28 facts from the 100 basic facts there are 72 facts left. By using the commutative property of addition, this leaves only 36 basic facts to learn. If for no other reason than this, the commutative property of addition is important.

When students know the 100 basic facts and know that in our number system only like units can be added, they have developed the basic understanding for adding all numbers. When they know the properties of the operation of addition they have learned the meaning of operation. Now they are not only technicians, but are on their way to becoming students of mathematics. The knowledge of place value prompts them to rename numbers when any place is overloaded because of addition. There is no more to learn about the operation of addition of whole numbers. Now all that remains in succeeding grades is to maintain the skill by practicing. To remain a professional in any field constant practice is needed. To maintain skill in adding, pupils must practice constantly.

RENAMING IN SUBTRACTION

Renaming is very important in the operation of subtraction. When the digits in the sum are smaller than the digits in the same place value of the addend, one must rename to get more like units.

$$\begin{array}{r} 3\ 12 \\ \cancel{4}\ \cancel{2} \\ -\ 2\ 5 \\ \hline 1\ 7 \end{array}$$

For years many teachers taught "borrowing." When subtracting 25 from 42 teachers would tell students that they could not subtract 5 from 2 so they should cross out the 4 and write a 3; then cross out the 2 and write 12. Then subtract 5 from 12 and 2 from 3. This was the shotgun approach. The teacher commenced teaching subtraction by beginning with the last step. No mention was made of place value and many students never knew why they crossed out and pushed over a 1 except that the teacher had told them to do it and it worked. Why it worked remained a mystery to them. Today we know that a student must understand how to rename 42 as 3 tens and 12 ones before he can understand subtraction. Students are taught first how to rename 1 ten as 10 ones. They are allowed to use concrete objects such as bundles of tens. They are given 4 bundles of ten and 2 ones. As the student breaks the rubber band on one of the bundle of tens and sees that 3 sets of ten and 12 ones is the same value as 4 sets of ten and 2 ones, it is convincing and impresses him.

Exercises, like the one shown here, must be designed after the concept stage so that students can give varied responses in renaming. In some they might fill in the number of ones, in others they fill in the

$$47 = 3 \text{ tens} \underline{\quad} \text{ones} \qquad 56 = \underline{\quad} \text{tens } 16 \text{ ones}$$
$$\underline{\quad} = 6 \text{ tens } 18 \text{ ones}$$

number of tens, and in still others they write the two-digit numbers that are the same as the sets of ten and the sets of ones. In renaming for subtraction, only 1 ten as ten ones is necessary. Never rename more than 1 ten. Therefore it is wrong to give exercises such as $56 = 3$ tens and 26 ones. It is true that another name for 56 is 3 tens and 26 ones, but this name is never used in subtraction and should not be used as an exercise when practicing ways of renaming in subtraction. A larger number than a ten in the one's place is never needed. Students must have this explained to them. After students are successful in renaming 1 ten for 10 ones, they should apply the skill in a subtraction problem that requires this skill. To begin, exercises should be designed in which the student is required to rename only a part of the problem, and then exercises should be added requiring renaming in all parts. The check should be placed next to the problem so that pupils become accustomed to checking an answer immediately to see if it is right or wrong.

4 ☐	check	☐ 10	check	☐ ☐	check		
5 3	27	7 0	48	8 3	4 9		
− 2 7	+	− 4 8	+	− 4 9	+		

Now students need to learn to rename 1 hundred as 10 tens. Again, exercises are designed to elicit various responses.

$$894 = \underline{} \text{ hundreds } 19 \text{ tens } 4 \text{ ones}$$
$$739 = 6 \text{ hundreds } \underline{} \text{ tens } 9 \text{ ones}$$
$$\underline{} = 8 \text{ hundreds } 17 \text{ tens } 4 \text{ ones}$$

Again, only 1 hundred is renamed as 10 tens. The largest number in the ten's place is a teen number. Never rename more than 1 hundred for subtraction. Now the skill should be applied to problems of subtraction that require that skill.

6 ☐	check	☐ 11	check	☐ ☐	check
7 8 6	291	8 7 7	563	9 3 8	475
− 2 9 1	+	− 5 6 3	+	+ 4 7 5	+

In some of the exercises the students supply only part of the renaming; in some they provide all the renaming. In each case they are required to check the problem immediately.

The last stage is to rename a hundred for 10 tens and a ten for 10 ones. Again, exercises are provided for skill practice.

$$479 = 3 \text{ hundreds } \underline{\quad} \text{ tens } 19 \text{ ones}$$
$$561 = \underline{\quad} \text{ hundreds } 15 \text{ tens } \underline{\quad} \text{ ones}$$
$$800 = \underline{\quad} \text{ hundreds } 9 \text{ tens } \underline{\quad} \text{ ones}$$
$$\underline{\quad} = 5 \text{ hundreds } 17 \text{ tens } 13 \text{ ones}$$

Then, students apply the skill in subtraction that requires renaming.

4 ☐ 13	check	☐ 12 ☐	check	☐ ☐ ☐	check
5̸ 6̸ 3̸	289	6̸ 3̸ 1̸	574	4̸ 0̸ 0̸	289
− 2 8 9	+ ___	− 5 7 4	+ ___	− 2 8 9	+ ___

When a student can rename a number such as 400 as 3 hundreds 9 tens and 10 ones, you know that he understands how to rename for subtraction. When students have learned how to rename for two steps such as 10 tens for a hundred and 10 ones for a ten, they are capable of transferring this skill to larger numbers with little difficulty.

Students should discover that the properties of commutative and associative addition do not apply in the operation of subtractions. If the sum and addend in a subtraction problem are changed, the whole problem is changed and the answer is different. To illustrate, in the problem $12 - 6 - 4$, the answer is 2. But if the grouping is changed to subtract first 4 from 6, then 2 from 12, the answer is 10.

To subtract successfully pupils must know the basic subtraction facts. In our number system you can only subtract like units, and in the set of whole numbers you can only subtract a smaller number from a larger number. In looking at subtraction problems, students must decide which sums have to be renamed to acquire more hundreds, tens, or ones so they can subtract like units. Once all these concepts are acquired, students merely need practice in subtraction in succeeding grades to maintain their computational skills.

OPERATING IN OTHER NUMBER BASES

In the upper-middle grades students learn to add and subtract numbers written in other number bases to review all the skills needed for addition and subtraction in base ten. To add or subtract in base five, students should construct the addition table for base five by filling in

+	0	1	2	3	4
0	0	1	2	3	4
1	1	2	3	4	10
2	2	3	4	10	11
3	3	4	10	11	12
4	4	10	11	12	13

the sums in the squares. In base five there are only 25 basic facts. Looking at the table they should see that 0 is still the identity element—when adding zero, the sum is the same as the other addend. Also, they should see that $3 + 2$ is the same as $2 + 3$, and that $4 + 1$ is the same as $1 + 4$, and so on. This reveals that the commutative property of addition is still valid. Then they can test to see if the associative property is still valid by adding $(3 + 2) + 4$ to see if the sum is the same as $3 + (2 + 4)$. After trying many combinations they see that the associative property of addition is still true for base five.

To add numbers named in base five, students should use the table.

Base Five

4 3

$+$ 2 4

———

1 2 2

In this exercise they first add the ones, 3 and 4. According to the table, the sum is 12 (one-two) and they record the 2 in the one's place and carry the 1 to the five's place. Now they add 1, 4, and 2 and the sum is 12 (one-two). Record this for the total sum of 122 in base five. This exercise involves using all the skills needed in adding whole numbers. Ones were added to ones, then renamed 12 (one-two) ones or 1 five and 2 ones. The fives were added and renamed 12 fives or 1 twenty-five and 2 fives. The problem can be checked by finding the name for the number called 43 in base five in base ten, and the name for 24 in base five in base ten. Add in base ten to see if this is the name for the same number called 122 in base five.

When subtracting numbers named in base five, the addition table in base five is again used. Here pupils need to use all the skills they have learned for subtracting with numbers named in base ten.

$$
\begin{array}{r}
\text{Base five} \\
3\,11 \\
\cancel{4}\cancel{1} \\
-\,1\,3 \\
\hline
2\,3
\end{array}
$$

Before subtracting 13 base five from 41 base five, they must rename 41 base five as 3 fives and 11 ones because 3 ones cannot be subtracted from 1 one in whole numbers. Now subtract 3 ones from 11 ones by looking at the table and seeing that the missing addend is 3. Next, subtract 1 five from 3 fives. Reinforcing skill in renaming can be done in another number base. The problem can be checked by renaming all the numerals in base five to numerals in base ten.

Students should not be required to memorize the basic facts in another number base. They should always use the addition table in that base. They will not be using other bases for any length of time and are simply using them now to practice skills already learned in base ten.

WAYS OF PRACTICING ADDITION AND SUBTRACTION

Punch-out arithmetic is a game that can be played for practice in addition and subtraction. The teacher tells the students she has some favorite numbers and writes 1, 2, 4, 8 on the chalkboard, then asks if they can tell her next favorite number. Those students who see that the pattern is established by multiplying the preceding number by 2 will answer correctly: 16, 32, 64, and so on. Now the students are told the

64	32	16	8	4	2	1	
				x	x	x	7
	x	x			x		50
	x				x	x	35
	x	x	x	x	x	x	63
x	x			x		x	101

rules of the game. Use any of these numbers, or all of them, but use them only once to make a given number. For example, to make 7, what numbers would you use? Some student will come to the board and mark columns 1, 2, and 4. Now have them make 50. As a student comes to the board to work out the problem, ask the other students to watch where he places his first x. He will put the first x in space 32, then an x in space 16, and finally an x in space 2. Number 35 can be placed on the outside. Students will say that x's should go in spaces 32, 2, and 1. After a number of examples, try number 63. For this number a student must place x's in spaces 32, 16, 8, 4, 2, and 1. To solve these problems students must keep adding and subtracting in their heads to get the number they started with. Students also should practice with larger numbers such as 101 so that they can use the columns with 64, then 32, then 4 and 1.

Some students may recognize the favorite numbers as the place values in base two. As they write the x's in the squares, they are writing the given number in base two. For example, 7 in base two is 111 or, decoded, 1 set of 4, 1 set of 2 and 1 set of 1.

Suppose that 1, 3, 9, 27, and 81 are chosen as favorite numbers. Now the rules are that any number can be used, or that all the numbers may be used, or that each number may be used twice. This means that 7 would be two x's in the 3 column and 1 x in the 1 column. We are using the numbers that are the place values in base three. The number 7 written in base three is 21, or 2 sets of 3 and 1 set of one. Again, students are adding and subtracting mentally.

Testing to see if an array of numbers forms a magic square is good practice in addition. If an array is a magic square, the sums of each of the rows, columns, and major diagonals is the same. Students are

4	3	8
9	5	1
2	7	6

asked to find the sum of each row and record the sums. Then they are asked to find the sums of each column and record these. Then they find the sum of each of the diagonals. In each case the sum is 15. Now they know that the array is a magic square. Students should notice that the middle number is 5, which is one-third the sum of each row, column, and major diagonal.

Next, ask the students to add some number such as 4 to each number in the preceding magic square to make a new array. Then they should test to see if this is still a magic square. They will discover it is

8	7	12
13	9	5
6	11	10

and that the middle number is now 9, which is one-third the sum of each row, column, and major diagonal.

Using the magic square they have just tested, ask them to subtract a number such as 5 from each number in the array to make a new array. Again, have them test the new array to find out if it is still a magic square. They find that it is, and they see that the middle number is

3	2	7
8	4	0
1	6	5

now 4 with 12 being the sum of each of the rows, columns, and major diagonals.

As a variation a four-by-four array can be used and tested to see if it is a magic square. Pupils must again add each row, column, and diagonal to see if the sums are the same. When they find that they are, they can then try to make other magic squares from this one by adding or subtracting a given number.

16	3	2	13
5	10	11	8
9	6	7	12
4	15	14	1

Box-car addition can be used to practice column addition. In performing box-car addition, start with the top addend and follow the arrows. Students must think of place value as well as the digits. In the example shown, start with 47, add 60 (which is 107), then add 3 (which is 110), then add 50 (which is 160 and then add 8 (which

is 168). Students are forced to think of the 6 in 63 as 6 tens and the 5 in 58 as 5 tens. They are not only practicing addition but also reviewing place value as they add.

Mental arithmetic is an important part of each mathematics period. The teacher should select a number such as 12 and instruct the students to follow her directions. Add 40, subtract 25, add 13, then add 100. What is the answer? Try to go faster and make the problems longer each day. The more work the students can do mentally without pencil or paper, the more accurate they will become in their computation.

Practice is needed to insure retention. Practice should be varied and should contain some extra twist or interest to keep the students involved. Teachers can share their ideas for drill and practice. Sometimes students themselves will devise new ways of practicing.

Teachers should constantly evaluate their students as they are practicing addition and subtraction to discover where they are making mistakes and to help them correct their weaknesses. The teacher's job is to analyze, then prescribe material to help each individual student improve his computation.

EXERCISES

1. In the following equations, decide if n represents an addend or a sum.

   a. $n - 13 = 27$ b. $67 + 89 = n$ c. $36 + n = 74$
   d. $82 - n = 37$ e. $n + 45 = 73$ f. $48 - 17 = n$

2. Solve for n in Exercise 1.
3. Name three properties of the operation of addition.
4. Rename 47 as ___tens and 17 ones.
5. In the following number sentences insert $<$, $>$, or $=$ to make each sentence true.

   a. $4 + 9 \bigcirc 8 + 3$ b. $37 - 14 \bigcirc 13 + 12$ c. $6 + 4 \bigcirc 20 - 10$
   d. $n + 4 \bigcirc n + 6$ e. $26 - 19 \bigcirc 10 - 3$ f. $81 + 20 \bigcirc 20 + 81$

6. Even after students know their facts, why is column addition still difficult?
7. When is it permissible to use the phrase "take away"?
8. In subtraction why do you never rename 67 as $40 + 27$?
9. The operation of addition is part plus part equals whole. What is the meaning of the operation of subtraction?

SELECTED READINGS

Biggs, E., *Mathematics for Younger Children*, Citation Press, New York, 1971.
Copeland, R. W., *How Children Learn Mathematics: Teaching Implica-

tions of Piaget's Research, The Macmillan Company, New York, 1970, pp. 86–103.

MARKS, J. L., C. R. PURDYA, and L. B. KENNEY, *Teaching Elementary School Mathematics for Understanding*, Chapter 6, McGraw-Hill, Inc., New York, 1965.

Mathematics for Elementary School Teachers, The National Council of Teachers of Mathematics, Chapters 3 and 5, Washington, D.C., 1966.

School Mathematics Study Group, *Studies in Mathematics, A Brief Course in Mathematics for Elementary School Teachers*, Volume IX, Leland Stanford University, Palo Alto, California, 1963, pp. 53–66.

SWENSON, E., *Teaching Arithmetic to Children*, Chapters 6 and 8, Crowell-Collier and Macmillan, Inc., New York, 1964.

Topics in Mathematics for Elementary School Teachers, Twenty-Ninth Yearbook of the National Council of Teachers of Mathematics, The Council, Washington, D.C., 1964, pp. 139–153.

Multiplication with Whole Numbers

INTRODUCTION

Multiplication was invented as a short method of adding equal addends. Instead of adding $4 + 4 + 4 + 4 + 4$, students can learn $5 \times 4 = 20$. This means that addition must be taught before multiplication. All topics as they are presented in standard textbooks are not necessarily prerequisites of the next topic. For example, subtraction is usually presented before multiplication in most texts. Subtraction is not a prerequisite of multiplication. A student can learn to multiply without knowing how to subtract. In fact, multiplication can be used as a relief for those students who are having difficulty with subtraction. Teachers should realize this and use their own judgment about when to teach multiplication.

Before students memorize the 100 basic multiplication facts they should understand the meaning of the operation. Meaning should always precede rote and drill. The meaning of multiplication can be taught by using four different models. Each student needs a good mental image. By being exposed to four different models he should find one that is meaningful to him.

The operation of multiplication has certain properties. These properties should be discovered by the students, after which they should learn their names. The names of the properties are needed only for communication.

Students who really understand the meaning of multiplication with the set of whole numbers will be able to transfer these ideas to other sets of numbers such as fractional numbers. Teaching students concepts and ideas that can be transferred from one operation to another is one of the main goals of mathematics instruction.

MULTIPLICATION IN THE
PRIMARY GRADES

Pupils show signs of readiness for multiplication in kindergarten and first grade. When pupils join sets that have the same number of objects, they are revealing readiness for multiplication. The teacher may ask how many sets there are, or how many members in each set.

What is the total when the sets are joined? Three sets of 2 is how much? Conveying the idea of 3 sets of 2 is preparing students for the concept of $3 \times 2 = 6$ at a later time. Pupils should hold up or otherwise display sets with the same number of members and respond by saying, so many sets of so many members. Ask them question by reversing the activity. Show me 4 sets of 3. The pupils then need to make four sets with 3 members in each set. Activities should be varied, using sums for the total set after joining to 20.

NUMBER LINE ACTIVITIES

In the first grade, after pupils have learned to use the number line for addition, they can use it for readiness in multiplication. A game called "cricket" can be played on the number line. A cricket always jumps the number of line segments that represents his name. Thus, a "2" cricket always jumps two spaces. If a "2" cricket is on zero and jumps 3 times to the right, where will he land? Students use their number line to count 2, 4, and 6. This exercise shows them that three twos are six. If a "5" cricket is on zero and jumps 4 times to the right, where does he land? This time pupils count 5, 10, 15, and 20. This exercise shows them that four fives are twenty. After they have selected some crickets themselves and told the number of jumps to make, vary the game. A "3" cricket might start on 4 and jump 2 times; where does he land? Now they must count by starting at 4 and then say 7, then 10.

Another game for multiplication readiness in the first grade can be played on the number line. The starting place is always zero. Point 12 is a hot dog stand. To get to the stand you must decide on the size step and how many steps you will take. For example, for each step of 6 units, I will take 2 steps. The first step lands on 6 and the second, on 12. The reward for getting to the hot dog stand is anything the pupils want to eat. A pupil may say he will take 4 units in a step and take 3 steps. His first step lands on 4, his second on 8, and his third on 12. Another pupil may choose a step of 2 units and take 6 steps. If a pupil decides on 5 units for a step, he should show that his first step would take him to 5, his second to 10, but his next step would be to 15, which means he oversteps the stand. Tell him you are sorry and wish him better luck next time. The game continues until all the whole number factors for 12 have been used. The units and steps should be recorded in a table on the board by the teacher as each pupil responds. The pupils then can see that 3 units of 4 steps is 12, 4 units of 3 steps is 12, 6 units of 2 steps is 12, and so on. The number line may be extended to 14 and the hot dog stand can become a balloon stand or a pet shop. Or the line may be shortened to 10 or some other choice may be made. Twelve is the best number, however, because it has the most factors.

After playing the game a few times, do not call on the brightest pupils any longer. Then, when all the whole number factors have been discovered, ask one of the bright ones to try to find another way to get to the hot dog stand. He may suggest using a half unit. When asked

UNITS	STEPS
6	2
3	4
4	3
2	6
12	1
1	12

how many steps from 0 to 1, he will draw two arcs. Then how many steps to 12? He will add by 2s 12 times and say 24. Some pupils may even say a quarter or fourth of a unit and respond with 48 steps. This game is fun for your brighter students and gives them a chance to work a little harder.

Cuisenaire rods also can be used to show readiness for multiplication Pupils can lay red rods representing 2 on top of a brown rod that represents 8. They will see that 4 red rods fit on the brown rod and thus that 4 sets of 2 are 8. Three light-green rods will fit on the blue rod. The light-green rod represents 3 and the blue rod represents 9. Three sets of 3 are 9. The red rods can be placed on the orange rod. Five red rods fit on the orange rod so 5 sets of 2 are 10. Problems can be posed such as, "How can you show 4 sets of 3?" Pupils will line up 3 light-green rods, then place them on an orange rod placed end to end with a red rod. The orange rod and the red rod, placed end to end, represent 12. This shows that 4 sets of 3 are 12.

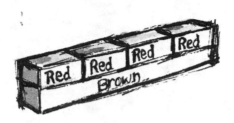

In most first grades, pupils are not introduced to the symbols for multiplication but instead use the idea of sets with equal numbers of members.

MULTIPLICATION SENTENCE

Beginning in the second half of second grade, pupils can be introduced to the *times* symbol $\times$ for multiplication and the multiplication sentence. How much are 4 sets of 3? Pupils answer 12 by showing the sets, using the number line, or using the rods. Then the teacher writes $4 \times 3 = 12$. She tells the pupils this is the mathematical way of writing 4 sets of 3 are 12. The first numeral tells the number of sets, and the second numeral tells the number of members in each set. The symbol $=$ means "is the same as," just as it did in addition and subtraction sentences. Pupils now should be using the model of sets to show the meaning of multiplication sentences. The teacher writes the sentence on the board and the pupils draw the picture to show the meaning of the sentence. When the teacher writes $3 \times 2 = 6$, pupils must draw 3 sets with 2 members in each set. If a pupil draws 2 sets with 3 members in each set he is wrong and should be corrected. At first the teacher should avoid sentences with 0 or 1 as one of the numerals. For variety, some of the larger units such as 4×8 should be given the students. The largest unit tried for most pupils should be 5×9 or 9×5.

Next, give students papers with sets of objects on them and have them write the multiplication fact below the picture. They must be cautioned to write the number of the set first, then the number of members in each set. They can find the total or product by counting the objects or by adding the equal addends.

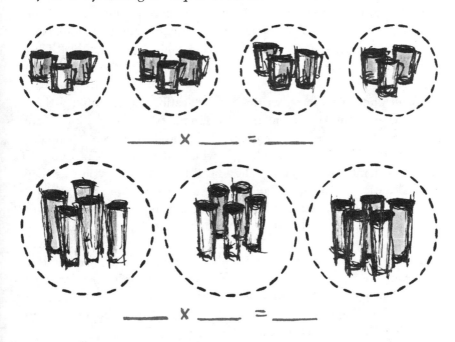

_____ X _____ = _____

_____ X _____ = _____

To introduce the factor 1 in multiplication the teacher should ask the pupils to draw a picture of $8 \times 1 = \square$. If they have been successful in the other activities they should draw 8 sets with one object in each set.

Now have them draw a picture of $1 \times 6 = \square$. This time they draw one set with 6 objects in the set. After they have performed several such exercises, ask if they can write the answer to $9 \times 1 = \square$ without drawing a picture.

When pupils have mastered 1 as a factor the teacher should ask them to draw a picture of $5 \times 0 = \square$. The only picture that can be drawn is an empty set. The pupils will see that the product is zero. Now ask them to draw a picture of $0 \times 4 = \square$. This is not possible. They cannot draw 0 sets with four members to a set. The product again is zero.

After pupils have been writing multiplication sentences for a time, the teacher should tell them that the numbers being multiplied are called factors and the answer is called the product. Given a sentence such as $3 \times 5 = 15$, they should tell which numerals are factors and which numeral is the product. They need this vocabulary just as they needed the words "addends" and "sum" in the operation of addition.

Some of the exercises should be designed so that pupils will discover the commutative property of multiplication as they proceed. Ask them to show $3 \times 5 = \square$ and then show $5 \times 3 = \square$. They should discover that while the number of sets and the number in each set are different, the product is the same. Soon they will see that the order of the factors may be changed but the product remains the same. They do not need to learn the name of the property at this time but they should begin to familiarize themselves with the concept.

EQUAL ADDEND AS MODEL

The next model of multiplication to be presented is the equal addend. Show your pupils that $3 \times 4 = 4 + 4 + 4$, or 12. The second factor is the number to be added and the first factor indicates how many times to add it. Have them show the meaning of 3×7 with equal addends. If a pupil writes $3 + 3 + 3 + 3 + 3 + 3 + 3$ he should be told that he is wrong, because the sentence says three seven's, which is $7 + 7 + 7$, or 21. All the combinations through 5×9 should be practiced with equal addends. Again, in the beginning units exercises with

0 and 1 as factors should be omitted. In some of the exercises pupils should show the equal addends and in others they should be given the equal addends and told to write the appropriate multiplication fact.

When pupils are working successfully with equal addends, introduce them to 5×0. They should explain or illustrate its meaning. If they write $0 + 0 + 0 + 0 + 0$, they will see that the product is 0. Now ask them to change the order of the factors to 0×5. What is the product? If a pupil should respond that 5×0 is 5, ask him the meaning of 5×0 so that he can correct his mistake. Try the same activity with an exercise such as 7×1. Here he should show the meaning of the fact as $1 + 1 + 1 + 1 + 1 + 1 + 1$, or 7. Now change the order of the factors to 1×7. What is the product?

NUMBER LINE AS MODEL

The next model of multiplication is the number line. To show 3×5 on the number line, point out 3 vectors, each 5 units long. The second factor tells the number to be added; the first factor tells how many times it should be added. Ask the pupils to draw vectors on a

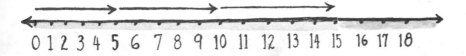

number line to show various combinations through 5×9. To vary the activity, draw the vectors on the number line and instruct the pupils to write the corresponding multiplication facts. Pupils who have been successful in using the number line in addition will have little difficulty using it for multiplication.

RECTANGULAR ARRAY AS MODEL

The last multiplication model is the rectangular array. A rectangular array contains an equal number of objects in each row. There are 4 rows

in the array shown here and 5 objects in each row. The first factor gives
the number of rows, and the second factor relates how many objects in

rows

$4 \times 5 = 20$

each row. Some arrays should be presented so that pupils can write
the appropriate multiplication fact; in others, the fact should be presented and the pupils told to draw the arrays. In an array like the one
pictured below the fact is $1 \times 8 = 8$. If the fact to be illustrated is

$1 \times 8 = 8$

8×1, the x's would be in one column of 8 with one in each row. Pupils
who are having difficulty should be asked to draw an array with one
of the factors 0. They will see that they cannot draw an array with 6
rows if there are no objects in each row. Therefore the product is 0.
A good exercise to show the commutative property of multiplication is
to prepare a paper and have pupils write the facts below the array.
Then have them turn the paper on its side and write the facts for the
arrays in that position. They will see that $3 \times 4 = 12$ and $4 \times 3 = 12$,
$2 \times 5 = 10$ and $5 \times 2 = 10$, and $1 \times 7 = 7$ and $7 \times 1 = 7$. This way,

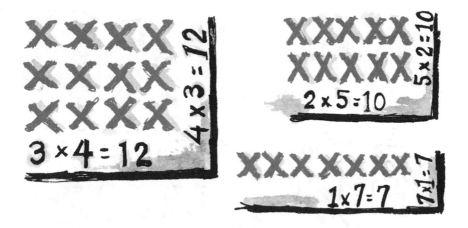

all pupils are involved and they are discovering that the order of the factors may be changed without changing the product.

10 AS A FACTOR

Using 10 as a factor can be taught before the rest of the basic multiplication facts. Pupils can illustrate the meaning of 3×10 by any of the four methods. If they choose the equal addends, they will write $10 + 10 + 10$, or 30. They will soon see that 3×10 means 3 tens. Because they have discovered that they can change the order of the factors, they will also know that 10×3 is 30. All the single digits can be used as factors with 10 as the other factor.

In the third grade, pupils can continue practicing the basic facts through 5×9 and the facts with 10 as a factor. Begin to test them to see which pupils know the facts without using any aids. Those who need aids such as drawing arrays, number lines, equal addends, or sets should be allowed to use them.

One way to practice the facts is to use lattice multiplication. Make squares for each digit in the factors. To multiply 325×76 draw a 3×2 array of squares and write the factors along the top and side. Pupils fill in the squares with the products. First, they multiply 7×5 and write 35 in the square. The 3 tens is written above the diagonal and the 5 ones below the diagonal. Now multiply 7×2. Write 14 in the square. Last, multiply 7×3 and write 21 in the square. Next, 6 is multiplied by 5 and 30 is written in the square, then 6×2 and 12 is written in the square. Last, multiply 6×3 and write 18 in the square.

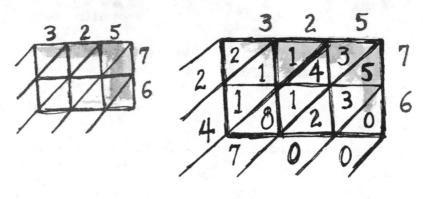

$$325 \times 76 = 24{,}700$$

The teacher can see immediately which facts the pupils know and which ones they still need to practice. Now the pupils add on the diagonal. First add the ones, which is 0. Write 0 below the square. Now add the tens, which is $5 + 3 + 2$, or 10. Record the 0 and carry the 1 to the next diagonal. Now add the hundreds, which is $1 + 3 + 4 + 1 + 8$, or 17. Record the 7 and carry the 1 to the next diagonal. Add the thousands, which is $1 + 1 + 1 + 1$, or 4. Record the 4. Add the ten thousands, which is 2. The product is 24,700. Pupils get a real feeling of confidence when they can multiply such large numbers, yet all they are doing is using the facts through 5×9 with their knowledge of addition.

DISTRIBUTIVE PROPERTY

Pupils can learn to use the distributive property of multiplication over addition to multiply two-digit numbers by one-digit numbers. In 3×14, they see that the array has been divided and that 14 has been renamed as $10 + 4$. How many x's on the left side of the line segment?

The answer is 30 because 3×10 is 30. How many x's on the right side of the line segment? The answer is 12 because 3×4 is 12. How many x's all together? The answer is 42 because $30 + 12$ is 42. Pupils can see that the number 14 was renamed as $10 + 4$ and that the factor 3 was

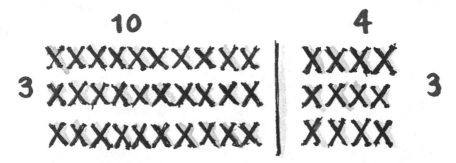

multiplied by each part of the indicated sum. Thus, $3 \times (10 + 4)$ or $(3 \times 10) + (3 \times 4)$ or $30 + 12$, which is 42. Once they grasp the idea that they always rename the two-digit number as 10 plus some number, they can then multiply by each part and find the product. Doing exercises like this in third grade give pupils practice with facts and also teaches them the meaning of compound multiplication.

The doubles were easy in addition and the doubles are easy in multiplication. Pupils soon learn that $2 \times 2 = 4$, $3 \times 3 = 9$, $4 \times 4 = 16$, $5 \times 5 = 25$, and so on. When the facts are extended beyond 5×9, first teach the doubles such as $6 \times 6 = 36$, $7 \times 7 = 49$, $8 \times 8 = 64$, $9 \times 9 = 81$, and $10 \times 10 = 100$. The few pupils who have difficulty with these can use one of the multiplication models to find the product.

DIFFICULT MULTIPLICATION FACTS

Now there are only a few facts left to be learned. They are 6×8, 7×8, 9×8, 6×7, 7×9, and 6×9. These are sometimes called the six monsters because some pupils have so much trouble with them. One approach is to use the facts they know to learn the unknown facts. For example, the pupil might be asked, what is 3×8? When he answers 24, ask him if he can use this to find 6×8. The usual response is, "You mean, I should add 24 and 24?" Answer "yes." Tell them if they know that 3 eights make 24, then 6 eights is 24 + 24, or 48. Now tell them if they know that 6 × 8 is 48, they should know 8 × 6. They will answer 48 because they have learned that the order of the factors can be changed without changing the product. Now ask them what is 3 × 7. How can you use this problem to find the answer to 6 × 7? Again, they see that by adding 21 and 21 they get a product of 42. This type of questioning can be put in exercise form for pupils to practice the skill involved and so learn to use it.

$$+\ \boxed{\begin{array}{l} 4 \\ 4 \end{array}} \times 9 = \boxed{\begin{array}{l} 36 \\ 36 \end{array}}\ + \qquad +\ \boxed{\begin{array}{l} 5 \\ 2 \end{array}} \times 8 = \boxed{\begin{array}{l} 40 \\ 16 \end{array}}\ +$$

$$\boxed{8} \times 9 = \boxed{72} \qquad\qquad \boxed{7} \times 8 = \boxed{56}$$

In exercises like the ones above, pupils can see that the sum of 5 × 8 and 2 × 8 is the product of 7 × 8.

Another approach is to use the doubles to learn the more difficult facts. If they know that 8 × 8 = 64, then 8 × 9 is 64 + 8, or 72. In other words, 8 nines is one more 8 than 8 eights. If they know that 6 × 6 = 36, then 6 × 7 is one more 6, or 36 + 6. Some pupils find that using doubles is a better method than using the easier facts such as 3 × 7, 3 × 8, and so forth.

After all the basic facts have been presented, pupils should fill out the multiplication table. Now they write the products in the table. The table shows that 2 × 6 is the same as 6 × 2, and 6 × 7 is the same as 7 × 6. Pupils should be encouraged to use the table when they are not sure of a fact. It is better that they look up the fact and write the correct answer than to write the wrong answer, which is simply practicing a wrong response. Each time they look up a fact they are reinforcing the answer in their minds.

Pupils should not be required to master the basic facts by the end of the third grade. Expose them to all the facts and teach them ways to find the products. Mastery of the facts can come at the fourth- or fifth-grade level. What is important at this stage is that they have a method by which to find the product. Also, it is important that they understand what multiplication means. They need many activities to help them

discover ideas about multiplication and to learn some of the properties
of multiplication.

x	0	1	2	3	4	5	6	7	8	9
0	0	0	0	0	0	0	0	0	0	0
1	0	1	2	3	4	5	6	7	8	9
2	0	2	4	6	8	10	12	14	16	18
3	0	3	6	9	12	15	18	21	24	27
4	0	4	8	12	16	20	24	28	32	36
5	0	5	10	15	20	25	30	35	40	45
6	0	6	12	18	24	30	36	42	48	54
7	0	7	14	21	28	35	42	49	56	63
8	0	8	16	24	32	40	48	56	64	72
9	0	9	18	27	36	45	54	63	72	81

Facts should be practiced in both the horizontal and the vertical
form. Pupils should learn that $7 \times 9 = \square$ is the same exercise as

$$\begin{array}{r} 9. \\ \times 7 \\ \hline \end{array}$$

After they have mastered the facts, write the exercises with missing
factors. If $7 \times 8 = 56$, what is $7 \times \square = 56$? Exercises can be presented
in a form such that students may give four different responses to the
same fact.

$$7 \times 8 = \square$$
$$7 \times \square = 56$$
$$\square \times 8 = 56$$
$$8 \times 7 = \square$$

Exercises like the ones above reinforce in pupils' minds the fact that
$7 \times 8 = 56$ and $8 \times 7 = 56$.

MULTIPLICATION IN THE
MIDDLE GRADES

During the middle grades the teacher could give a pretest to deter-mine which basic facts the children do not know. The next step is to give them exercises to help them learn these facts. The multiplication table should be available to students so that they can look up the facts they are not sure of. Always stress that it is important to write the cor-rect response. They should not guess but instead look up the fact or use one of the methods they have been taught while learning the meaning of multiplication.

PROPERTIES OF MULTIPLICATION

Stress the properties of multiplication that have been discovered. Teach pupils the names of the properties. Can you multiply if you are given only the number 7? The answer is, "no." To multiply you need two numbers. Multiplication is a binary operation. What other opera-tion do you know that is binary? They will say addition and subtraction. What is 3×5? What is 5×3? Can you always change the order of the factors without changing the product? When the students say "yes," tell them that this characteristic is called the *commutative property of multiplication*. What happens when 0 is one of the factors? Students should know from experience that the product is 0. This is called the *property of zero*. Zero is an important number in multiplication. It is the only number that can be used as a factor which produces a product of zero, or itself. Zero is really a hero. When 1 is a factor, what is the product? Students will say that the product is the same as the other factor. One is the *identity element of multiplication*.

Next, try an exercise with three factors. How would you multiply $2 \times 5 \times 7$? Some students will multiply 2×5 to get 10, then multiply by 7 to get the final product, 70. Others may say they multiplied 5×7 to get 35, then multiplied by 2 to get the final product of 70. Then is $(2 \times 5) \times 7$ the same as $2 \times (5 \times 7)$? In the first exercise 5 is associ-ated with 2; in the second exercise 5 is associated with 7. This is called the *associative property of multiplication*. Students should notice that in $(2 \times 5) \times 7 = 2 \times (5 \times 7)$ the factors did not change order. On the left the factors are in the order of 2, 5, and 7; on the right side they are in the same order: 2, 5, 7. The only thing that has changed is the parentheses, which show that the grouping has changed. Grouping is needed because only two numbers can be multiplied at one time. This is the way to express the selection of the two factors to be multiplied first.

The properties of multiplication can be used to show how to use short-cuts in multiplication. Asked to multiply $25 \times 37 \times 4$, students will give the answer, 3700, without using a pencil. When asked how they did it they say they multiplied 25×4, then by 37. What gives you the right to change the problem? They answer that the properties of multiplication gives them the right.

$25 \times 37 \times 4$	original problem
$25 \times 4 \times 37$	commutative property of multiplication
$(25 \times 4) \times 37$	associative property of multiplication
100×37	binary operation of multiplication
13700	binary operation of multiplication

Students should realize that the short-cut utilizes the properties of multiplication. There is no black magic in mathematics. Short-cuts are possible only because there are properties of mathematics that allow them. Impress this on the students until they understand.

What is the answer to $8 \times 7 \times 0 \times 9$? The answer is 0 because 0 is one of the factors. Any number times 0 yields the product 0. If $a \times b = 0$, what do you know about the numbers represented by the letters a and b? Students should realize that a could be 0, b could be 0, or both a and b could be 0. Exercises should be designed to reinforce the idea that when 0 is a factor, the product is always 0.

MULTIPLES OF 10 AND 100

Before students learn compound multiplication they must learn to multiply with the multiples of 10 and 100. The multiples of ten are 10,

20, 30, 40, 50, 60, 70, 80, and 90. To multiply 3×40, think of 40 as 4×10. Now you have $3 \times 4 \times 10$. The 3 and 4 are associated so the sentence becomes $(3 \times 4) \times 10$. The 3×4 is 12 and 12 times 10 is 120. If students know their basic facts and know how to multiply by 10, they can then multiply by the multiples of 10. Do not teach students to annex a zero. In multiplying 3 times 4 tens, the answer is 12 tens. Exercises should be given in which students respond in tens.

$$5 \times 7 \text{ tens} = \_\_ \text{ tens} \qquad 6 \times \_\_ = 24 \text{ tens}$$
$$\_ \times 3 \text{ tens} = 27 \text{ tens}$$

When multiplying 5×7 tens, the 5 is 5 ones. This means that ones times tens equal tens. The next exercise should be designed so that the numeral is used for 7 tens. For example, $5 \times 70 = \_\_\_$. Here students are encouraged to think that 5 times 7 tens is 35 tens, then to write 350. If some have difficulty, ask them to show what 5×70 means with equal addends. When they write $70 + 70 + 70 + 70 + 70$, they see the 0 in the one's place and that the answer is 350. After they are successful multiplying with multiples of 10 they should be given exercises with multiples of 100.

$$3 \times 4 \text{ hundreds} = \_\_ \text{ hundreds}$$
$$6 \times _____ = 42 \text{ hundreds}$$
$$\_ \times 8 \text{ hundreds} = 32 \text{ hundreds}$$

Next, exercises should be written in numeral form using 4 hundreds.

$$3 \times 400 = \_\_\_\_$$
$$6 \times \_\_ = 4200$$
$$\_ \times 800 = 3200$$

Notice that in multiplying 3×400 it is necessary to rename 400 as 4×100, then to think $3 \times 4 \times 100$. Then associate 3×4 to get 12 and multiply 12×100.

To practice the multiples of ten, students can learn square multiplication of teen numbers. To multiply 13×17 the factors are renamed as

$10+3$ and $10+7$. Then the multiplication is shown in squares. First multiply 10×10 and write 100. Then multiply 3×10 and write 30. Next, multiply 10×7 and write 70. Last, multiply 3×7 and write 21. What is the product? Students discover that they must add the four

$\times$	10	7
10	100	70
3	30	21

products: $100+30+70+21$ to get the product 221. Students are really using a double distributive. In order to multiply 13×17 rename 13 as $10+3$ and 17 as $10+7$; then the distributive property allows it to be stated as 10×10 and 10×7. Next, by the distributive property multiply 3×10, then 3×7.

$$13 \times 17 = (10+3) \times (10+7)$$
$$= (10 \times 10) + (10 \times 7) + (3 \times 10) + (3 \times 7)$$
$$= \quad 100 \quad + \quad 70 \quad + \quad 30 \quad + \quad 21$$
$$= \quad 221$$

Students must learn by experience that every time they are dealing with one factor which has two or more digits they are using the distributive property of multiplication. It is the distributive property that explains what is happening in compound multiplication.

COMPOUND MULTIPLICATION

Students should learn first to multiply a factor with many digits times a factor with one digit. They should use the long form to do the problem in order to see all the steps involved. Also, they need to see how place value plays an important part in multiplication. Multiply-

Long Form

```
      458
     ×9
    ─────
      7 2....9 ones × 8 ones
      4 5 0....9 ones × 5 tens
    3 6 0 0....9 ones × 4 hundreds
    ─────────
    4 1 2 2
```

ing 458 by 9, think of 458 as 4 hundreds, 5 tens, and 8 ones. Nine ones times 8 ones is 72 ones. Next, 9 ones times 5 tens is 45 tens, or 450. Last, 9 ones times 4 hundreds is 36 hundreds, or 3600.

Using the short form of multiplication students must "carry" or add an unseen number to a product. In 458×9, using the short form, mul-

Short Form

```
      458
     ×9
    ─────
    4 1 2 2
```

tiply 9×8 and get 72 ones. Record the 2 in the one's place and carry the 7 tens. Then multiply 9 ones times 5 tens to get 45 tens. Add the 7 tens, which is 52 tens. The 2 is recorded in the ten's place and the 5 is carried to the hundred's place. Nine ones times 4 hundreds is 36 hundreds plus 5 hundreds is 41 hundreds. Record 41. To explain this to students, a teacher must realize how many separate steps there are in this problem. Students need practice with supplementary facts before they can master multiplication involving one factor with many digits.

Supplementary facts like the ones displayed here are needed to help students learn to add a number to a product. This is the skill used in "carrying" in multiplication. This skill should be practiced in drills separate from the problems. It is always difficult for students to add an unseen number to a product.

$(7 \times 8) + 6 = \square$ $(6 \times 7) + 4 = \square$ $(92 \times 8) + 6 = \square$

The next stage is to use factors containing more than one digit. Now the problems are getting very difficult because so many steps are involved in one problem. One mistake in any of the steps makes the whole problem wrong. This stage requires great concentration. The long form should be practiced first so that students will be aware of the numbers being multiplied. In multiplying 679 by 58, the distributive

Long Form

679
×58

7 2	.....8 ones × 9 ones
5 6 0	.....8 ones × 7 tens
4 8 0 0	.....8 ones × 6 hundreds
4 5 0	.....5 tens × 9 ones
3 5 0 0	.....5 tens × 7 tens
3 0 0 0 0	.....5 tens × 6 hundreds

3 9,3 8 2

property is used twice. First, 8 ones is distributed over 9 ones, 7 tens, and 6 hundreds. Then 5 tens is distributed over 9 ones, 7 tens, and 6 hundreds. In the long form students must keep in mind the place value of each digit. They must also realize when multiplying ones times tens that the product will be in tens. When multiplying tens times hundreds, the product is in thousands. Also, in the long form, there are six different exercises in multiplication as well as column addition.

Using the short form of multiplication, students must multiply and carry the unseen number. In multiplying 679 by 58 by the short form, three steps are combined in one to arrive at the first partial product,

Short Form

679
×58

5 4 3 2
3 3 9 5

3 9,3 8 2

5432. This operation requires a great deal of concentration and is very difficult. The next partial product, 3395, results from another three steps combined in one. The 5 in 3395 is placed in the ten's place because the multiplication is by tens. A pupil who is still weak in multiplication and weak in addition will find this an impossible task. Those not mathematically inclined should not be obliged to do compound multiplication as soon as other students. Let them continue to practice supplementary facts that are a combination of multiplication and addition such as $(4 \times 9) + 5$.

VARIOUS WAYS OF CHECKING

Students always should be encouraged to check their work. In the case of compound multiplication, most students consider the task a gruesome one. Most of the time they are given only two choices. One is to multiply by changing the order of the factors; the other is by long division. This is not much of a choice. There are other methods of checking. One of them is lattice multiplication. Most students find this

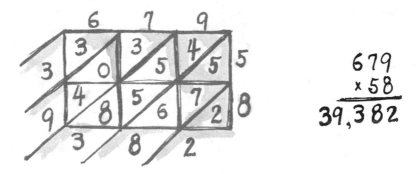

method fun. Teachers also like this method because all the parts of the problems are shown. Any mistakes in multiplication can be seen immediately by looking at the products in the squares. If mistakes are made in adding on the diagonal, students probably need more practice in addition.

Another method for checking is called "casting out nines." In this method, add the numbers represented by the digits of the numeral. Continue to add until the sum is a one-digit number. If the one-digit is 9, change it to 0. The one-digit sum represents the remainder of

Check by Casting Out Nines

```
6 7 2.....15.....6
                     ✕
✕5 3..... 8.....8

 2 0 1 6            4 8.....12.....3
 3 3 6 0
 3 5,6 1 6.....21.................3
```

the number if divided by 9. When adding the numbers represented by 6, 7, and 2, the sum is 15. Now add 1 and 5 to get the sum of 6. This means 672 divided by 9 leaves a remainder of 6. Now add 5 and 3. The sum is 8. This means 53 divided by 9 leaves a remainder of 8. Now multiply 6 ✕ 8 to get the product 48. Add 4 and 8 to get 12. Now add 1 and 2 to get 3. If the problem checks, the product, 35,616, should come out to 3 when the nines are cast out. Add 3, 5, 6, 1, and 6. The sum is 21. Then add 2 and 1 for the sum 3. The problem checks. The only difficulty with this check is that if you missed a numeral in copying or changed the order of the digits, the number could have the same answer when you cast out nines. In other words, if you copied 672 as 627, the remainder would be 6 for each number. Students enjoy casting out nines and this method can be used as a check in all four operations. For example, to check 4002 − 689, add the numbers 4, 0, 0,

```
  4 0 0 2.....6.....6
−   6 8 9....23.....5
  3 3 1 3....10.....1
```

and 2 to get 6. Now add 6, 8, and 9 to get the sum 23. Then add 2 and 3 to get the sum 5. Subtract 5 from 6; the remainder is 1. Add the numbers of the answer, 3, 3, 1, and 3 to get a sum of 10. Adding 1 and 0, the sum is 1. The problem checks because the 1 appears in both places.

One of the activities used to practice multiplication can also include another operation such as addition. In the table here the words "part"

sum		13	17		20	24
part	7	5				
part	8			8		
product			72	56	36	140

are used because both addition and multiplication are involved and it is not possible to write *addend* and *factor*. Students are given two numbers to fill in the other two numbers. For example, given 7 and 8 in the parts, students find the sum and product using the two numbers. They fill in 15 as the sum and 56 as the product. Given 13 as the sum and 5 as one part, they must subtract to find the other part, which is 8. Then 5×8 is 40. If the sum is 17 the product is 72, they must find the two numbers whose sum is 17 and whose product is 72. The numbers are 8 and 9. If the product is 56 and one part is 8, the other part must be 7. Then the sum is 15. If the sum is 20 and the product is 36, the students must find two numbers whose sum is 20 and whose product is 36. This is more difficult. At first, one pupil may answer 4 and 9. It is true that 4×9 equals 36, but the sum of 4 and 9 is 13. This student is "president of the half-right club." Another student may say 6 and 6. Again, it is true that 6×6 is 36 but the sum of 6 and 6 is 12. Now we have a "vice-president of the half-right club." After much thinking, someone will say 18 and 2. This is correct because the sum of 18 and 2 is 20 and the product is 36. Pupils need brain twisters like this to pose a challenge to them. If the sum is 24 and the product is 140, hint that pupils should look at the 0 in 140. The answer is 14 and 10.

Another way to practice multiplication is by using the square game used in addition. Give the class two factors and two products. What times 7 is 56? The answer, 8, is written in the square next to 7. What times 7 is equal to 35? The answer, 5, is written in the square below 7.

Then, what is the product of 5 × 8? The product, 40, is written below the product 56. What is the product of 8 × 8? The product, 64, is written next to the product 35. Now the difficult one: What is the product of 56 × 40? The product, 2,240, is written in the small square, the space for the grand product.

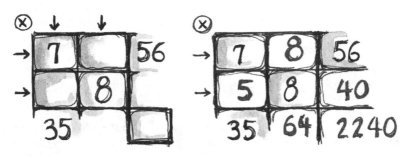

To check, What is the product of 35 × 64? The product is 2240. The problem checks.

MULTIPLICATION IN OTHER BASES

For some students a good way to practice the techniques of multiplication is to multiply numbers represented by numerals in other bases. The first step is to know the basic facts in that number base. There are twenty-five basic facts in base five, shown in the following table.

×	0	1	2	3	4
0	0	0	0	0	0
1	0	1	2	3	4
2	0	2	4	11	13
3	0	3	11	14	22
4	0	4	13	22	31

Ask the students to fill in the table with the products. When multiplying 4 × 4, think of 4 sets of 4 being grouped in fives. The answer is 31 base five. These facts are used in compound multiplication. Also, the students must remember how to add in base five. In the problem 423 × 34 in base five, he must first multiply 4 ones times 3 ones. The table shows

Base Five

```
    4 2 3
  × 3 4
  ───────
  3 3 0 2
2 3 2 4
───────
3 2,0 4 2
```

that the product is 22. The one 2 is recorded and the other 2 is carried. Then multiply 4 ones times 2 fives. The table shows that this product is 13. Then add 2, which totals to 20. The 0 is recorded and the 2 is carried. Next, 4 ones times 4 twenty-fives. The table shows that the answer is 31. Now 2 is added to 31 and 33 is recorded. This is the first partial product. Now 3 fives times 3 ones is 14. The four is recorded in the five's place and the 1 is carried. Three fives times 2 fives is 11. The 1 is added to 11 and the sum is 12. The 2 is recorded and the 1 is carried. To complete, 3 fives times 4 twenty-fives is 22. The 1 is added to 22 and the sum is 23, which is recorded. Now the two partial products are added. In the one's place will be 2 and in the five's place will be 4. Now add 3 and 2, which is 10. Record the 0 and carry the 1. Now add 3 and 3 and 1, which is 12. The 2 is recorded and the 1 is carried. Now add 2 and the 1 and record the 3. When multiplying in another base, students are reviewing all the steps of multiplying in base ten. He must go slower and think about each step. No one can multiply in base five or any other base as fast as in base ten. Multiplying in other bases emphasizes the importance of the facts and the need to use the basic facts and renaming to perform the operation.

SUMMARY

The most important property taught in the unit on multiplication is the distributive property of multiplication over addition. It is used in multiplying a two-digit number by a one-digit number such as 12×4. This involves multiplying 4×2, then 4×10, or multiplying tens and ones with nothing to carry. When multiplying 132×3, the property is used again. Here we multiply 3×2, then 3×20 and 3×100. This problem involves multiplying hundreds, tens, and ones, with nothing to carry. Now, in 17×4, multiply 4×7 and 4×10. This time there is something to carry from ones to tens. Next, give students exercises such as 132×4, where the 4 is distributive over 2 ones, 3 tens, and 1 hundred. Here there is carrying from tens to hundreds. Finally, in 164×3 the 3 is multiplied by 4 ones, 6 tens, and 1 hundred and there is double carrying involved. Because the distributive property is a unifying concept, third graders can do all the exercises shown above, whereas in the traditional programs before the distributive property was taught, they could do only the first two exercises. Now the property is used to explain compound multiplication. Later, students will use the property in multiplying fractional numbers. The same property is valuable in performing simplification in algebra. This shows how various skills are developed from the application of a single idea, in this case, the application of the distributive property of multiplication over addition.

EXERCISES

1. Draw a rectangular array to show that $3 \times 7 = 21$.
2. Using adding equal addends, show what 5×8 means.
3. $3 \times (10 + 4) = (3 \times 10) + (3 \times 4)$ illustrates which property?
4. How can a student use the fact that $3 \times 8 = 24$ to help him find 6×8?
5. Multiply 748×96 using lattice multiplication.
6. $8 \times 0 = 0$ illustrates which property?
7. What is the number 1 called in the operation of multiplication?
8. What properties of multiplication are common to addition?
9. Show how multiplying 47×6 illustrates the distributive property.
10. Why doesn't a pupil have to know subtraction before he learns to multiply?

SELECTED READINGS

BANKS, J. H., *Learning and Teaching Arithmetic*, Chapter 7, Allyn and Bacon, Inc., Boston, 1964.

COPELAND, R. W., *Mathematics and the Elementary Teacher*, 2d ed., W. B. Saunders Company, Philadelphia, 1972, pp. 132–145.

Mathematics for Elementary School Teachers, Chapters 4 and 6, The National Council of Teachers of Mathematics, Washington, D.C., 1966.

School Mathematics Study Group, *Studies in Mathematics, A Brief Course in Mathematics for Elementary School Teachers*, Vol. IV, Stanford University Press, Palo Alto, Calif., 1963, pp. 79–103.

Topics in Mathematics for Elementary School Teachers, Twenty-Ninth Yearbook of the National Council of Teachers of Mathematics, The Council, Washington, D.C., 1964, pp. 59–94.

Division with
Whole Numbers

INTRODUCTION

Division is difficult to learn and to teach because, like subtraction, it is an inverse operation. In multiplication the factors are given and the product is the unknown, but in division the product and one factor are given; one factor is the unknown. The operation of addition is prerequisite to multiplication; the operation of subtraction is a prerequisite of division. Division was invented as a short method for subtracting equal addends. All division problems can be done by subtraction but the process is very often long and tedious.

Teachers should be aware of the fact that long division is difficult for so many pupils because there are so many parts to the process. The various parts depend on knowledge of place value, multiplication, and subtraction. Weakness in any one of the three areas is enough to cause failure more often than success. Present elementary mathematics texts include all the prerequisites for long division. No longer is the shot-gun approach used, in which students began long division before they understood what they were doing. For over thirty years many teachers taught long division by instructing pupils to round off, estimate, multiply, and subtract. In many cases students did not understand the words and consequently did not know what they were expected to do. As a result they found themselves trying to memorize a maze that sometimes would get them through a problem but most often would not. The approach today is to teach all the necessary steps before starting division.

The basic division facts come from the knowledge of the multiplication facts. A multiplication sentence with a missing factor is another way of writing a division fact. This makes learning the facts of division fairly simple for all students who have the multiplication facts well in mind.

Perhaps some day long division will be left for the high school grades and other concepts can be taught in the elementary grades. Even with that happy thought in mind we are still left with the reality of trying to do a better job in teaching division in the elementary grades.

DIVISION IN THE PRIMARY GRADES

Readiness for division begins in the primary grades and involves using sets of objects. A good beginning activity is to have each pupil select 12 objects such as discs. Ask them to make 4 piles with the same number of objects in each pile. When the task is completed, each pupil should have 3 objects in each pile. The teacher approaches the idea of division by asking the question: Twelve divided into 4 equal sets shows how many in each set? Other activities can be performed with the same 12 objects, such as having pupils make 2 equal piles to see how many objects are in each pile. Then make 3 equal piles with the 12 objects and 6 equal sets. The object of these activities is to help pupils understand that they start with the whole number set of 12 and divide it into many equal subsets to find the number of members in each set.

Readiness for multiplication should be combined with readiness for division. Arrange 3 sets of 4 on your desk. How many objects are there? Divide 12 objects into 4 equal sets. How many members in each set? Pupils are being led to understand that in one activity they start with equal sets and form a larger set. This is the model of multiplication. In the other activity they start with the larger set and are told the number of equal sets to form, so they must find the number of members in each set. This is the model of division.

Beginning in the second grade pupils can learn the symbols of the operations. The sentence $3 \times 4 = \square$ is read: Three times four is equal to what number? Or, three sets of four is how much all together? The *equal* symbol has been taught in addition and subtraction and the *times* ($\times$) symbol is taught as the symbol of multiplication. The sentence,

$12 \div 4 = \square$ is read: Twelve divided by 4 is what number? The symbol $\div$ is taught as the symbol of division and is called *divide*.

The sentence starts with a set of 12, and the 4 can be either the number of equivalent sets, or the number of members in the equivalent sets. If 4 is the number of equivalent sets, you are finding the number of members in each equivalent set. This is the partitioning application of division, which is more difficult for pupils. If 4 is the number of members in each equivalent set, then you are finding the number of sets.

SETS AS MODEL OF DIVISION

In these first exercises pupils should draw sets on paper to represent the sentence they see on the chalkboard. They should use the standard models for the numbers 0, 1, 2, 3, 4, 5, 6, 7, 8, 9, and 10, which they were taught when they were learning the whole numbers.

$$8 \div 4 = \square$$

Pupils first draw the model for the number 8, then divide the set into 4 equal sets by using closed curved lines. They can then see that each subset contains 2 objects. The missing factor in the sentence is 2. At first, the larger set should not contain more than 12 objects. In the beginning the teacher directs the activity by telling all the pupils to draw 8 objects and then asks them to divide the set into 4 equal parts. Draw their attention to the first number in the division fact which tells them how many objects there are in the larger set. The second number in the division fact tells them how many equal subsets there are or how many there are in each equal set.

When pupils can successfully draw the objects to represent the division sentence, reverse the activity. Now the teacher draws the picture of the division fact on the board or on papers that are given to the pupils and they write the division sentence that goes with each drawing. To start this activity the teacher should ask: "How many objects are

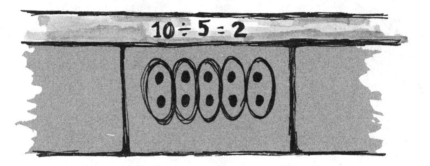

there all together? How many equal subsets are there?" How many objects in each subset? Write the sentence that goes with the drawing. It is important to keep a visual model along with the abstract sentence.

NUMBER LINE AS MODEL OF DIVISION

The number line can also be used as an aid in showing the meaning of division. Assume that the pupils know how to use the number line for substraction problems. They also should know the vector or arrow

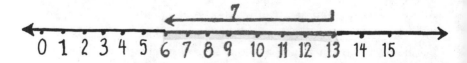

points toward zero on the number line in subtraction. This point can be reviewed in an exercise such as $13 - 7 = 6$, where the arrow or vector starts on 13, goes to the left or toward zero 7 units, and lands on 6. For the division fact $12 \div 4 = \square$, pupils start on 12 and draw vectors or arrows that are 4 units long until the last one lands on 0. This means that one vector goes from 12 to 8, the next from 8 to 4, and the last from 4 to 0. Pupils count the number of vectors, which gives them the missing factor. It is far easier for pupils to look at the number line and

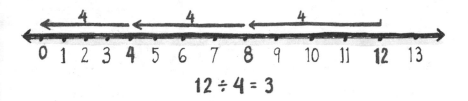

$$12 \div 4 = 3$$

write the sentence than it is for them to draw the vectors on the number line.

A game that can be played on the number line to illustrate division is called having a "cricket convention." All the crickets in the world are having a convention, and they are all standing on number 12. All claim they can make it to zero if they start to jump, going to the left. Remember, a cricket jumps the same number of spaces each time according to the number in his name. A 2 cricket always jumps two spaces in a single jump. Can you show some of the crickets who are telling the truth by drawing arcs on the number line to show the way they jump? The pupil who says the 4 cricket will show that he first lands on 8, then on 4, and finally on zero. Cricket 4 is telling the truth. He takes 3 jumps to get to zero. The 6 cricket will land first on 6, then on 0. He takes 2 jumps to get to zero. The 1 cricket really has to jump because he takes 12 jumps to get to zero. If some pupil suggests that the 5 cricket is telling the truth, ask him to show the jumps. He will see the cricket land first on 7, then on 2. What happens if it jumps again? Some pupils will say that it will jump over zero and land on the other side. You may even find a pupil who knows that the cricket will land on negative 3. This cricket is not telling the truth because it does not land on zero.

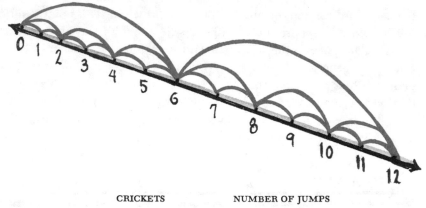

CRICKETS	NUMBER OF JUMPS
4	3
6	2
1	12
3	4
2	6
12	1

After all the crickets such as 6, 1, 2, 4, 3, 12 have been named, the teacher can relate the game to the solution of division facts. What is 12 divided by 4? Think of 12 on the number line with a 4 cricket. How many jumps does the cricket take to reach zero? Then 12 divided by 4 is 3. The convention can be held on various numbers such as 14 or 20, but 12 is the best number because 12 has the most whole number factors.

The number line activities show that division is a short method of subtracting equal addends. Start with 18 and subtract 6 as many times as possible. The pupils will write $18 - 6 = 12$; $12 - 6 = 6$; $6 - 6 = 0$. How many times did you subtract 6? Then 18 divided by 6 is 3.

MISSING FACTORS

After students have started to learn the multiplication facts through 5×9 in the second and third grades, they can begin to learn the basic division facts up to a dividend or product of 45. Four times what is 24?

Pupils who know that 4×6 equals 24 should be able to find the missing factor. Then $24 \div 4$ is what? This is the same question written as a division fact. They are finding the missing factor when given the product, 24, and one factor, 4. In multiplication, the sentence reads, 4 sets of what equal 24? In the division sentence it says 24 is divided into 4 equal sets containing how many members? The question is the same and can be written as either a multiplication sentence with a missing factor or as a division sentence. Exercises should be designed so that pupils can fill in the missing factor, then find the same missing factor in a division sentence. The exercises shown below are examples.

FACTOR		MISSING FACTOR		PRODUCT
3	$\times$	□	=	21
4	$\times$	□	=	20

PRODUCT		FACTOR		MISSING FACTOR
21	$\div$	3	=	□
20	$\div$	4	=	□

In the early stages the words *product* and *factor* should be used in both multiplication and division exercises. The words *dividend, divisor,* and *quotient* will be taught in the middle grades.

Facts involving zero should be omitted at this time. You cannot divide by zero in our number system but this should not be explained until the middle grades. The number 1 can be used as a factor in the division problems as well as in the multiplication problems.

The next stage is to design exercises of multiplication sentences with a missing factor and ask pupils to write the division sentence that asks the same question. Reverse exercises also should be administered in which pupils are given the division sentences and asked to write the multiplication sentence. Include some exercises which require pupils to draw a picture of the sentence. Teachers should remember that they and their pupils must be able to draw a picture of the skill being taught so that pupils can understand clearly the operation in question. If they cannot draw such a picture, then they do not understand what they are doing. Encourage picture drawing to prevent the work from becoming mechanical. Teach the division facts concurrently with the multiplication sentences to help pupils understand that division is the inverse of multiplication.

EVEN DIVISION

Even division yields a remainder of zero. To say that 12 is divisible by 6 means that 12 divided by 6 comes out even with a remainder of 0. In the third grade, when pupils learn the concept of multiples, they are learning that multiples are products with one of the factors given. The multiple of 3 are all the products that have 3 as a factor. When we ask for the divisors of 12 we are asking for all the factors that have 12 as one of its multiples, or all the factors which divide into 12 evenly with a remainder of zero. The factors of 12 are 1, 2, 3, 4, and 6. Until virtually the end of third grade pupils will be concerned only with even division.

UNEVEN DIVISION

Uneven division yields some remainder besides 0. When dividing a set of objects into equal sets, some objects are left over. Choose a set of objects such as 17. Ask pupils to divide the set into 3 equal piles. They will see that they have 5 in each pile and 2 left over. This means that 17 divided by 3 is 5 with a remainder of 2. Activities should be planned in which pupils are given various numbers of objects to divide into equal sets with some objects left over.

The cricket game on the number line illustrates uneven division. If a cricket convention is arranged on 20 and all claim that they can jump to the left and land on zero, some of the crickets are not telling the truth. Can you find some of the crickets that are not telling the truth? As the pupils name crickets they should show where the cricket lands on the last jump. The cricket cannot jump over zero. The name of the cricket, the number of jumps, and the landing place should all be recorded on the board in a table. If the 6 cricket is chosen, a pupil can show that it first lands on 14, then on 8, and finally on 2. If it jumps again it will jump over 0 and land on the other side. The 8 cricket would

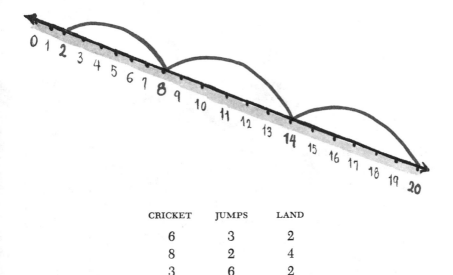

CRICKET	JUMPS	LAND
6	3	2
8	2	4
3	6	2
11	1	9

land first on 12, then on 4. It makes two jumps and lands on 4. It is not telling the truth because it cannot make it to zero. All this activity should be recorded on the board. After a number of crickets have been named and the activity has been recorded, the pupils can look at the table and see that the number the cricket lands on is always smaller than the size of the cricket. The exercises from the table can then be phrased as division exercises; i.e., $20 \div 6 = 3$ r2 means 20 divided by 6 is 3 with a remainder of 2. The number of jumps and the landing place are recorded in the answer. Twenty divided by 6 is the same as starting at 20 on the number line and having a 6 cricket jump to the left. He jumps 3 times and lands on 2, so the answer is 3 r2. The number of jumps is called the quotient and the landing place is called the remainder. The 6 is the divisor and the 20 is called the dividend.

Another activity involves the circular number line. Sometimes teachers call this a Martian number line. The number line can be divided into 5 equal pieces and the numbers 0, 1, 2, 3, and 4 are recorded.

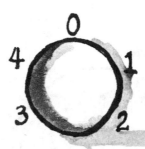

Each pupil should have his own number line sketched on a piece of paper. Starting on zero and moving clockwise, where do you land if you take six steps? The answer is 1. Starting on zero and moving 12 steps, where do you land? This time the answer is 2. Start on zero and move 20 steps. Where do you land? The answer is zero. Start at zero and move 36 steps. Where do you land? This is a difficult one. The answer is 1. After the activity has continued for about five minutes some of the pupils will be giving all the answers correctly and very quickly. Others will be still counting each step and taking more time. When over half the class has found a quick method of finding the answers, the teacher should ask one of the pupils to tell the others how he does the work. The pupil will probably say that 5, 10, 15, 20, 25, 30, 35, and so on, all land on zero. He is saying that all the multiples of 5 land on zero on the number line. When you are moving 36 steps you know that 35 lands on zero, so 36 lands on 1. The number line was divided into 5 equal parts for the first activity because pupils can count by fives easier than by other numbers. Using the number line, show 13 divided 5. Take 13 steps on the number line to find where you land. This is the remainder. How many times do you go around the number line? This is the quotient. Thirteen divided by 5 means how many 5s are there in 13? The answer is 2 with 3 left over. Pupils should be given many exercises using 5 as the divisor and show how they arrive at their answers by using the circular number line.

After working a number of division problems with 5 as the divisor, pupils should see that the remainders are always 0, 1, 2, 3, and 4. Then ask: "Is it possible to have a remainder greater than 4 when dividing by 5?" If a pupil says "yes," ask him to state a problem to illustrate. He will soon see that if the remainder is 6 he can go around the circle once more and would have a remainder of 1. Try to impress the idea early that the remainder must always be less than the divisor. If it is not clear, make another set the size of the divisor.

When working with division problems with divisors represented by other one-digit numbers, such as 6, pupils can make circles and divide them into as many equal parts as the divisor demands. Have them use the circular number line to find the answers to their problems. This will lead the pupils to think of the multiples of 6 when they divide by 6. For example, $27 \div 6 = \square$. Here pupils must think of the numbers times 6 that yield a product less than or equal to 27. They find one fact to be $4 \times 6 = 24$ and another to be $5 \times 6 = 30$; so $27 \div 6$ is 4 with a remainder of 3. This thought process should be encouraged and developed through the exercises that the pupils are given.

Dividing with multiples of ten also can be taught in the third grade. What is 3 tens divided by 3? This means there are 3 sets of tens divided into 3 equal sets. How many in each set? The exercise should be written in two forms:

$$\begin{array}{r} 10 \\ 3\overline{)30} \end{array} \quad \text{and} \quad 30 \div 3 = 10.$$

Exercises can be designed to show the relationship between dividing by tens and dividing by ones. If a pupil knows that $9 \div 3 = 3$, then $90 \div 3 = 30$. Pupils must be encouraged to think of 160 as 16 tens. Then 16 tens divided by 4 is 4 tens. Twenty-four tens divided by 4 is 6 tens.

$$16 \div 4 = \square \qquad 8 \div 2 = \square \qquad 6 \div 3 = \square \qquad 24 \div 4 = \square$$
$$160 \div 4 = \square \qquad 80 \div 2 = \square \qquad 60 \div 3 = \square \qquad 240 \div 4 = \square$$

Once they are successful with exercises such as these, they can divide with other two-digit numbers. When dividing 39 by 3, think of

39 as $(30 + 9)$; then divide by 3. Now there are two problems. One is $30 \div 3$, the other is $9 \div 3$. This is the distributive property of division over addition. The quotient is $10 + 3$ or 13. It is hard to teach pupils

$$
\begin{array}{ccc}
13 & & 10 + 3 \\
3\overline{)39} & \text{or} & 3\overline{)30 + 9}
\end{array}
$$

to rename the two-digit number with multiples of the divisor. The tens part of the renaming must be a multiple of 3; the ones part of the renaming must be a multiple of 3. In dividing 93 by 3, rename 93 so that the tens part and the ones part each are multiples of 3. Now divide $90 + 3$ by 3 in two steps, first the tens, then the ones. With directions like this, pupils can begin to do division problems in which the quotient has a two-digit numeral for an answer. For the slower students, pictures can be drawn of the sets of tens and the sets of ones. They then can draw circles around the objects in the set to show the division.

In the primary grades the objective is to teach the meaning of division. This must be done with concrete experiences. Then make the connection to the missing factor of multiplication. Experience with even and uneven division with one-digit divisors begins. Seeds are planted early; time is needed to bring the concept to full bloom. The purpose of the primary grades is to plant the seeds; mastery will come later in the middle grades. The creative teacher will devise many games to help pupils see what the operation of division means. Activities must be varied and planned so that the students succeed.

DIVISION IN THE MIDDLE GRADES

The first prerequisite of learning long division is to know all the basic multiplication and division facts. There is no hope of succeeding in long division if these facts are not fully mastered. Every teacher in the middle grades will find a few students who still have trouble with some of the facts. Practice must be provided for these students.

Games are a good technique for practice. A large chart can be made of cardboard with the factors from 0 to 10 written across the top and side with blank squares for the products. Small squares are made to fit on the chart. On one side of the small square will be a multiplica-

×	0	1	2	3	4	5	6	7	8	9	10
0											
1											
3											
4											

etc.

tion fact such as $7 \times 8 = ?$ or a missing factor sentence such as $7 \times ? = 56$. Students are given a certain number of cards with blank sides up. They take turns playing a card. If they have a card that has a green mark in the corner, they may play two cards instead of one. If they have a card with a red mark in the corner, they must draw an extra card from the pile left over and forfeit their play. Many variations can be devised and other games invented. Students should play with other players of about the same ability. Pupils who know all the facts can act as judges for a game to determine whether the plays made are correct.

A three-minute speed test on the 100 basic facts is good practice for students who are not sure of them. Keep a record of the number of problems they work correctly each time they take a test to show their rate of improvement over the year.

Students should be motivated to use the multiplication chart for both the multiplication and the division facts. A teacher who smiles and says, "Look up the facts you are not sure of," is using the positive approach. Each time a student looks up a fact and records the correct response he is reinforcing his grasp of the facts. Positive responses will insure success much quicker than frowns and nagging. All students want to succeed but some have more difficulty in memorizing or understanding. They need encouragement and understanding.

Place value of digits is an important prerequisite for division. Students should be able to look at 467 and see that the number is made up of 46 tens and 7 ones, as well as 4 hundreds, 6 tens, and 7 ones. For those who have difficulty with place value in the middle grades, using money to illustrate the renaming involved is one of the best methods to help them understand. They must always remember that 1 hundred is the same as 10 tens; 1 thousand is the same as 10 hundreds. Often the slower students must learn to build the number. Here it is necessary to start with 4 hundreds, 6 tens, and 7 ones. Next, write the number with tens and ones only as 46 tens and 7 ones, and then write the three-digit numeral. The pupils must practice changing the hundreds into tens before they can say that there are 46 tens and 7 ones, merely by looking at 467. Give them exercises like this for drill and include thousands as well as tens and hundreds.

The use of inequality sentences can teach the students to think about what number is closest to the missing factor in division. For example, in dividing 17 by 5 most of us ask: What is the largest whole number times 5 that is less than or equal to 17? We can answer the question only if we know the multiplication facts of 5. Students must practice using sentences that require this type of thinking before they start long division. This is another prerequisite of division. The symbol $\leq$ means *less than or equal.*

Find the largest whole number to make the sentence true.

$$\square \times 9 \leq 47 \qquad\qquad \square \times 8 \leq 51$$
$$5 \times \square \leq 39 \qquad\qquad 7 \times \square \leq 60$$

Find the largest multiple of 10 to make the sentence true. (Multiples of 10 are 10, 20, 30, 40, 50, 60, 70, 80, and 90.)

$$\square \times 7 \leq 387 \qquad\qquad \square \times 9 \leq 569$$
$$8 \times \square \leq 436 \qquad\qquad 6 \times \square \leq 510$$

Find the largest multiple of 100 that makes the sentence true. (Multiples of 100 are 100, 200, 300, 400, 500, 600, 700, 800, and 900.)

$$\square \times 4 \leq 2,768 \qquad\qquad \square \times 5 \leq 4,358$$
$$8 \times \square \leq 5,867 \qquad\qquad 9 \times \square \leq 7,380$$

Slower students should be encouraged to list all the multiples of 10 or 100—and then pick out the largest one to make the sentence true. They should practice multiplying by multiples of 10 and 100. What is 7×800? What is 7×90? As difficult as these exercises with inequality may seem to the slower pupils, they must continue to try to find a way to answer them for they need to master this technique. There is no easy way or short-cut. Those who cannot solve inequality sentences should be given more work in multiplication and place value. They are not ready for long division and should not yet attempt it.

Division should be introduced dramatically to involve students and help them understand what occurs when they divide. One way is to start the lesson by throwing out on the table 367 tongue depressors. Give some student in the class a bunch of rubber bands and ask him to start bundling the tongue depressors into sets of 9. As he bundles, have another student show the number left each time he bands a group by performing the subtraction on the board. The pupil at the board will write $367 - 9 = 358$; $358 - 9 = 349$; $349 - 9 = 340$, and so on. The other students should check the work on the board to be sure it is correct. Soon some student will say that it is not necessary to do all this work. If 10 bundles make 90, 20 bundles make 180, and so on. Now the student can stop bundling and the class should begin discussing just how many sets of 10 there should be. One of the brighter students will say 40 because 40×9 is 360. With this type of introduction students see that the work could be done by subtracting 9s until they run out of depressors. But by thinking in terms of multiples of 10s they can save themselves a lot of work. Now start explaining how the largest multiple of 10 will be used in the division process.

VARIOUS METHODS OF LONG DIVISION

The scaffolding or ladder approach to long division is used in the early stages to help students think about the place value of each digit. In this method students use the whole divisor and the whole dividend. They can work the problems in many ways.

```
                                                            4 3
                                                             3
        4 3              4 3              4 3               4 0
      9) 3 8 7          9) 3 8 7         9) 3 8 7          9) 3 8 7
       3 6 0 | 4 0       1 8 0 | 2 0      9 0 | 1 0         3 6 0 → 9 × 4 0
        2 7              2 0 7            2 9 7              2 7
        2 7 | 3          1 8 0 | 2 0      9 0 | 1 0          2 7 → 9 × 3
          0 | 4 3          2 7 | 3        2 0 7                0
                           2 7            9 0 | 1 0
                             0 | 4 3      1 1 7
                                          9 0 | 1 0
                                          2 7
                                          2 7 | 3
                                            0 | 4 3
```

Any student who can look at 387 divided by 9 and say that the largest multiple of 1 is 40 because 40 × 9 is 360 and 360 is less than 387 is on the road to the short method of long division. Others may have to think of 20 and use it twice. Still others may be more secure at first using 10 over and over again. In each case they arrive at the correct answer. Some teachers prefer that the partial products be written in the quotient because students do not make a mistake when they carry the answer up to the quotient, as they might with the scaffolding method. In the early stages of learning division the teacher should continue to ask questions about the largest whole number, the largest multiple of ten, and the largest multiple of 100. Exercises should be prepared so that students can answer questions as they work the division problems. An example of such an exercise is given below.

$$8) \overline{5 3 8}$$

1. Can you use a multiple of 100 for the quotient?   _____
2. Is 8 × 100 larger or smaller than 538?   _____
3. Can you use a multiple of 10 for the quotient?   _____

4. What is the largest multiple of 10 you can use?   _____
5. Why can't you use 70 in the quotient?   _____
6. Why do you subtract 480 from 538?   _____
7. What is the largest whole number $\times$ 8 that is less than or equal to 58?   _____
8. What is the remainder?   _____

Fewer problems should be given but the students·should answer the questions for each problem to show that they understand what they are doing. This will provide them with a mental model to use as they solve problems independently.

The scaffolding method, once mastered by the slower student, is difficult to transfer to the standard method of division. For this reason it is best to start all students with the standard method, allowing them at first to write partial quotients above the line.

Teachers should find time to spend five minutes alone with a student who is having difficulty with division to determine where his trouble lies. If the trouble is mistakes in multiplication, other work should be recommended to clear up the deficiency. If the trouble is mistakes in subtraction, more work on subtraction should be given. Remember that 100 minutes of instruction on long division with the teacher at the chalkboard demonstrating how to solve the problems is not going to answer the questions of every student. Part of the time given to mathematics each day must be spent working with individual students or in small groups. Show-and-tell method of instruction will not teach those who are having real difficulties.

One of the worst mistakes made by many teachers in the middle grades is introducing problems with two- and three-digit divisors too soon. At first, confine problems to those with one-digit divisors, while increasing the dividend. Everyone can perform more accurately when multiplying with one-digit divisors and a dividend in multiples of 10,

$$9\overline{)56} \qquad 9\overline{)407} \qquad 8\overline{)3,489} \qquad 7\overline{)64,803}$$

100, and 1000. For example, 7×400 is much easier than 23×30. Everything that is practiced with one-digit divisors will apply to larger divisors.

In some exercises the steps used in the division problem should be reviewed before the division problem is attempted to see if the students can perform each of the steps. For example, in dividing 517 by 8 the following exercises should be given. If the students can multiply 80×6, 8×4, and subtract 480 from 517, they should be able to divide 517 by 8.

1. $80 \times 6 = \square$ 2. $8 \times 4 = \square$ 3. $\begin{array}{r} 5\,1\,7 \\ -\,4\,8\,0 \\ \hline \end{array}$ 4. $8\overline{)5\,1\,7}$

If any mistakes are made in the first three exercises, they will not be successful with the division.

Exercises should be designed so that students can look at various answers to a problem and pick the one that seems the most sensible or reasonable. Which of the answers shown here is the most reasonable?

1. $6\overline{)1\,8\,4\,5}$ a. 37 r3   b. 307 r3   c. 3070 r3

Students should look at the problem and see that they can use a multiple of 100, so the answer will be in the hundreds and therefore could not be 37 or 3070. Another approach to the same type of exercise is to give a division problem and ask whether the quotient will be a one-, two- or three-digit number. Students must learn to look at a problem and estimate the answer before they start to work. Only in this way can they become aware of answers that do not make sense. For years mathematics teachers mistakenly asked only for answers and never asked students to analyze the problem before they started to find the answer.

ZERO IN QUOTIENT

Students have trouble with zero in the quotient because they are concerned only with finishing the problem—not with whether the answer is reasonable. In the exercise 1845 divided by 6, students should see that they can use multiples of 100. After they have decided that 300 is the largest multiple of 100 that can be used, they multiply 300 by 6 to get the product, 1800, and the remainder, 45. The next question is, What is the largest multiple of 10 that can be used? The answer is

0, or no multiple of 10 because 6×10 is greater than 45. The next question is, How will you show in the quotient that there are no multiples of 10? The answer should be that a zero is written in the ten's place. What will happen if you fail to write the zero in the ten's place? The answer is that the quotient will be 37 instead of 307. Is 37 a sensible or reasonable answer when you knew in the beginning that a multiple of 100 could be used? This type of questioning must be used throughout the drill and a zero should be written in the ten's place on the blackboard for the entire class to see. Students must be required to check all division problems immediately. They check by multiplying the quotient times the divisor, then adding the remainder to the result. If the result is not the same as the divisor, they must try to find their error. It is more useful to assign 10 division problems for the class to estimate first, then work and check the answers, than to assign 30 division problems and require that only the answers be found. Estimating and checking are just as important as solving the problem. Help students understand the importance you attach to estimating and checking.

TWO- AND THREE-DIGIT DIVISORS

Before assigning problems with two- and three-digit divisors, practice multiplying two- and three-digit numbers times multiples of 10 and 100. What is 23×20? What is 37×300? Work on mental computation—doing most of the work without pencil and paper. Hand out a sheet containing problems such as 45×40, 56×400, and 67×500. Ask them to write down the products without doing any figuring on paper. This type of work should cover several days and students should keep track of the number they estimate correctly each day to see if they improve as they practice.

The next set of exercises should be designed so that they can estimate the number of tens or hundreds that will be needed. Ask them to write which answer is most reasonable in each case.

1. $23 \times ?$ is less than or equal to 56 tens? 2 tens? 3 tens? 4 tens?
2. $14 \times ?$ is less than or equal to 72 hundreds? 4 hundreds? 5 hundreds? 6 hundreds?

To answer the questions, students must think: 23×2 tens is 46 tens, 23×3 tens is 69 tens. Therefore, 2 tens is the best answer. In the next exercise the students must think that 14×4 hundreds is 56 hundreds, 14×5 hundreds is 70 hundreds, and 14×6 hundreds is 84 hundreds. Therefore, 5 hundreds is the best answer. This skill being practiced is used in the short process of long division.

Most students have had experience in rounding off numbers to the nearest tens, hundreds, and thousands long before they come to the unit on long division. Rounding off should be reviewed once again before they go much further in division. When rounding off to the nearest tens, look at the one's place. If the digit is 5 or less, leave the ten's digit as it is. This means that 31, 32, 33, 34, and 35 rounded off to the nearest tens is 30. If the digit in the one's place is greater than 5, the digit in the ten's place is increased by one. Thus, 36, 37, 38, and 39 rounded off to the nearest ten would be 40. When rounding off to the nearest hundreds, look at the ten's place to see if the digit is less than or greater than 5. The only time it is necessary to look at the one's place in rounding off to the nearest hundreds is when the digit in the ten's place is 5; if there is any digit in the one's place larger than 0, the ten's place becomes more than 5 and would round off to the next larger digit in the hundred's place. Exercises should be designed for students to practice rounding off to the nearest tens and the nearest hundreds.

When starting long division with a two-digit divisor, the teacher should help students break the problem up into small parts so that they can see and understand each step. In the example that follows, the problem is stated and the questions to ask are listed. Students should work the problem as they answer the questions for each step. This may seem like a long and involved process but it provides students with a mental model to be used for all problems.

$$32 \overline{)913} \qquad\qquad\qquad \text{Check}$$

1. What is 32×100? _____
2. Can you make 100 sets of 32 with 913 objects? _____

3. How many tens in 913? _____
4. Draw a line under the digits 9 and 1 in the dividend.
5. Can you make 20 sets of 32 with 913 objects? _____
6. What is 30×32? _____
7. Is 2 tens the largest multiple of 10 you can use? _____
8. Write 2 tens in the ten's place of the quotient over the dividend.
9. Multiply 2 tens $\times$ 32 and write the number of tens below the 91 tens.
10. Subtract 64 from 91 and write the remainder.
11. Stop and check your subtraction by adding 64, and the remainder, to see if the sum is 91.
12. Write the 3 ones next to the 27 tens in the remainder.
13. Do you think 9 sets of 32 is less than or equal to 273? _____
    Think $9 \times (30 + 2) = (9 \times 30) + (9 \times 2) = ?$
14. If 9 sets is too large, what will you try next? _____
15. What is 32×8? _____
16. Write the 8 in the one's place of the quotient and write the product beneath 273.
17. Subtract 256 from 273 and check your answer by adding.
18. Is the remainder less than the divisor? _____
19. Write a small letter r next to the one's place of the quotient; then write the remainder.
20. Check your answer by multiplying the quotient times the divisor and adding the remainder.

Students should be given about six problems to complete along the lines of those just listed. The teacher and students should work the first long division problem, then the students should work the other five by themselves. Now the teacher has time to turn to the slower students and give them extra help.

In the next set of exercises students can use the idea of rounding off the divisor to make multiplication easier. Again, the exercises should be planned with a series of questions that will lead the pupils through each step. To teach a skill as difficult as long division, the steps must be written to program the student to respond correctly; thus the steps in the process become a part of his working scheme.

$$27\overline{)1\,6\,0\,8}$$ Check

1. What is 100×27? ____
2. Can you make 100 sets of 27 with 1,608 objects? ____
3. How many tens in 1,608? __
4. Draw a line segment under the digits 1, 6, and 0 in the dividend.
5. Round off 27 to the nearest ten. __
6. Thirty times what is less than or equal to 160 tens? __
7. Write the digit 5 in the ten's place of the quotient above the digits in the dividend.
8. Multiply 5 tens $\times$ 27 and write the product under 160 tens.
9. Subtract the product from 160 and check by addition.
10. Write the 8 from the one's place to the right of the digits 2 and 5.
11. What is 8×27? ____ What is 9×27? ____
12. Can you make 9 sets of 27 with 258 objects? ____
13. Write the digit 9 in the one's place of the quotient.
14. Write the product of 9×27 below 258 and subtract. Check the subtraction by addition.
15. Is the remainder less than the divisor? ____
16. Write the small letter r next to the one's place of the quotient then write the remainder.
17. Check your work by multiplying the quotient times the divisor and adding the remainder.

After students have worked a few exercises, they are ready to try division problems without the questions. Those still having difficulty will need the teacher's help with the steps that are still giving them difficulty.

It is very easy for a teacher in the upper middle grades to lose patience with students who still do not understand division after she has worked with them for several days. We need to remind ourselves constantly that division is a very difficult process and that the concentration required, besides the skills involved, is tremendous for the average or below-average students. To establish empathy with slower students, the teacher should try dividing with numerals written in some base other than ten. He will become as confused as the slow students and see why they find the work very tedious and unexciting.

There is no law in mathematics that says that everyone must work problems by the short method. The important idea is to help students find some method that is meaningful to them so that they can savor the success that goes with finding the right answer. If a student cannot round off and needs to use the whole divisor, he should proceed in this way.

A very bright boy in eighth grade once said that he had enjoyed sixth grade the most. When asked why he said, "Mr. B. was a great teacher but he did not understand mathematics very well. He let the ones who did understand teach the others. And do you know something? You never really understand long division until you teach it!" Too often teachers forget that many bright students in mathematics would like to help the slower ones—and they are well able to do so. We should let them experience the thrill that goes with helping others. Often those who can compute easily gain a great deal by teaching others because by teaching they gain insight into the meaning of the computation that they could not acquire in any other way.

SUMMARY

Division is a difficult operation and few teachers have found a way to make it exciting. The prerequisites of the process must be checked. Students must practice all the steps in the operation before they start to put the steps together.

Textbooks do not provide enough exercises to prepare pupils for the final process. Teachers must provide this instruction themselves. By listening and watching students, teachers should be able to decide where they need help. One thing we surely know is that the old show-and-tell method that illustrated the last stage of long division without taking up the intermediate steps never taught the average or below-average students. Division must be approached in steps, by looking at the parts involved and by teaching students to perform the parts oper-ations successfully, thus preparing them for the final stage.

EXERCISES

1. Name three prerequisites of long division.
2. Multiplication is the short method of adding equal addends. Division is the short method of what operation?
3. What question do you ask yourself when you divide 17 by 5?
4. Illustrate with the numbers 7 and 56 that a multiplication sentence with a missing factor is another way of writing a division fact.
5. Why is it important for the slower learner to stay with division problems that have only one digit in the divisor?
6. Show how the distributive property may be applied in the example $396 \div 3$.
7. What is even division?
8. Which should be emphasized first in long division, estimating the answer or finding the answer?

SELECTED READINGS

Banks, J. H., *Learning and Teaching Arithmetic*, Allyn and Bacon, Inc., Boston, 1964, pp. 255–270.

Dumas, E., *Math Activities for Child Development*, Allyn and Bacon, Inc., Boston, 1971, pp. 1960–1990.

Marks, J. L., C. R. Purdy, and L. B. Kenney, *Teaching Elementary School Mathematics for Understanding*, 3d ed., McGraw-Hill Book Company, New York, 1970, pp. 126–138.

Mathematics for Elementary School Teachers, The National Council of Teachers of Mathematics, Washington, D.C., 1966, Chapters 4 and 6.

School Mathematics Study Group, *Studies in Mathematics, A Brief Course in Mathematics for Elementary School Teachers*, Vol. IX, Stanford University Press, Palo Alto, California, 1963, pp. 107–124.

Van Engen, H., and E. C. Gibb, *General Mental Functions Associated with Division*, Iowa State Teachers College, Cedar Falls, Iowa, 1956.

Number Theory

INTRODUCTION

Students can play a better game of mathematics when they know more about the properties of the numbers involved in the game. Number theory is that part of mathematics that deals with the study of the properties of integers. Only a part of number theory is taught in elementary mathematics, the part concerned with the set of whole numbers. The sets of odd and even numbers and primes and composites are subsets of the set of whole numbers and the properties of these sets, too, must be learned in elementary mathematics. Rules of division are part of the study of number theory. In teaching the "why" of mathematics, students must have, first of all, a knowledge of the properties of the whole numbers. Later in their study of mathematics we extend this knowledge to the properties of the integers.

NUMBER THEORY IN THE PRIMARY GRADES

In the first grade pupils learn that the set of numbers written in base ten which end in 0, 2, 4, 6, 8, in the one's place are called even numbers. The set of numbers written in base ten which end in 1, 3, 5, 7, 9, in the one's place are called odd numbers. As addition and subtraction are taught in the first and second grades, attention should be drawn to the pattern that develops when adding and subtracting odd and even numbers. As exercises are assigned in addition and subtraction, pupils should label the addends and sums according to whether they are odd numbers or even numbers. Looking at exercises similar to the following, pupils should begin to make some generalizations about the sums of odd and even numbers, odd and odd numbers, and even and even numbers.

$$6 + 4 = \boxed{10} \qquad \boxed{7} + 5 = 12 \qquad 8 + \boxed{5} = 13$$

$$\underline{E} \quad \underline{E} \quad \underline{E} \qquad \underline{O} \quad \underline{O} \quad \underline{E} \qquad \underline{E} \quad \underline{O} \quad \underline{O}$$

$$12 - 5 = \boxed{7} \qquad 14 - \boxed{6} = 8 \qquad \boxed{15} - 7 = 8$$

$$\underline{E} \quad \underline{O} \quad \underline{O} \qquad \underline{E} \quad \underline{E} \quad \underline{E} \qquad \underline{O} \quad \underline{O} \quad \underline{E}$$

Questions like the following are helpful: When you add an even number to an even number, what kind of number is the sum? When you add an odd number to an odd number, what kind of number is the sum? When you add an even number to an odd number, what kind of number is the sum? In subtraction, if the sum is even and the addend is odd, what kind of number is the missing addend? In subtraction, when the sum is an odd number and the addend is an odd number, what kind of number is the missing addend? In adding two numbers, if the sum is an even number, can you tell whether the addends were odd or even? (No, you cannot.) In adding two numbers, if the sum is odd what do you know about the addends? (One is even, the other is odd.) Pupils should become aware of what to expect when they add 8 and 7—an odd or an even number. The sum must be an odd number and the answer therefore cannot be 14. Ask the pupils to label the parts of the exercises odd or even and ask them questions. You are thus planting the seed for generalizing the addition and subtraction of odd and even numbers in the third grade.

In the third grade pupils should be given pieces of tag board made of squares to represent some of the odd and some of the even numbers.

The first question to ask is, "How do the shapes representing the odd numbers differ from the shapes representing the even numbers?" It is important that pupils notice that the shapes representing the odd numbers have an extra square attached. All even shapes are large squares or rectangles. The even shapes are made up of sets of 2. This means that 4 sets of 2 is an even number, 100 sets of 2 is an even number, and 17 sets of 2 is an even number. Any number of sets of 2 is an even number. Written in general terms, letting n stand for any number, $2n$ (2 times n) is a symbol for all even numbers. This general way of writing even numbers will come much later in mathematics but teachers must realize that in the third grade the generalization can be presented so that pupils can begin to understand it. The odd shapes are made up of sets of 2 plus one extra square. Therefore, 6 sets of 2 plus 1 is an odd number. Written in general terms, letting n stand for any number, $2n + 1$ (2 times n plus 1) is a symbol for all odd numbers.

ADDING EVEN AND ODD NUMBERS

Now the shapes of odds and evens should be used to illustrate the model for adding odds and evens. Put the 2 shape with the 4 shape. What kind of shape does it make? Does this show that $2 + 4 = 6$? Does it also show that adding an even number to an even number results in an even number? What kind of shape can you make with the odd shape that represents 3 and the even shape that represents 6? When adding an odd number and an even number, what kind of number is the sum? What kind of shape is made with the odd shape that represents 5 and the odd shape that represents 7? When adding an odd number to an odd number, what kind of number is the sum? After many activities such as this, make the addition table for odd and even numbers. Students should tell what the sums are when adding even to even, even

+	E	O
E	E	O
O	O	E

to odd, odd to even, and odd to odd. Using the table, see if the pupils can tell what kind of number the sum would be when adding 3 odd numbers, 5 odd numbers, and 7 odd numbers. After the brighter students have announced that the sums are all odd numbers, explaining that adding an odd number of odd numbers gives an odd number for a sum, illustrate this fact using shapes.

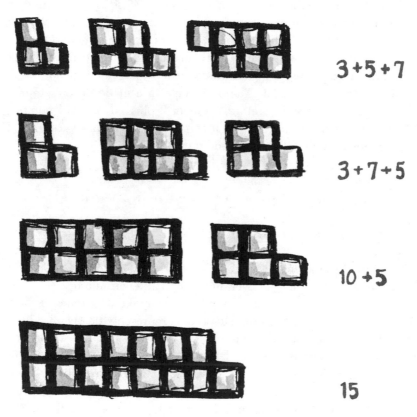

3 + 5 + 7

3 + 7 + 5

10 + 5

15

Beginning with the exercise $3 + 5 + 7$, ask the pupils to take the shapes and put them on their desks in the order of the addends. Now write $3 + 7 + 5$ and ask the students to switch the shapes to match the order of the addends of the new phrase. Now write $10 + 5$ on the board and ask the students to join the shape representing 3 with the shape representing 7 to see that it makes the shape representing 10. This shows again that odd plus odd is even. Now write the sum 15 and ask the students to join the 5 shape to the 10 shape to see that an odd plus an even is an odd sum. The exercise started with 3 odd numbers and the sum is the shape of an odd number. Doing the exercise in steps also illustrates that addition is easier when adding the numbers that make ten. The addends 3 and 7 can change order because of the commutative property of addition. In one exercise, a lot of mathematics can be covered.

Using the table for the addition of odds and evens, students should tell what kind of number the sum would be if you add 4 odd numbers, 6 odd numbers, and 8 odd numbers. Some of the students will soon generalize. When adding an even number of odd numbers, the sum is even. Slower students can be assigned an exercise using the shapes. The teacher might write $1 + 3 + 5 + 7$ on the board and ask the students to put the shapes of the numbers on their desks in the order in which they are written. By joining the shapes students will see that the sum is represented by an even number.

Next, their attention should be drawn to what happens when they add an odd number of even numbers, such as 5 even numbers. Is the sum an odd or even number? What happens when adding an even number of even numbers, such as 4 even numbers? Is the sum an odd or an even number? Some students generalize by replying that evens in addition always produce evens. This is true.

Now is the time to see if students are able to predict the kind of number a sum will be in column addition. Give them a set of column addition and ask them to tell whether the sum is even or odd. They should not add the numbers to find the sum.

	6	7	20	9	2
	8	11	8	7	3
+	5	10	12	5	5
	1	3	7	1	1
	E	O	O	E	O

When the sums have been labeled odd or even and the work has been checked, ask the students to see if they can discover any patterns. What do you look at in the column to decide whether the sum is odd or even? The answer should be, count the number of odd numbers. If the number of odd numbers is odd, the sum is odd; if the number of odd numbers is even, the sum is even. As one student said one day after an exercise like this, "It is simple. Evens don't count so just concentrate on the odds." Students who learn to look for patterns and are able to make some judgments about an answer before they solve it are really learning how to play the game.

SUBTRACTION OF ODD AND EVEN NUMBERS

The table for the generalization of addition of odds and evens can also be used for the generalization of subtraction. Pupils have already learned that subtraction is the inverse of addition as an operation. In subtraction, the sum and one addend are given and the missing addend must be found. This now can be reinforced with the generalization of odds and evens. In the sentence $12 - 7 = \square$, the sum is even and the addend is odd. What must be true of two addends if the sum is an even number? Pupils should reply that the addends are either both odd or both even. Now if the sum is even and one addend is odd, what must the other addend be? The only correct answer is *odd*. In the sentence $17 - 8 = \square$, the sum is odd and the addend is even. What must be true of two addends if the sum is odd? Again, from the table it is apparent that one of the addends is odd and the other addend is even. When the sum is odd and one addend is even, what must the other addend be? The only answer is that the other addend is odd. Pupils should use their knowledge of subtraction in analyzing subtraction sentences to tell whether the parts of the sentence are odd or even. This is excellent reinforcement just at the time in third grade when pupils are apt to become mechanical in their computation.

SQUARE NUMBERS

After multiplication has been introduced in the third grade and most of the pupils are able to multiply the doubles such as 2×2, 3×3, and

4×4, they can begin looking for a pattern in adding odd numbers and discover square numbers. The following four sentences should be written on the chalkboard. Ask the pupils to look at the sentence and tell what kind of numbers are written on the left side of the equations. They

$$1 = 1$$
$$1 + 3 = 4$$
$$1 + 3 + 5 = 9$$
$$1 + 3 + 5 + 7 = 16$$

should say that all the numbers on the left side of the equations are odd numbers and that they are consecutive odd numbers. What kind of numbers are on the right side of the equations? Now the pupils should notice that the numbers alternate odd, even, odd, even. Why do the sums on the right side of the equations alternate odd, even, odd, even? Some pupil will say that when adding odd and odd, the sum is even but when adding odd, odd, and odd, the sum is odd. This brings them back to the concept that an odd number of odd numbers yields a sum that is an odd number. Now ask them to write the next sentence following the pattern established by the four sentences. Most of them will be able to say that $1 + 3 + 5 + 7 + 9 = 25$. How many addends are in the second sentence? The answer is two and the addends are 1 and 3. How can you find the sum of 4 by using multiplication? The correct answer this time is 2×2. In the next sentence how many addends are there? (There are 3.) How can you find the sum of 9 by using multiplication? (Multiply 3×3.) How many addends in the next sentence? (There are 4.) How can you find the sum of 16 by multiplying? (Multiply 4×4.) What is the sum when you add the first five consecutive odd numbers? (The sum is 25.) How can you find the sum of 25 by multiplying? (Multiply 5×5.) Now get ready for a braintwister. What is the sum of $1 + 3 + 5 + 7 + 9 + 11 + 13 + 15 + 17 + 19$? You will be amazed at the number of pupils who will respond 100 almost immediately. When asked how they got the number so quickly, they will say they multiplied 10×10. Those students who responded immediately with 100 have discovered the pattern. Pupils should be told that the set of numbers running 1, 4, 9, 16, 25, ... are called square numbers. Square numbers are numbers whose factors are twins. Is 36 a square number? Why? Pupils will say "yes" because 6×6 equals 36. Is 24 a square number? The answer is "no" because the factors of 24 cannot be twins. Third-grade students can discover square numbers because they have the facts needed to make the discovery. No one can find a pattern in mathematics unless he possesses the knowledge to understand the pattern. Once a student knows about odd and even numbers and addition and some multiplication, he can discover a new set of numbers called square numbers.

NUMBER THEORY IN THE MIDDLE GRADES

In the fourth grade pupils extend their knowledge of multiplication and begin to learn all the multiplication facts. Besides reviewing the generalizations about adding and subtracting odd and even numbers, extend the generalization about odd and even numbers to multiplication.

MULTIPLICATION OF ODD AND EVEN NUMBERS

Every even number has 2 as a factor. This means that every even number can be written as $2 \times$ some number. The other factor can be

$2 \times 7 = 14$

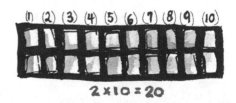

$2 \times 10 = 20$

either odd or even. Show a shape using squares to represent the number 14. Students will have to draw 7 sets of 2 squares. The shape will be the shape of an even number for there will not be any squares left over. Draw a shape to represent the number 20. This shape will show 10 sets of 2. Drawing shapes should convince students that all even numbers have a factor of 2. Now ask them to take the shape that represents 3 and put 5 of them together. Will the shape represent an even or odd number? By drawing the shapes for odd numbers and using an odd

number of these shapes, the final shape will always be an odd shape. This exercise proves that when multiplying an odd number by an odd number, the product is always an odd number. After drawing a few shapes to show the results of multiplying odds and evens, the table for multiplying odd and evens should be made. As students fill in the

$\times$	E	O
E	E	E
O	E	O

products they will realize that the only way to come up with a product that is an odd number is to use all odd factors. If you multiply 4 numbers and the product is an odd number, what do you know about the factors? You know that all the factors are odd numbers. When you multiply 3 numbers and the product is even, what do you know about the factors? The only fact you can be certain of is that at least one of the factors is even. This means that one of the factors could be even and the other two factors odd, or two of the factors could be even and one of the factors odd, or all three of the factors could be even. Why is 62 or 64 a poor guess for the product of 9×7? The product cannot be even because both the factors are odd numbers. Why is 57 a poor guess for the product of 7×8? The product of 7×8 cannot be an odd number because one of the factors is even. As they begin to generalize about the multiplication of odds and evens, students will realize that this is another method of finding answers in multiplication.

DIVISION OF ODD AND EVEN NUMBERS

The multiplication table can also be used to discuss the division of odds and evens. In the sentence $56 \div 7 = \square$ the product is even and the known factor is odd. What must be true about the missing factor? The missing factor must be even because one of the factors must be even if the product is even. In the sentence $63 \div 7 = \square$ the product is odd and the known factor is odd. What must be true about the missing factor? The missing factor must be odd because all the factors are odd if the product is odd. Questioning like this reinforces the idea that division is the inverse of multiplication. In division the product and one factor are given and the missing factor must be found. Students must use their knowledge of the meaning of division when analyzing the division sentence to determine whether the missing factor is odd or even.

FACTORING

Factoring is a very useful notion in mathematics. For instance, a counting number, x, is called a factor or divisor of another counting number, z, if there is another counting number, y, such that x times $y = z$. For example, 2 is a factor of 6 because $2 \times 3 = 6$. Two is also a divisor of 6 because $6 \div 2 = 3$. The number 4 is not a factor of 6 because there is no counting number times 4 that yields the product 6.

To speak of the factors of 12 means all the counting numbers that are factors of 12. One is a factor because $1 \times 12 = 12$. Two is a factor because $2 \times 6 = 12$. Three is a factor because $3 \times 4 = 12$. Four is a factor because $4 \times 3 = 12$. Six is a factor because $6 \times 2 = 12$. Twelve is a factor because $12 \times 1 = 12$. Therefore, 1, 2, 3, 4, 6, and 12 are all factors of 12.

PRIME AND COMPOSITE NUMBERS

One way to begin the unit on prime and composite numbers is to write certain numbers on the chalkboard and ask the students to factor the numbers using counting numbers. In the exercise shown below they

8	12	9		2	7	13
2×4	3×4	3×3		1×2	1×7	1×13
4×2	6×2	1×9		2×1	7×1	13×1
1×8	1×12	9×1				
8×1	4×3					
	2×6					
	12×1					

should observe that the numbers 8, 12, and 9 on the left side of the line segment all have many sets of factors. The only factors of 2, 7, and 13 on the right side of the line segment are 1 and the number itself. In choosing the numbers for factorization an effort should be made to place both odd and even numbers on both sides of the line. Then when students are asked to point out the difference in the numbers on the two sides of the line segment, they will not say that even numbers are on one side and odd numbers on the other. The only relationship you want them to see is that the numbers on the left side have many sets of factors besides 1 and the number itself. The only factors of numbers on the right side of the line segment are 1 and the number itself. Numbers such as 2, 7, and 13 are called *prime* numbers. A prime number has only two distinct factors—itself and 1. Numbers such as 8, 12, and 9 are called *composite* numbers. Composite numbers have other factors besides themselves and 1. The number 1 is a counting number but is not considered prime or composite. The definition of prime numbers states that the factors must be distinct. In the case of 1, the factors are 1 times 1, which are the same factor. If the number 1 were included in the set of primes, it would lead to many special cases and additional statements that would have to be made about primes and prime factorization.

The sieve of Eratosthenes is used to determine which counting numbers are primes. Eratosthenes was a Greek mathematician and his method was to list numbers, then cross out all numbers that were not prime. You can list as many numbers as you wish. For example, to find all the primes in the set of numbers from 1 through 50, list the numbers in a rectangular array. First cross out the number 1 because it is not

prime. Next, cross out all the multiples of 2 except 2. This means all numbers with 2 as a factor. Next, cross out all numbers with 3 as a factor except 3. Now cross out all number that have 5 as a factor except 5. Last, cross out all numbers with 7 as a factor except 7. The numbers that have not been crossed out are prime numbers. If you want to determine the prime numbers between 1 and 100, extend the array to 100 and follow the same procedure. Students should list all the primes they found in the array and study them. Primes are 2, 3, 5, 7, 11, 13, 17, 19, 23, 29, 31, 37, 41, 43, 47. The only even prime is the number 2. Why is it that no other even number is a prime? Students should reply that the other even numbers all have 2 as a factor so therefore would have other factors besides themselves and 1. Are all odd numbers prime? They should answer "no" and give an example such as 9, which is odd but not prime. All the prime numbers listed except 2 end in 1, 3, 7, and 9. Why is it that some of the prime numbers do not end in 5? The answer to this question should be that all numbers ending in 5 have 5 as a factor.

PRIME FACTORIZATION

When students know some of the primes and the definition of prime numbers they are ready to learn prime factorization. Prime factorization (sometimes called complete factorization) involves factoring a composite number until all the factors are prime numbers. For example, $8 \times 9 = 72$ is one way to factor 72. This is not the prime factorization of 72 because the factors 8 and 9 are not prime numbers. One of the ways to show prime factorization is to use a factor tree. In the examples shown below, 72 is factored in three different ways but the results are the same in each.

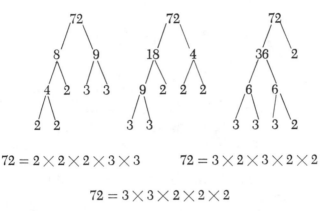

$$72 = 2 \times 2 \times 2 \times 3 \times 3 \qquad 72 = 3 \times 2 \times 3 \times 2 \times 2$$

$$72 = 3 \times 3 \times 2 \times 2 \times 2$$

The prime factorization of 72 is $2 \times 2 \times 2 \times 3 \times 3$. The factors may be in a different order but the factorization is the same if there are three factors of 2 and two factors of 3. Students who are familiar with exponents could write the factorization as $2^3 \times 3^2 = 72$. This shows that regardless of whether you begin with the factors 8×9, 18×4, or 36×2, the final factorization in prime form will be the same. Students should practice finding the prime factorization of many composite numbers. In most of their work they will need only to know the primes 2, 3, 5, 7, 11, 13, and 17.

MULTIPLES OF A NUMBER

All this work in learning how to find the prime factorization of a composite number is leading up to the least common multiple of two or more numbers. Before teaching the least common multiple of counting numbers, students must first understand what multiple means. Teach-

ers should not assume that their pupils remember or know the concept.
Multiples of 2 are {2, 4, 6, 8, 10, 12, 14, 16, . . .}. The three dots at the
end of the set show that this is an infinite set and that the multiples of
2 go on and on. The set of multiples of 2 consists of all the products that
have 2 as a factor. The word *multiple* implies special products of a given
number and other factors. Students should practice listing some of the
multiples of various numbers such as 2, 3, 6, 12, 24, ...

LEAST COMMON MULTIPLE

Some of the multiples of two given numbers should be listed. For
example, the multiples of 8 and 12 should be listed in two sets.

Multiples of 8 are {8, 16, 24, 32, 40, 48, 56, 64, 72, 80, 88, . . .}

Multiples of 12 are {12, 24, 36, 48, 60, 72, 84, 96, 108, . . .}

Students now should look at the two sets and list the multiples that the
two sets have in common. They see that 24, 48, and 72 are in both sets.
If the sets were extended, what do they think would be the next multiple the two sets would have in common? Many of the students will say
96. They see that the multiples in common are forming the set of multiples of 24. What is the smallest least common multiple of the two
sets? The answer is easy. It is 24. By working through a problem like
this students will come to understand multiple, common multiples, and
least common multiple. This is one method of finding the least common multiple but it is not the most efficient method.

Another method of finding the least common multiple (L.C.M.)
involves prime factorization. For example, to find the L.C.M. of 15 and
42 using prime factorization, write the prime factorization of 15, then
of 42. Now they should think of these factors as members of sets. In

$$15 = 3 \times 5 \qquad\qquad A = \{3, 5\}$$
$$42 = 2 \times 3 \times 7 \qquad\qquad B = \{2, 3, 7\}$$
$$\overline{\text{L.C.M.} = 3 \times 5 \times 2 \times 7} \qquad \overline{A \cup B = \{3, 5, 2, 7\}}$$

the example sets A and B represent the sets with the factors of 15 and
the factors of 42. Do not repeat members when forming the union of the

two sets. To find the least common multiple, do not repeat factors. The factor 3 in the product 15 and the product 42 is written only once. The least common multiple $3 \times 5 \times 2 \times 7$, or 210, is a multiple of 15 because 15×14 is 210. It is also a multiple of 42 because 42×5 is 210. Students should see immediately that the method of using prime factorization is far easier than the method of writing the multiples out until you find the least common multiple of two or more members.

When the same factor occurs more than once in the prime factorization some students have difficulty in writing the least common multiple. They must think of each of the factors as being different. For example, to find the least common multiple of 8 and 12, 2 occurs more than once as a factor. The 2s might be given a subscript to show that they are different. The prime factorization of 8 is $2 \times 2 \times 2$ and to show that the 2s are different the subscripts 1, 2, and 3 are used. The

$$
\begin{array}{l}
8 = 2_1 \times 2_2 \times 2_3 \\
12 = 2_1 \times 2_2 \times 3 \\
\hline
\text{L.C.M.} = 2_1 \times 2_2 \times 2_3 \times 3 \quad \text{or } 24
\end{array}
$$

same idea is used with the factors of 12. The least common multiple must contain three factors of 2 and one factor of 3. If the prime factorization is written in exponential form, the least common multiple is made up of one of each kind of factor and the highest exponent of each factor. For example, $8 = 2^3$ and $12 = 2^2 \times 3$. Then the least common multiple has the factors 2 and 3 and the highest exponent of each. The least common multiple is $2^3 \times 3$, or 24.

Often students will ask why they are learning to find the least common multiple. Tell them that the method of finding the least common denominator in the set of fractional numbers is the same as the method of finding the least common multiple in the set of counting numbers. It is easier to learn the method in the familiar set of counting numbers than to learn it in the more unfamiliar set of fractional numbers.

Students should be given some exercises in finding the least common multiple of three and four numbers. The method is the same. First, find the prime factorization of each number, then join the factors without repeating common factors. Some exercises should include a situation in which one number is prime and the other number is composite. For example, find the least common multiple of 11 and 8. The answer is 88 and there is no need for any factoring. If one of the numbers is prime and the other number composite, but the prime number is not a factor, the least common multiple is the product of the two numbers. Another exercise might ask for the least common multiple of 5 and 15. Here the prime number is a factor of the composite number so the least common multiple is not the product of the two numbers. The least common multiple is 15. If both the numbers are prime numbers, how do you find the least common multiple? Students should learn that they need multiply only the two numbers. As various exercises are assigned, ask the students to analyze the numbers first to determine if they are prime or composite. Then they use their knowledge of prime and composite numbers to decide how much work they must perform to find the least common multiple.

GREATEST COMMON FACTOR

Now they should learn how to find the greatest common divisor or factor of two or more numbers. The first method is to list all the factors of the numbers given. For example, what is the greatest common factor or divisor of 12 and 42?

Factors of 12 are 1, 2, 3, 4, 6, 12
Factors of 42 are 1, 2, 3, 6, 7, 14, 21, 42
Greatest common factor is 6

All the factors of 12 are listed first. Start with 1 and 12 to the far right: $1 \times 12 = 12$. Now write 2×6, then 3×4. Then with the factors of 42, begin with 1 and 42, then 2 and 21, 3 and 14, and finally, 6 and 7. Look at the two listings and you can see that 6 is the greatest common factor. Ask the students first to write all the common factors. They will write 1, 2, and 6. Now ask them which is the greatest common factor. Listing all the factors is difficult and students often omit some of them.

Another method of finding the greatest common factor (G.C.F.) or the greatest common divisor (G.C.D.) is to use the prime factorization method. For example, to find the G.C.F. of 12 and 42, write the prime factorization of each number first. Then by observation find the factors

$$12 = 2 \times 2 \times 3 \qquad\qquad A = \{2_1, 2_2, 3\}$$
$$42 = 2 \times 3 \times 7 \qquad\qquad B = \{2_1, 3, 7\}$$
$$\text{G.C.F.} = \quad 2 \times 3, \text{ or } 6 \qquad A \cap B = \{2_1, 3\}$$

common to both. In this case 2 and 3 are factors of both numbers. Using sets A and B to list the factors as members of sets, then using the operation of intersection, we see that 2 and 3 are the members of the new set. The G.C.F. is the product of the common factors. In this case the G.C.F. is 6 because $2 \times 3 = 6$.

Plan G.C.F. exercises to include one prime number and one composite number. If the prime number is not a factor of the composite number, the greatest common factor is 1. If the prime number is a factor of the composite number, the greatest common factor is the prime number. For example, the G.C.F. of 7 and 8 is 1 because 7 is not a factor of 8 and thus the only common factor is 1. In another example, the G.C.F. of 3 and 12 is 3 because the prime number 3 is a factor of the composite number 12. Students should look at the numbers before they begin work to determine whether they need to go through the work of finding the prime factorization of the numbers or if they can find the greatest common factor simply by observation.

When they are successful in finding the least common multiple of two or more numbers and in finding the greatest common factor of two or more numbers, they should find the L.C.M. and the G.C.F. for the same set of numbers. For example, find the greatest common factor and the least common multiple of 8 and 12, using the prime factorization method.

They first find the prime factorization of each number:

$$8 = 2 \times 2 \times 2 \qquad\qquad A = \{2_1, 2_2, 2_3\}$$
$$12 = 2 \times 2 \times 3 \qquad\qquad B = \{2_1, 2_2, 3\}$$
$$\text{L.C.M.} = 2 \times 2 \times 2 \times 3, \text{ or } 24 \qquad A \cup B = \{2_1, 2_2, 2_3, 3\}$$
$$\text{G.C.F.} = 2 \times 2, \text{ or } 4 \qquad\qquad A \cap B = \{2_1, 2_2\}$$

Also, have them write sets A and B with the factors as members of the sets, then find the union and intersection of the two sets. When they find that the L.C.M. is 24 and the G.C.F. is 4, ask them to multiply 4 × 24, then 8 × 12. They should be surprised to find that both products equal 96. Ask them why this happens. Tell them to count the total number of factors in both factorizations of 8 and 12. How many of these factors were used in the L.C.M.? How many of the factors were used in the G.C.F.? Now they should look at the union and intersection of the two sets. Because members in the union are not repeated, some members of the two sets are omitted. These members appear in the intersection as the members they share in common. By following through on some exercises like the one just described students will grasp the relationship between finding the least common multiple of two or more numbers and finding the greatest common factor.

Students are apt to wonder why they are learning how to find the greatest common factor or divisor of two or more numbers. Tell them that this is a method of finding the greatest common factor of the numerator and denominator of fractional numbers, which they will use when they simplify fractions.

DIVISIBILITY TESTS

Consider the number 3,567,830. Can you tell whether 2, 3, 4, 5, 6, 9, or 10 are divisors without actually dividing? There are tests which enable us to tell some of the divisors of a number merely by looking at the numeral. These tests are called divisibility tests.

Students know that the set of whole numbers can be divided into two subsets: (1) the set of even numbers, and (2) the set of odd numbers. The even numbers are those numbers which can be expressed as $2 \times n$, where n is a whole number. Odd numbers are those numbers which have a remainder of 1 when divided by 2. Therefore, they can be expressed as $(2 \times n) + 1$, where n is a whole number. Have students study a table like the one shown on this page to see if they can

n	1	2	3	4	5	6	7	8	9	10	11	12
$2 \times n$ (even)	2	4	6	8	10	12	14	16	18	20	22	24

recognize any sort of pattern in the numerals that name even numbers. When they recognize the pattern, state the following conclusion: A whole number written in the decimal system (base ten) is even if the last digit is one of the digits 0, 2, 4, 6, 8. If the last digit is not one of these numbers, then it is an odd number. This is the divisibility test for even numbers, written in the decimal system.

Now ask them to see if they can find a pattern that enables them to tell at a glance if a number written in the decimal system is divisible by 5. Illustrate with another table so that all students can see that all

n	1	2	3	4	5	6	7	8	9	10	11	12
$5 \times n$	5	10	15	20	25	30	35	40	45	50	55	60

numbers that have 5 as a factor end in 0 or 5. The test for divisibility by 5 is stated as follows: A whole number expressed in the decimal system is divisible by 5 if, and only if, the last digit is 0 or 5.

Ask the students what fact is true about all products with 10 as a factor. Most will know that the last digit for the product is 0. Thus, the test for divisibility by 10 is stated as follows: A whole number expressed in the decimal system is divisible by 10 if, and only if, the last digit is 0.

Now ask if it is possible to tell whether a number written in the decimal system is divisible by 3 simply by looking at the last digit. Are the numbers 0, 3, 6, 9, 12, 15, 18, 21, 24, and 27 all divisible by 3? Notice that each of the digits 0, 1, 2, 3, 4, 5, 6, 7, 8, and 9 appear as a last digit in this list. Are the numbers 4, 7, 10, 13, 16, 19, 22, 25, 28, and 31 divisible by 3? The answer is "no." Again, all the ten digits appear as a last digit of the numbers. This shows that you cannot tell whether a number is divisible by 3 simply by looking at the last digit. A table can be devised for the students to divide the given number by 3 to see if 3 is a divisor or if 3 is not a divisor. If 3 is a divisor they should write Y for yes; if 3 is not a divisor they should write N for no.

Number	27	86	111	51	143	96	231
Divisible by 3	Y	N	Y	Y	N	Y	Y
Sum of the digits	9	14	3	6	8	15	6

Do you notice anything about the sum of the digits which seems to be true for all numbers which are divisible by 3? When students see that the sum of the digits is divisible by 3 when the number is divisible by 3, they understand the test for divisibility by 3. Have them check the rule on other numbers such as 78 and 169.

Some students may wish to discover why the test for divisibility by 3 is true. They can do this by answering a series of questions:

If two numbers such as 9 and 12 are each multiples of 3, is the sum divisible by 3?

If two numbers such as 9 and 7, where only one of the numbers is a multiple of 3, are added, is the sum divisible by 3?

Now ask the students to look at a number that has been renamed and expanded:

$$
\begin{aligned}
63 &= (6 \times 10) + 3 & (1) \\
&= (6 \times (9+1)) + 3 & (2) \\
&= (6 \times 9) + (6 \times 1) + 3 & (3) \\
&= (6 \times 9) + (6 + 3) & (4) \\
63 &= \quad 54 \quad + \quad 9
\end{aligned}
$$

In step 1 is $(6 \times 10) + 3$ the same as 63?

In step 2 how was the number 10 renamed?

In step 3 what property was used?

In step 4 can you associate 6 with 3 in the operation of addition?

Is the number 6×9 divisible by 3?

Is the number $6 + 3$ divisible by 3?

Then is $(6 \times 9) + (6 + 3)$ divisible by 3?

Is 63 divisible by 3?

$6 + 3$ is the sum of the digits of what numeral?

The answers to these questions prove that the test for divisibility by 3 is true.

The test for divisibility by 9 is the same as the test for divisibility by 3. If the sum of the digits of the number is a multiple of 9, or divisible by 9, the whole number is divisible by 9. For example, by looking at 37,251 it is possible to tell it is divisible by 9 because $3 + 7 + 2 + 5 + 1 = 18$ and 18 is a multiple of 9.

Many students have learned to tell if a year is leap year by looking at the last two digits. If they are a multiple of 4 it is a leap year. For example, 1968 was a leap year because 68 is a multiple of 4 ($4 \times 17 = 68$). This is the test for divisibility of 4—look at the last two digits on the right of a number to find out if they are divisible by 4. Students who want to know why this test is true must look at the place value of the digits in the decimal system. Consider the number 1968. The 9 digit is in the hundred's place. The total value of the digit 9 is 9×100. The number 100 is a multiple of 4, therefore 9×100, or 900, is a multiple of 4. The digit 1 is in the thousand's place. The total value of the digit 1 is 1×1000. The number 1000 is a multiple of 4. The digit 6 is in the ten's place and the total value of the digit 6 is 6×10. The number 10 is not a multiple of 4. The only way the total value can be a multiple of 4 is for the face value of the digit 6 to be a multiple of 4. The total value of the digit 8 in the one's place is 8. If the sum of the total value of the ten's place and the one's place is a multiple of 4, then the whole number is a multiple of 4. The whole mathematical argument is based on the premise that if a is a multiple of 4 and b is a multiple of 4, then $a + b$ is a multiple of 4. Going back to 1968, we know that 1000 is a multiple of 4; we also know that 900 is a multiple of 4. So if 68 is a multiple of 4, then $1000 + 900 + 68$ is a multiple of 4.

The number 6744 is divisible by 2 because the first digit is 4. The number is also divisible by 3 because $6 + 7 + 4 + 4 = 21$ and 21 is a multiple of 3. The number 6744 is divisible by 6 because it is divisible by both 2 and 3. The number is not divisible by 9 because the sum of the digits is 21 and 21 is not a multiple of 9. It is also not divisible by 5 or 10 because the one's digit is neither 0 nor 5. It is divisible by 4 because the last two digits to the right, 44, are a multiple of 4. Students should practice looking at numbers written in the decimal system to decide by which numbers they are divisible. Remember that divisibility is a property of a number, whereas the test of divisibility depends on the properties of numerals. The number 9 is divisible by 3 no matter how the number 9 is written.

DIVISIBILITY TESTS IN OTHER BASES

Students in the upper middle grades have had experience in writing numbers in other bases besides base ten. They should study to see whether the tests for divisibility hold true when numbers are written in other bases. Is 34_{five} a name for an odd or an even number? Students will say, "Three-four in base five is the number we call 19 in base ten; therefore it represents an odd number." The test for divisibility by 2 in the decimal system does not work in base five for the numeral because the last digit is 4 and the number is not even. Is there any way to tell whether a number written in base five is odd or even without translating it to base ten? To answer this question students should work several exercises.

BASE FIVE	BASE TEN	
3 4	1 9	odd
3 1	1 6	even
1 2 3	3 8	even
3 1 1	8 1	odd
2 4 2	7 2	even

Now that the students have taken the numerals in base five and written the name for the number in base ten, labeling the number odd or even, they should look for some patterns in the base five numerals. What do you notice about the base five numerals when they represent an odd number? What do you notice about the base five numerals when they represent an even number? Some students will find one pattern and others will see a different pattern. Some will say that they count the number of odd digits in the numeral. If the number of odd digits is odd, the numeral represents an odd number. Others will say that they add the digits. If the sum of the digits is even, the number represented is even; if the sum of the digits is odd, the number represented is odd. Both the patterns are true in base five. For example, 113,421 in base five represents an even number because it contains four odd digits and also because the sum of the digits is 12.

To follow through on the divisibility tests in other bases, students should practice on numbers written in base seven to see if they can find patterns to determine whether the number represented is odd or even without translating back to base ten. Students will find the same patterns in base seven numerals that developed in base five numerals. Then they can try numerals written in base 3. Again they will see the same patterns develop in numerals written in base 3 as in base 5 and base 7. This should incline them to believe that numerals written in odd bases such as bases 3, 5, 7, 9, 11, and so on, follow the same patterns that reveal whether a number is divisible by 2.

Now ask students to take numbers written in base 6 to see if they can find a pattern to help them determine whether the numeral represents an odd or an even number without translating to base ten. The pattern discovered will be the same divisibility rule used in base ten. When the last digit is 0, 2, 4, the number is even; when the last digits are 1, 3, 5, the number is odd. Now ask them to try numbers written in base 4 to look for a pattern to determine odd and even numbers. Again the same divisibility rule that exists in base ten is valid. If the last digits are 0, 2, the number is even; if the last digits are 1, 3, the number is odd. Some students will come to the conclusion that if a number is written in an even base such as base 2, 4, 6, 8, 10, 12, they can determine whether a number is divisible by 2 by looking at the last digit. Looking for patterns in other number bases will impress upon students that there are some properties that are numeral properties.

Tests for divisibility in the decimal system will be useful to students when they must find all the factors of a number. They can tell by looking at a numeral if 2, 3, 4, 5, 6, 9, and 10 are factors because they know the tests. The more a student knows about the properties of numbers the more knowledgeable he will become in operating with numbers. The number 51 looks as though it might be a prime number; but if a student knows the divisibility rule for 3 in the decimal system, he can tell it is divisible by 3 and therefore is not prime.

SUMMARY

Students who become interested in prime numbers should be encouraged to read other books to find out more about primes. Prime numbers such as 5 and 7, whose difference is 2, are called twin primes. Pupils can list all the twin primes between 1 and 100, then those between 100 and 200. They should compare the number of twin primes between 1 and 100 with those between 100 and 200. Mathematicians believe that there is an infinite number of twin primes, but they become quite scarce as the numbers get larger.

Christian Goldbach, an eighteenth-century mathematician, found, when working with prime numbers, two patterns that he could not prove were always true. Nor could he find any numbers for which the patterns were not true. These patterns are called Goldbach's conjectures.

Conjecture 1: Every even number greater than 2 is the sum of two prime numbers.

Conjecture 2: Every odd number greater than 7 is the sum of three prime numbers.

Exercises should be designed so that students can test the conjectures with certain numbers. Challenge them to find any numbers that make the conjectures false. Or challenge them to prove that the statements are true for all numbers because up to this time no one has been able to supply such proofs. Challenges like this make mathematics an open-ended subject.

Another problem using prime numbers is to show that if n is greater than 1, there is at least one prime number between n and $2n$. Test for at least 5 different numbers greater than 1.

The study of the properties of whole numbers and counting numbers will provide students with greater depth and perception so that when they are faced with a problem they will not simply grind out an answer according to a set pattern like technicians but will observe and apply their knowledge to solving problems that they have never seen before. The more mathematics they know, the more creative they become in solving problems. Pupils can transfer knowledge from one set of numbers to another set of numbers only if they understand completely the concepts they are using. Number theory supplies much of this understanding.

EXERCISES

1. Write the set of multiples of 8 that are less than 54.
2. Write the set of prime numbers greater than 12 and less than 30.
3. Write the prime factorization of 108.
4. Find the least common multiple of 16 and 24, using the prime factorization method.
5. Find the greatest common factor of 18 and 54, using the prime factorization method.
6. What do you observe about the numbers when you find the least common multiple of 11 and 77?
7. When you add seven odd numbers will the sum be an even number or an odd number?
8. If the product of two numbers is an even number, what do you know about the factors?
9. Which two whole numbers are neither prime nor composite?
10. What are the factors of 12?

SELECTED READINGS

FEHR, H. F., and T. J. HILL, *Contemporary Mathematics,* Chapters 7, 8, and 9, D. C. Heath and Company, Boston, 1966.

SWAIN, R. L., and E. D. NICHOLS, *Understanding Arithmetic,* Chapter 5, Holt, Rinehart and Winston, Inc., New York, 1965.

Topics in Mathematics for Elementary School Teachers, Twenty-Ninth Yearbook of the National Council of Teachers of Mathematics, Unit 5, The Council, Washington, D.C., 1964.

The Meaning of
Fractional Numbers

INTRODUCTION

Man has always invented mathematics according to the needs of the world he is living in at the time. Today new kinds of mathematics are invented each day because in our scientific world the need for them is arising constantly. After the operations for the set of whole numbers was invented, man found that when performing division with two whole numbers the answer was not always a whole number. Four divided by 2 is 2 because 2×2 equals 4; but when 2 is divided by 4, what number times 4 yields the product 2? The need to find answers to problems not involving whole numbers led man to invent fractional numbers.

After fourth grade it is a very rare student who will confuse adding like units in a problem such as $47 + 28$ by adding 2 tens to 7 ones, or 8 ones to 4 tens. The slowest students in mathematics have learned that in our number system it is possible to add only like units, such as ones to ones, tens to tens, and so on. Yet every teacher of mathematics in the sixth, seventh, eighth, and ninth grades knows that every year when she asks students to add $2/5 + 3/4$ some of the bright students and most of the slow students will say the sum is five ninths. If students had really been taught the meaning of fractional numbers in the primary grades they would know that it is not possible to add fifths to fourths any more than they can add tens to ones. It is quite a different thing for a student to say he cannot work a problem because he does not know how to add fifths to fourths than for him to go ahead and come up with a wrong answer. All this means is that the teaching of the meaning of fractional numbers in the elementary grades has not been adequate for all students, slow or bright.

MEANING OF FRACTIONAL NUMBERS
IN THE PRIMARY GRADES

Geometric shapes usually are used to introduce primary-grade pupils to fractional numbers. Therefore, some work with geometric shapes should precede the introduction of fractional numbers. Pupils learn today that the words "triangle," "square," "rectangle," and "circle" refer to the set of points that make up the figure. All geometric shapes have an inside and an outside. Use wire shapes to represent the shapes so that pupils can familiarize themselves with them.

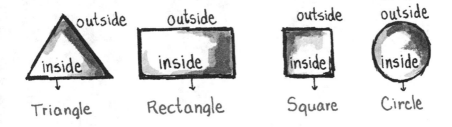

A rectangular region, like any geometric region, is the union of the interior of the figure and the geometric figure itself. The geometric

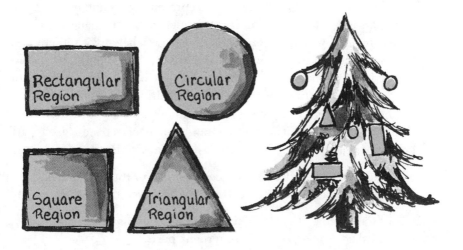

region represents a whole unit. The whole unit is then divided into congruent parts. The concept of congruent figures should be taught to pupils early. Congruent figures are two or more plane figures that have the *same size* and *shape*. Triangles can be made in various sizes and so can all the other geometric plane figures. The only time the triangles are congruent, however, is when they are of the same shape and size.

The same size means that one figure can fit evenly on top of the other figure. Pupils should match figures that are the same size and the same shape and those that have the same shape but are of different sizes. We will go into this whole matter more deeply in the chapter on teaching geometry in the elementary grades (Chapter 10).

After they have had some practice matching geometric figures, pupils should be given several pieces of paper representing rectangular regions, all of the same size. These pieces of paper represent congruent rectangular regions. One piece of paper should be labeled with a letter *A*. This shape will represent a whole unit. Another piece of paper should be folded so that the paper has two congruent parts. The parts should be separated by cutting on the fold and each part should be labeled with the letter *B*. A third piece of paper should be folded so that there are 4 congruent parts. The parts should be separated and each part labeled with the letter *C*. Following is a lesson with the papers.

How many parts called *B* are needed to cover the part called *A?*
How many parts called *C* are needed to cover the part called *A?*

Hold up one of the *B* parts. This is one of how many *B* parts? Then the part called *B* is one of two congruent parts.

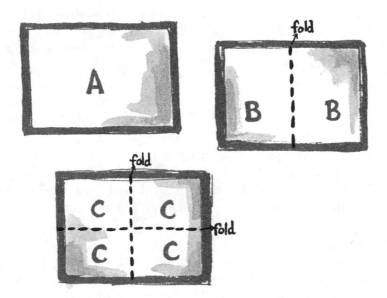

Hold up one of the *C* parts. This is one of how many *C* parts? Then the part called *C* is one of four congruent parts.

Hold up two *B* parts. These are two of how many *B* parts? Then the two parts called *B* are two of two congruent parts.

Which is larger, one *B* part or two *B* parts?

Then which is larger, one out of two congruent parts, or two out of two congruent parts?

Then two *B* parts are of the same size and shape as which other figure on your desk?

Then two *B* parts are the same size and shape as one *A* part.

Which is larger, one *A* part or one of two congruent *B* parts?

Show that the answer is correct by holding up the *A* part and one of the two *B* parts.

The four *C* parts are the same size and shape as which other figure on your desk?

Then four *C* parts are the same size and shape as the one *A* part.

Which is larger, one *A* part or one of the four congruent *C* parts?

Show that the answer is correct by holding up the *A* part and one of the four *C* parts.

The lesson just described teaches pupils to see the relationship of the congruent parts to the whole part. All students are involved in the activities, which is better than having a teacher demonstrate at the chalkboard or flannel board. There should be many such activities to ready pupils for fractional numbers before they learn to write the symbol called a fraction. The question, "How many out of how many?" should be asked over and over in different situations. How many *C* parts make a *B* part? Then two out of how many is the same as one out of how many? Now pupils must show that two of the four parts are the same as one of the two parts. This type of activity readies pupils for equivalent fractions, which come later. The seed must be planted early so that the experience is there when it is time to teach the various ways in which a fractional number can be written. A variety of figures should be used, such as triangles, squares, and circles. Pupils should fold or divide the figure to make congruent parts.

The next activity stage is semi-concrete. Here pupils are given geometric figures drawn on paper. The figures are divided into congruent parts with some of the parts shaded. Pupils should look at

How many congruent parts? _   How many congruent parts? _
How many shaded parts? _   How many shaded parts? _
The shaded parts are _ of _.   The shaded parts are _ of _.

each figure and count the number of congruent parts. Then they should count the number of shaded parts. Now record how many shaded parts there are compared to all the parts. When pupils respond 3 out of 5 and 4 out of 8, they are beginning to see a fractional number as a part of the whole. Similar questions should be asked about the non-shaded parts. Pupils should see that the sum of the shaded parts and the non-shaded parts makes up the whole piece. It is important to plan the exercises so that pupils learn first to notice the total number of congruent parts. Then direct their attention to the special parts, such as the shaded or the non-shaded. Now make a statement that relates the special parts to the whole or total number of parts. Again, all this takes place before the symbol called "fraction" is presented. The meaning of the symbol must be taught before the symbol is introduced. Also, beginning in first grade, students should work with whole units divided into many different numbers of congruent parts. It is foolish to work only with halves, fourths, and thirds. If a student can understand halves, fourths, and thirds, he can understand fifths, sixths, eighths, ninths, and tenths. In fact, the real meaning of fractional numbers cannot be taught until a student's comprehension goes beyond halves and fourths.

Pupils need to use all they have been taught in mathematics to learn the meaning of fractional numbers. To help them prepare to draw pictures of fractional numbers they will have to use their knowledge of solving number sentences and how to measure with a ruler.

$$\square + \square + \square = 6$$

The first step is to have them solve the number sentence square + square + square = 6. They should remember that the same number must be used to replace like frames. Most pupils will know that the answer is $2 + 2 + 2 = 6$ by the time they reach the unit on fractional numbers. Now they should be told that the rectangle below the sentence is 6 inches long. Ask them to use a ruler to divide the length into three equal segments. After they find 2 inches and mark a dot, and again locate 4 inches with a dot, they should be told to draw vertical line segments to divide the rectangular region into 3 congruent parts. Now ask them to show, by shading, 2 of 3 congruent parts. This same activity can be repeated with a rectangle whose side is 5 inches long. Pupils divide the rectangular region into 5 congruent parts. Circles can be drawn and given to the pupils to divide into halves and fourths by using the ruler. In exercises like these pupils are drawing pictures to match instructions such as 3 out of 7. They will discover that the second number, such as 7, tells the total number of congruent parts; the first number, such as 3, tells the number of congruent parts being considered. This activity reverses the process of selecting shaded congruent parts as part of the total congruent parts.

SYMBOL FOR FRACTIONAL NUMBERS

Now it is time to introduce the symbol for fractional numbers. Ask first- and second-graders how they would write 1 out of 2, or what we usually call one half? You will be amazed at the creative answers you receive. Some pupils will use a wavy line as shown in the drawings,

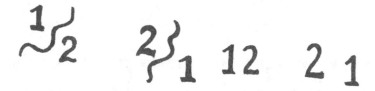

others will write the numerals next to each other the way we write 12; some will write the 2 first, then the 1. Give pupils credit for all these efforts and tell them that man invented a way of writing fractional numbers many years ago. We all have to use the method because people all over the world understand this method of writing fractional numbers.

$$\frac{1}{2} \begin{array}{l} \rightarrow \text{ Number of special parts} \\ \rightarrow \text{ Number of congruent parts altogether} \end{array}$$

Once the fraction, one half, is written on the chalkboard, pupils should discuss the fraction. How many digits or symbols are used? What separates the symbols? Where do you write the total number of congruent parts, above or below? Where do you write the number of special parts, such as shaded parts, above or below? Now that you know how the fraction, one half, is written, explain what this fraction means. Pupils should look at three fourths and say that the 4 means the total

$$\frac{3}{4}$$

number of congruent parts and that the 3 means the number of parts considered or shaded. Then write many different fractions for them and let them explain what each fraction means.

Now that they know how to write a fraction, they should be given many drawings and required to write the fraction that represents the parts being considered. Sometimes they should be asked to write the fraction that represents the shaded parts; at other times they should be asked to write the fraction that represents the unshaded parts. The

Fraction for shaded parts ____
Fraction for unshaded parts ____

Fraction for shaded parts ____
Fraction for unshaded parts ____

slower ones should be helped by saying, "First count the congruent parts in the drawing. Then count the shaded parts." Ask, "Where do you write the total number of parts? Where do you write the number of shaded parts?"

The next stage is to have the pupils make drawings of the fractions written on a piece of paper. Tell them the parts do not have to be exactly congruent and allow them to do free-hand drawing so that the work does not become too tedious. They can show the number of considered parts by shading. Encourage them to use various kinds of geometric shapes for their drawings instead of always using rectangular shapes.

Students in the primary grades need help in learning how to read fractions. Words such as halves, thirds, fourths, fifths, sixths, sevenths, eighths and ninths must be taught. In teaching pupils to read fractions teachers should point out that the denominator of the fraction is an ordinal number: third, fourth, fifth, and so on. The only exception is 2, which is called half instead of second. The numerator of the fraction is a whole number: zero, one, two, and so on. Therefore, 3/5 is read "three fifths." Have them read the fractions aloud to hear them say five sixths, seven eighths, two ninths.

SETS TO SHOW FRACTIONAL NUMBERS

After students have a grasp of fractional numbers with geometric shapes and can write a fraction, they should be given exercises with sets of objects. Draw eight circles on the chalkboard and shade three of them. Tell the pupils that the whole set represents the whole number 1. This is one set. How many circles in the set? How many circles are shaded? What fraction will represent the shaded circles out of all the circles in the set? A few pupils should respond three eighths. Write the fraction on the board. Now the rest of the pupils can see that the 8 tells how many circles there are in the set and the 3 tells how many circles should be considered because they are shaded. Assign other exercises with sets of 10 circles and direct the class to shade one half of the circles in the set. Some will shade one half of each circle, others will shade 5 of the 10 circles, and some will not know what to do. Then the teacher must go back and say, "What does one half mean?" They should say that one half means that something is divided into two congruent parts and only one part is considered. Now draw a dotted line around one half of the circles. In other words, divide the set of circles into two subsets, each with the same number of circles. Now how many circles are there in each subset? This means that one half of 10 is 5. Divide a set of 12 triangles into two subsets with the same number of triangles in each subset. What is one half of 12?

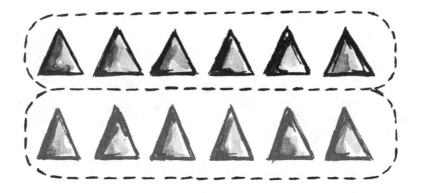

Here is a braintwister: Take the set of squares and divide them into 3 equal subsets. What is two thirds of the set of 12? In each subset there are 4 squares and in two subsets there are 8 squares.

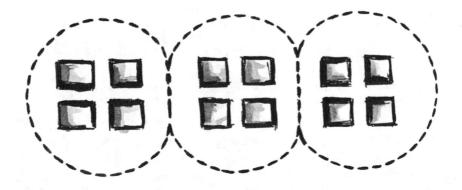

It is not necessary in the primary grades to introduce the symbolism of writing, for example, 2/3 × 12. At this point pupils are learning to use the concept of fractional numbers with sets of objects as well as with geometric shapes.

NUMERATOR AND DENOMINATOR

In the third grade pupils have learned place value to the thousands. They know that each digit in a numeral has a place value as well as a total value. The place value of a digit answers the question, "How many what?" In the unit on the meaning of fractional numbers pupils should learn the names for the parts of a fraction. They need to know that a fraction is a symbol standing for numbers that are called fractional numbers. Everyone, including the teacher, will become careless and say "fraction" when they mean "fractional number" but the distinction should be made. The top symbol in a fraction is called a numerator. The word *numerator* comes from the word *number*, which means *how many*. The bottom symbol in a fraction is called a *denominator* and comes from the word *denomination*. The word *denomination* asks the question, *How many what?* Therefore, the denominator in a fraction plays the same role as place value in whole numbers. If pupils really understand the role of the numerator and the denominator, they will then be able to learn to operate with fractional numbers with little difficulty.

ZERO IN FRACTIONAL NUMBERS

Besides reviewing with drawings of fractional numbers less than 1, and writing fractions that go with the drawings, some new ideas must be presented. Ask pupils to try to make a drawing of the fraction 0/4. Some will draw a rectangular region, divide it into 4 congruent parts, and then stop. Does this drawing show that zero fourths of the region are shaded? The answer is "yes." There are 4 congruent parts and none of them is shaded. So zero fourths means something has been divided into 4 congruent parts and none of the parts is considered. Make a drawing of 0/2. This time the pupils will draw a geometric shape and divide it into two congruent parts. Again, none of the parts will be shaded. The drawing shows 0/2 of the shaded parts. Is there any difference in the meaning of 0/4 and 0/2? The answer is "yes" because one means that some whole unit was divided into halves. Is there anything similar about the two fractions 0/4 and 0/2? This answer is also "yes" because both fractions stand for zero parts being considered. If you have zero objects, or if you have 0/4 objects, do you have the same amount? The answer is "yes" because 0/4 is another name for zero.

The next idea to present concerns what happens when the denominator is zero. Can you make a drawing of 5/0? The answer is "no" because the denominator says to divide a whole unit into zero congruent parts and this cannot be done. When the denominator is 0 the symbol does not stand for any number and is a meaningless symbol.

PROPERTY OF ONE

What does the fraction 2/2 mean? Pupils should say it means that some whole unit has been divided into two congruent parts and that both parts are being considered. What is another number for 2/2? The answer should be one whole unit or the number 1. Then what does 4/4 mean? After several questions like these pupils should begin to see that when any number is divided by itself it stands for the whole number 1. This is another one of the basic rules of the game called mathematics—the property of one. The property of one states that any number divided by itself except for zero, is 1. This property is a very important one in fractional numbers.

NUMBER LINE TO SHOW FRACTIONAL NUMBERS

After these ideas have been discussed with the class the pupils are ready to use a number line in the unit on fractional numbers.

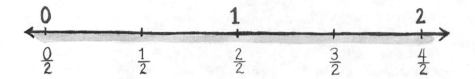

The line segment from 0 to 1 represents one whole unit and the line segment from 1 to 2 represents another whole unit. When the line segment from 0 to 1 is divided into halves, the dot at the midpoint of the line segment represents the fractional number 1/2. Then 3/2 means that you are considering the half units and that there are three of them. The fractional number 2/2 is the same as the number called 1. The fractional number 0/2 indicates that the unit has been divided into halves but you are not considering any of the parts. The fractional number 4/2 means that you are talking about half units and considering four of them. Pupils can see on the number line that 4/2 is another name for the whole number 2. Which is greater, 1 or 2? Everyone knows that 2 is greater than 1. On the number line in horizontal form, the farther you go to the right, the larger the numbers become. Which is greater, 3/2 or 1/2? The answer again is easy because 3/2 is to the right of 1/2 on the number line and therefore is greater. Pupils must understand that the number line is another geometric way of representing fractional numbers.

In order to show the fraction 3/5 on the number line, how must you divide the whole unit from 0 to 1? Pupils should say that the unit must be divided into 5 congruent parts because the denominator is 5. Now they should divide the whole unit into fifths and write the fractions 0/5, 1/5, 2/5, 3/5, 4/5, 5/5 in the correct places. It is important that they divide the line segment into fifths even if the divisions are not exactly alike. It is also important that they write the fractions by the

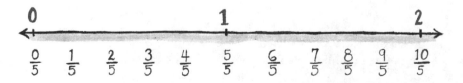

dots on the number line. Which is greater, 3/5 or 4/5? Which is less, 3/5 or 1/5? As they give their answers have them indicate the positions of the fractions on the number line. This type of exercise should be repeated for sixths, thirds, fourths, and eighths. Have the brighter students extend the number line to the whole number 2 and write the fractions between 1 and 2 as well as between 0 and 1.

EQUIVALENT FRACTIONS

The number line can be used to show equivalent fractions. Equivalent fractions are fractions that name the same number. For example, 2/4 and 1/2 are equivalent fractions because they name the same num-

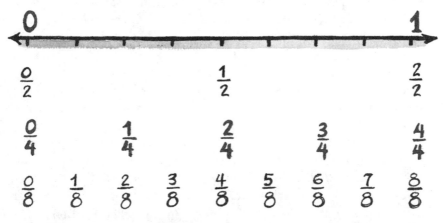

ber. Each pupil should be given a number line containing only a 0 and a 1. They should then take another piece of paper and make a strip the

length of the unit from 0 to 1 on the number line. The strip of paper should then be folded into two equal parts according to the length. This strip should be placed just above the number line. At the place where the fold meets the strip of paper they should make a dot. The fraction 1/2 should be written below the dot, the fraction 0/2 below the dot at 0, and the fraction 2/2 below the dot at 1. The same strip of paper should then be folded into fourths. Place the strip of paper over the number line with one end on the dot labeled 0 and the other end matching the dot labeled 1. At the first fold to the right of 0, have the pupils make a dot and label this 1/4. At the next fold make a dot and label this 2/4, at the next fold label the dot 3/4, and at the end of the strip label the dot 4/4. Now go back and label the dot under the 0, 0/2; and under this fraction 0/4. Repeat the whole exercise by folding the strip of paper into eighths. When they finish they will have a number line on which the unit from 0 to 1 has been divided into eighths, fourths, and halves. Using the number line. pupils should supply two other names for the point called 1/2, three additional names for the point called 1, and one other name for the point called 1/4. Now they should be told that the fractions 1/2, 2/4, and 4/8 are called equivalent fractions because they name the same number. They are simply different names for the same amount. If some students have trouble understanding equivalent fractions, try using money to illustrate the concept. A dollar bill represents the whole unit. Name a piece of money that is the same as 2 quarters. Is 2/4 the same as 1/2? Whether you have two quarters or one half of a dollar, the amount is the same. The difference is in the number of coins. The same is true of the fraction 2/4. There are two pieces, each one fourth of the unit, and in the fraction 1/2 there is one piece of a unit that is divided into halves. Looking at the number line, name an equivalent fraction to 3/4.

The same number line should be used for exercises involving the order of the fractional numbers. Which is greater, 3/8 or 1/2? How can you tell? Which is less, 3/4 or 7/8? How can you tell? Pupils should be constantly reminded to refer to the number line, which will show them that the larger fraction is farther to the right than the smaller fraction. Which is greater, 3/8 or 5/8? Do you have to look at the number line to find out? These questions help pupils to see that if the two fractions being compared have the same denominator, they need only look at the numerator to tell which is larger or smaller.

Distribute number lines to your students and have them fill in some of the fractions that name points on the number line. By observing some of the fractions already named on the number line, they should be able to figure out which fractions are missing.

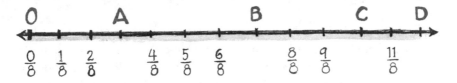

What fraction goes with the letter *A* on the number line? With the letter *C*? With the letter *B*? With the letter *D*? Pupils should be able to see that 3/8, 7/8, 10/8, and 12/8 are the missing fractions.

INEQUALITIES OF FRACTIONAL NUMBERS

To explore the order of fractional numbers a bit further, give pupils a number line marked with halves, thirds, and fourths. They should first

study the number line and then fill in <, >, or = to make the sentence true.

$$\frac{1}{3} \bigcirc \frac{1}{4} \qquad \frac{1}{2} \bigcirc \frac{2}{3} \qquad \frac{3}{4} \bigcirc \frac{2}{3}$$

$$\frac{3}{2} \bigcirc \frac{5}{3} \qquad 1 \bigcirc \frac{3}{4} \qquad \frac{1}{3} \bigcirc \frac{1}{2}$$

Exercises like these help pupils see for the first time that one third is less than one half, three fourths is greater than two thirds, and so on. The number line becomes a model for them to use when they are thinking about the order of some of the so-called common fractions.

Pupils should be given problems that will help them reason out the answers from knowledge they have gained about fractional numbers by drawing geometric figures, and working with sets of objects and the number line. One of these problems should ask them to state which is greater, 2/9 or 2/7, without making any drawings or using the number line. Let some students answer while the others judge whether or not the responses are correct. The answer should be, if a unit is divided into ninths, and the same size unit is divided into sevenths, the parts from the division into sevenths are larger than the parts from the division into ninths. Therefore, two sevenths is larger, or greater than two ninths. In other words, if the denominators are different but the numerators are the same, look at the denominators to determine which fraction is greater and which is less. This type of discussion helps pupils understand what 2/7 really means. Can you have 2/7 if there is not a 1/7? Is 2/7 simply a shorter way of saying 1/7 plus 1/7? Then 2/7 always means 2 one sevenths. The unit is sevenths and there are two of them. Is this similar to whole numbers when we say, for example, in the number 47, that the digit 4 is in the ten's place and that there are 4 tens? In whole numbers the unit or place value is shown by position whereas in fractional numbers the denominator indicates the unit. Class activity such as this is necessary since many students reach high school without realizing that 2/7 is the short way of writing $2 \times 1/7$. The seed must be planted early, then gradually and carefully cultivated in each succeeding grade.

Pupils in the primary grades can comprehend much more about fractional numbers than many teachers realize. But pupils must be given opportunities to become involved. As they draw pictures and number lines, they are establishing models that develop meaning for them. We all learn as we perform ourselves, not as others demonstrate for us.

MEANING OF FRACTIONAL NUMBERS IN THE MIDDLE GRADES

In the fourth grade, teachers should determine which students understand fractional numbers less than 1. Give them some geometric shapes divided into congruent parts. Shade some of the parts to see if they can write the fraction representing the shaded parts. Have them draw pictures that represent fractions. Use the number line to see if they can find the dot that represents the fractions 1/2, 1/4, 3/4, 7/8, and so on. Have them divide sets of objects into 2/3 of a set, 3/4 of a set. See if they understand the order of fractions. Can they tell which is greater when comparing 5/7 and 6/7? Can they compare 5/8 and 5/6 and 1/3 and 1/2? Do they know the names of the parts of the fraction? Can they tell what the denominator means and what the numerator means?

By reviewing for a few days teachers can determine which students must go back and relearn material presented in the primary grades and which students are ready to go on with more advanced concepts. It is useless to try to force the ones who do not have the background to learn more about fractions, and it is just as needless to spend a long time reviewing with those who do have the background. Grouping in mathematics is difficult and very demanding of a teacher, but it must be done. By the time students reach fourth grade there is a wide spread in their abilities.

The group that needs to relearn the material on fractional numbers should be given activities described in the section for primary grades, redoing the activities in the hope that with more exposure to the material some of them will understand.

FRACTIONS LARGER THAN ONE

Mixed form or mixed numerals should be presented to students after they have had experience with fractions larger than 1 on the number line.

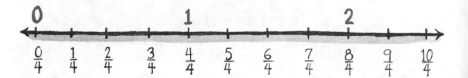

How do you know that the fraction 5/4 is greater than 1? Some will say that 5/4 is to the right of 1 on the number line. Others will say that 5/4 is to the right of 4/4 on the number line. It is the comparison with 4/4 that is important here. The fraction 5/4 is 4/4 plus how much more? The answer should be 1/4. Then can you write 5/4 as $4/4 + 1/4$? What is another name for 4/4 on the number line? Then can you write 5/4 as $1 + 1/4$? When you write 5/4 as $1 + 1/4$ you are using a whole number, 1, and a fraction, 1/4. The symbol $1\frac{1}{4}$ means $1 + 1/4$ and is called a mixed numeral because you are using a whole number and a fraction to write one number. How would you write 7/4 as a mixed numeral? Can you write the fraction 3/4 as a mixed numeral? Why not? With sufficient questioning of this type, pupils soon will see and be saying that the numerator is not large enough. The numerator must indicate that you have more than 1. How can you tell by the numerator if the fraction is naming 1? The answer should be that the numerator is the same as the denominator. How can you tell that 6/4 can be a mixed numeral? The denominator is 4 and the numerator must be greater than 4 for a fraction to be a mixed numeral. In this case the numerator is 6 and the denominator is 4, so the numerator is greater than the denominator and the fraction can be a mixed numeral. After a class lesson using this type of questioning, students should be given exercises to indicate which fractions could be mixed numerals.

$$\frac{3}{5}, \ \frac{7}{4}, \ \frac{6}{6}, \ \frac{11}{9}, \ \frac{3}{7}, \ \frac{8}{5}, \ \frac{10}{10}, \ \frac{5}{8}, \ \frac{13}{9}$$

Now ask them to name the fractions they selected as mixed numerals. The slower students should be shown that 9/8 is one whole unit divided into eighths with one eighth left over. They should use both the number line and geometric drawings as aids. On the number line they can see

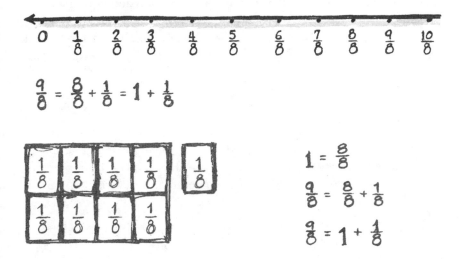

$$\frac{9}{8} = \frac{8}{8} + \frac{1}{8} = 1 + \frac{1}{8}$$

$$1 = \frac{8}{8}$$

$$\frac{9}{8} = \frac{8}{8} + \frac{1}{8}$$

$$\frac{9}{8} = 1 + \frac{1}{8}$$

that 9/8 is 1/8 beyond 8/8, or 1. With the geometric drawing they can see that 8/8 is a whole unit and that 8/8 plus 1/8 is 9/8, or $1 + 1/8$.

When students can name fractions in mixed form they are ready to perform the reverse and name the numbers written in mixed numerals as fractions. How many fourths are the same as one? How many fourths are the same as 2? How many fourths are the same as $2 + 3/4$? Then $2\frac{3}{4}$ can be named as what fraction? In renaming $3\frac{4}{5}$ as a fraction you are going to think of renaming the whole number in terms of what fraction? Why did you pick fifths instead of sevenths or thirds? How many fifths are the same as 3? How many fifths are the same as $3\frac{4}{5}$? Questions like these draw students' attention to the fraction part of the mixed numeral first. Before you can rename a mixed numeral as a fraction your attention must be on the denominator of the fraction in the mixed numeral. Next, your attention must focus on the whole number part of the mixed numeral. The whole number part must be renamed in terms of the fraction represented by the denominator of the fraction. Last, you add the fraction part of the mixed numeral to the fraction obtained when you renamed the whole number part of the numeral. This means that there are three steps in renaming mixed numerals as fractions. Questions must be asked to get the students involved in reacting to the three steps. As a first step, exercises should be designed in which a whole number is given and students name the whole number in terms of a given fraction.

> Rename 3 in terms of thirds. _
> 2 is how many fourths? _
> How many sixths are the same as 5? _

Next, exercises should be assigned that involve renaming a mixed numeral as a fraction. In the beginning stages the mixed numeral should carry a plus sign to remind students to add the fraction part.

Rename the mixed numerals as follows:

$$2 + \frac{3}{5} = \qquad 5 + \frac{1}{6} = \qquad 7 + \frac{3}{4} =$$

$$2\frac{3}{7} = \qquad 3\frac{2}{3} = \qquad 8\frac{1}{2} =$$

After doing some exercises like these, start a discussion in which pupils can tell how they arrived at the fractions. Some students will say that they multiplied the denominator by the whole number, then added the numerator. Now let them explain why the method works and why it is a short-cut. Guide their explanations so that they will realize that $2\frac{3}{7}$ means $7/7 + 7/7 + 3/7$ and that the whole number 2 can be written as 14/7. Instead of adding 7/7 twice, you can multiply 2×7 to find the number of sevenths.

So far we have made no mention of *proper* and *improper* fractions. The English used to call improper fractions *vulgar* fractions. In elementary mathematics today there is no need to make the distinction between so-called proper fractions and improper fractions. If teachers feel that they must because of achievement testing, or for some other reason, they should tell their pupils that fractions whose numerator is smaller than the denominator are sometimes called proper fractions; fractions whose numerator is the same size or greater than the denominator are sometimes called improper fractions. No great fuss should be made over the distinction.

After working with mixed numerals students should understand that all whole numbers can be written in fraction form. The whole number 1 can be written in an infinite number of ways as a fraction, such as: 2/2, 3/3, 4/4, 5/5, and so on. This means that all whole numbers are a subset of the fractional numbers. Whole numbers are included in the fractional numbers, but fractional numbers are not included in the set of whole numbers. This may seem confusing to teachers who were taught that fractions are different from whole numbers, but it will not be confusing to students who understand the property of one.

ORDERED PAIRS

In the middle grades, teach students that fractional numbers can be written as ordered pairs as well as fractions. The symbol (1, 2) is an ordered pair. The first member of the ordered pair is the number that names the number of parts being considered; the second number of the ordered pair names the number of total congruent parts. This means that (1, 2) and 1/2 are simply two different ways of writing the same fractional number. Students should practice writing fractions in ordered pairs, then writing ordered pairs as fractions. They need this knowledge when they work with fractional numbers in some books. It should be pointed out that (3, 4) is different from (4, 3). In the case of (3, 4) the ordered pair stands for the number named by the fraction 3/4 and in the case of the (4, 3) ordered pair it stands for the number named by 4/3. There is a considerable difference between the fractional numbers 3/4 and 4/3. The order of the numbers in the pair is very important and cannot be changed without representing a different number.

EQUIVALENT FRACTIONS

Equivalent fractions are fractions that name the same number. All equivalent fractions that name the same number form an equivalence class. The number usually takes its name from the "simplest" member of the equivalence class. In the example shown here the equivalence class is named by one-half. The ability to convert a fraction to an equivalent form is a necessary prerequisite for all but the most simple computations involving fractions.

$$\left\{ \frac{1}{2}, \ \frac{2}{4}, \ \frac{3}{6}, \ \frac{4}{8}, \ \frac{5}{10}, \ \frac{6}{12}, \ \frac{7}{14} \cdots \right\}$$

By the middle grades most pupils should be comfortable in deriving equivalent fractions by using drawings and the number line. They have seen and can make drawings to show that $1/2 = 2/4$, $1/3 = 2/6$, $3/4 = 4/8$, and so on. This ability should be tested before they begin studying other ways of deriving equivalent fractions. If some pupils cannot show either by drawing or by the number line that $1/2 = 2/4$, then this work must be repeated for them. Follow the directions given in the primary-grade section of this chapter.

One effective way to start teaching other ways of deriving equivalent fractions is to write the fraction $1/2$ on the board. Pupils should supply other names for the fraction and their answers should be written on the chalkboard:

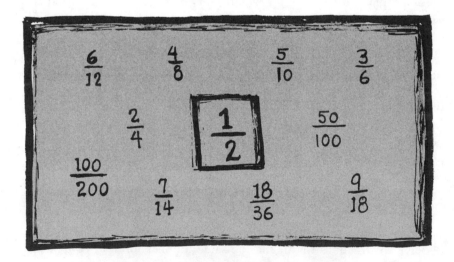

Then the students should study the names and try to discover a pattern. Many will say, "The denominator is twice as large as the numerator." After a pattern has been found, one half could be presented in another way. Is one half equal to 7 divided by seven plus seven? (Yes it is.)

$$\frac{1}{2} = \frac{7}{7+7}$$

Is one half equal to 13 divided by thirteen plus thirteen? (Yes it is.)

$$\frac{1}{2} = \frac{13}{13+13}$$

Then can you now fill in the missing numbers in the following problems?

$$\frac{1}{2} = \frac{15}{15+} \qquad\qquad \frac{1}{2} = \frac{}{17+17}$$

$$\frac{1}{2} = \frac{1\frac{1}{2}}{1\frac{1}{2}+} \qquad\qquad \frac{1}{2} = \frac{8}{+}$$

By filling in the numbers the pupils are seeing that one half means 2 of some number in the denominator and 1 of the same number in the numerator. This leads to the next stage. If $\frac{1}{2} = \frac{7}{7+7}$ then does $\frac{1}{2} = \frac{1 \times 7}{2 \times 7}$? The answer is yes because $7 + 7$ means 2×7 and 7 means 7×1. Now looking back at the various names for one half, pupils will see that they all can be found by multiplying both the numerator and the denominator by the same whole number. Thus

$$\frac{1 \times 2}{2 \times 2} = \frac{2}{4} \qquad \frac{1 \times 3}{2 \times 3} = \frac{3}{6} \qquad \frac{1 \times 8}{2 \times 8} = \frac{8}{16}, \text{etc.}$$

To name equivalent fractions of 2/3 you can multiply both numerator and denominator by the same whole number. Thus

$$\frac{2}{3} = \frac{5+5}{5+5+5} = \frac{2 \times 5}{3 \times 5} = \frac{10}{15}$$

Teachers who have never used the intermediate stage of adding like numbers to show equivalent fractions before they get to the stage where students are asked to multiply both numerator and denominator by the same number should try it. Many pupils for the first time will understand why they can multiply by the same number without changing the value of the number. The logic is quite simple. The addition of equal addends can be performed by multiplying.

In working with fractional numbers, most often it is necessary to find a particular equivalent fraction, not just any equivalent fraction. For example, we want to find another name for one half in the sixth family. This means $1/2 = n/6$. The n in the numerator means that we want to find how many sixths are the same as one half. By looking at the denominators we see that 2×3 is 6. The numerator also must be multiplied by 3. Both numerator and denominator must be multiplied by

$$\frac{1}{2} = \frac{n}{6} \qquad \frac{1 \times 3}{2 \times 3} = \frac{3}{6}$$

the same number. Similarly, the unknown can be in the denominator

$$\frac{2}{3} = \frac{10}{n} \qquad \frac{2 \times 5}{3 \times 5} = \frac{10}{15}$$

so here we must concentrate on the numerator. Looking at the fractions we see that $2 \times 5 = 10$. The denominator also must be multiplied by 5. Therefore, $2/3$ and $10/15$ are equivalent fractions that name the same number.

Students should look at several examples of equivalent fractions and point out some relationships they see in the numerators and de-

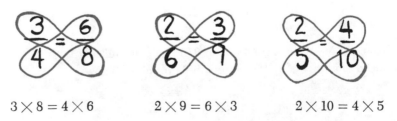

$3 \times 8 = 4 \times 6$ $\qquad$ $2 \times 9 = 6 \times 3$ $\qquad$ $2 \times 10 = 4 \times 5$

nominators of the equivalent fractions (see diagram). In the case of $3/4 = 6/8$ some students will see that 3×8 is the same as 4×6. The same relationship exists in the other examples, such as $2 \times 9 = 3 \times 6$ and $2 \times 10 = 4 \times 5$. This means that fractions which are equal or name the same number are always equal to the cross multiplication of the numerator of one fraction by the denominator of the other fraction. The usual convention is to start with the numerator on the left and multiply it by the denominator on the right; then multiply the denominator on the left by the numerator on the right.

In practice, to determine whether fractions are equal, students should also be able to explain why the fractions are not equal. In the following examples they should tell which fractions are equal and which are not equal. Then they should explain why they said they were equal or not.

$$\frac{2}{7} \overset{?}{=} \frac{3}{9} \qquad\qquad \frac{4}{5} \overset{?}{=} \frac{16}{20}$$

not equal because
$2 \times 9 \neq 7 \times 3$

equal because
$4 \times 20 = 5 \times 16$

$$\frac{8}{11} \overset{?}{=} \frac{30}{44} \qquad\qquad \frac{5}{9} \overset{?}{=} \frac{15}{27}$$

not equal because
$8 \times 44 \neq 11 \times 30$

equal because
$5 \times 27 = 9 \times 15$

Thus, 2/7 is not equal to 3/9 because 2×9 is not equal to 3×7. And 4/5 is equal to 16/20 because 4×20 is equal to 5×16.

ORDER OF FRACTIONAL NUMBERS

The test for equality of fractions can also be used for inequality. In specifying the order of fractions, students can use the cross multiplication technique. Is 2/5 equal to, greater than, or less than 3/8? To de-

$$\frac{2}{5} \;\bigcirc\!\!\!> \; \frac{3}{8} \qquad\qquad \begin{aligned} 2 \times 8 &= 16 \\ 5 \times 3 &= 15 \\ 16 &> 15 \end{aligned}$$

termine the order, multiply 2×8, then 5×3. The product 16 is greater than the product 15; therefore the fraction 2/5 is greater than the fraction 3/8. The cross multiplication was started with the numerator on the left side times the denominator on the right side. Is 3/7 greater than, less than, or equal to 4/9? To test, first multiply 3×9 then

$$\frac{3}{7} \;\text{\textcircled{<}}\; \frac{4}{9} \qquad\qquad \begin{array}{c} 3 \times 9 = 27 \\ 4 \times 7 = 28 \\ 27 < 28 \end{array}$$

7×4. Is $28 > 27$ or is $27 < 28$? Twenty-eight > 27. Therefore, 3/7 is less than 4/9. Some students will want to know why this technique works, so now you can go back to equivalent fractions. Find the fraction in the 63 family that names the same number as 3/7. Find the fraction in the 63 family that names the same number as 4/9. After the students

$$\underline{\hspace{2.5cm}} \qquad \frac{3}{7} \times \frac{9}{9} = \frac{27}{63} \qquad \frac{4}{9} \times \frac{7}{7} = \frac{28}{63} \qquad \frac{27}{63} < \frac{28}{63}$$

multiply 4/7 by 9/9, the equivalent fraction is 36/63. The other equivalent fraction is $4/9 \times 7/7$, or 28/63. Now they are comparing two fractions in the same family and can see that 27/63 is less than 28/63. They also see that the numerators 27 and 28 are the same numbers they get for products in the cross multiplication method. So cross multiplication is a short way of comparing fractions without having to find equivalent fractions each time.

FRACTIONS INDICATE DIVISION

Fractions are also a way of indicating division. The fraction 3/4 means the number 3 divided by the number 4. It can be written $3 \div 4$ as well as in fraction form. When the divisor is greater than the dividend, as in this case where 4 is greater than 3, the quotient will be less than 1. When you divide 3 by 4 the quotient is 0.75. In $8 \div 4 = 2$ the check is $2 \times 4 = 8$. Also, for $3 \div 4 = 0.75$ the check is $4 \times 0.75 = 3$.

$$8 \div 4 = 2 \qquad\qquad 3 \div 4 = 0.75$$
$$\text{Check: } 2 \times 4 = 8 \qquad\qquad \text{Check: } 4 \times .75 = 3$$

Students should understand that fractions can stand for division as well as parts of a whole unit. This concept of a fraction is sometimes ignored in the middle grades so that when students reach junior high mathematics their understanding of fractions is limited. In our number system any fraction can be expressed as a decimal number by dividing the numerator by the denominator. A decimal number is in any number expressed in base ten numeration. For example, the fraction 9/4 expressed as a decimal number is $9 \div 4 = 2.25$. The numeral 2.25 is a decimal number written in our base ten. Assign students exercises that involve changing fractions to decimal numbers. If a student looks at 5/6 and says, "I do not know which number is the divisor," he should be told to read the fraction as 5 divided by 6. As he hears this he realizes he is dividing by 6; therefore 6 is the divisor. When in doubt, students should be encouraged to read the symbol aloud and to listen to what they are saying.

DECIMAL FRACTIONS

Decimal fractions are a special subset of fractional numbers in base ten. All fractions that have a power of 10 as a denominator can be expressed as a decimal. The powers of 10 are 10, 100, 1000, 10,000, and so on. This means that 3/10 can be written in a shorter way as 0.3. The digit 3 is in the tenth's place and stands for three tenths. The fraction 17/100 can be written as 0.17. The fact that our numeration system is based on groupings of ten provides us with another way of writing fractions with denominators that have powers of ten.

Review the base value chart so that students can see that the places to the right of the one's place are expressed as fractions with denominators that are powers of ten. The concept of 10 hundredths as equal to one tenth needs extra work. A piece of paper should be cut into ten vertical strips. Each strip represents one tenth of the whole. Now one of the strips should be cut into ten congruent pieces. Students need to see that 10 of the smaller pieces make up one of the strips. Therefore, when they see 0.17, they understand it represents one tenth and 7 hundredths. But the one tenth can also be expressed as 10 hundredths, which together with the 7 hundredths, is equal to 17 hundredths. Slower students will not understand the concept of decimals on first exposure and will require a great deal of practice in working with strips of paper and seeing a unit divided into tenths and hundredths.

SIMPLIFYING FRACTIONS

Students should learn to simplify fractions in the unit on the meaning of fractions. To simplify a fraction means to find another name for the fraction so that the only common factor of the numerator and the denominator is 1. To simplify 6/12, students should write 6 in prime factorization, then 12 in prime factorization to find the greatest common

$$\frac{6}{12} = \left(\frac{6}{6}\right)\frac{\times 1}{\times 2} = \frac{1}{2} \qquad \begin{array}{l} 6 = 3 \times 2 \\ 12 = 2 \times 2 \times 3 \\ \hline \text{G.C.F.} = 3 \times 2 \text{ or } 6 \end{array}$$

divisor or factor (see example). When they see that 6 is the greatest common factor they write 6/12 as $6 \times 1/6 \times 2$. The 6s in the numerator and denominator can be divided by 6 to arrive at 1/2, which is in the simplest terms because the greatest common factor is 1.

In simplifying fractions students will use the knowledge they acquired in number theory. If either the numerator or denominator is a prime number, all they need do is to look at the composite number to see if the prime number is a factor of the composite number. If it is,

$$\begin{array}{c} \frac{7}{21} \xrightarrow{\rightarrow \text{prime}} \\ \xrightarrow{\rightarrow \text{has 7 as}} \\ \text{factor} \end{array} \qquad \frac{7}{21} = \left(\frac{7}{7}\right) \frac{1}{3} = \frac{1}{3} \qquad \frac{6}{8} = \left(\frac{2}{2}\right)\frac{\times 3}{\times 4} = \frac{3}{4}$$

then the prime number is the greatest common factor and can be divided out. If both numerator and denominator of the fraction are composite numbers, then the students must use prime factorization and find the greatest common factor, then divide this factor out. If both numerator and denominator of the fraction are prime numbers, the fraction is in the simplest form. Also, if either the numerator or denominator is a prime number and the other number is a composite number that does not have the prime number as a factor, the fraction is in simplest form. Students need to analyze the numerators and denominators of the fractions first to see if they are prime or composite, then decide if they need to find the greatest common factor. If they do, they should use the method taught in number theory. Emphasize over and over again that you can divide out a number in both numerator and denominator because of the property of one. The term "canceling" or "cancellation" is simply another way of saying that the property of one has been used. All these relationships should be volunteered by the students as the teacher puts fractions on the chalkboard, questions them about the numerators and denominators, and leads them to explain when they must find the greatest common factor and when they must not.

SUGGESTIONS FOR DRILL AND PRACTICE

One of the methods of practicing equivalent fractions is to write a fraction in the middle of a piece of paper, then have students write as many other names for the fraction as they can.

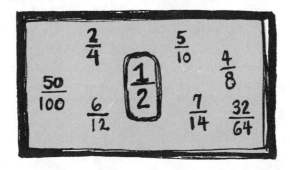

Another way to practice equivalent fractions is to make up bingo cards with fractions written in their simplest form. Some of the fractions on the cards might be 1/2, 2/3, 3/4, 5/6, 5/8, 1/7, 5/9, and so on. Then, on pieces of paper equivalent fractions to these simplest fractions

should be written, such as 2/4, 6/8, 6/9, 5/10, 3/21, 12/32, 15/27, and so on. As the equivalent fraction is called out, students put a piece of paper over the square of the fraction named in simplest form. For example, if 5/10 is called, all students who have 1/2 on their cards should cover it up.

Another game is concentration. Nine large pieces of paper should be taped to the chalkboard. On one side are written fractions in simplest form. The blank sides are toward the group. Students are given 5 or 6 pieces of paper containing equivalent fractions. A student chooses one of his fractions, such as 6/12, and picks one of the large papers on the board. If the sheet he selects has an equivalent fraction, he gets to pick another. If not, the paper is turned over and another student gets a turn.

SUMMARY

Students must really understand the meaning of fractional numbers before they can learn to work with them. In the primary grades, pupils should be involved in activities that create meaning for them. The activities should include using geometric shapes, sets of objects, and the number line.

The concept of equivalent fractions is very important and should be stressed. Students must see that a fractional number can have an infinite number of names. The way to generate some of the equivalent fractions is by using the property of one. This property is introduced in the set of fractional numbers and is very important.

Early in their exposure to fractions, pupils learn that a fractional number is a part of a whole unit. Before they finish elementary mathematics they should also know that a fraction is a way of indicating division.

For years the meaning of fractional numbers was poorly taught because the topic always occurred at the end of each textbook and most teachers did not get to the topic until the end of the year, then in the rush to complete the work, did not give students a chance to become involved. They merely demonstrated and illustrated on the chalkboard. In current texts fractions are introduced earlier and more time can be spent on them and many meaningful activities can be devised to help students understand them.

EXERCISES

1. Write five equivalent fractions of the fraction 3/4.
2. What three models can be used to show the meaning of fractional numbers?
3. State the property of one.
4. How is the property of one used to generate equivalent fractions?
5. Show how you can tell whether five ninths is greater than, less than, or equal to seven elevenths.
6. Write the ordered pair $(3, 7)$ as a fraction.
7. How is the property of one used in simplifying 8/28?
8. Why is $3/4 = (7+7+7)/(7+7+7+7)$ true?
9. How can you show whether $7/9 = 8/11$ is, or is not, a proportion?
10. Do $(3, 4)$ and $(4, 3)$ represent the same fraction? Explain.

SELECTED READINGS

GROSSNICKLE, F. E., L. J. BRUECKNER, and J. RECHZEH, *Teaching Elementary School Mathematics,* Chapter 13, Holt, Rhinehart and Winston, Inc., New York, 1968.

School Mathematics Study Group, *Mathematics for the Elementary School: Units EB11 and EB12,* Yale University, New Haven, Conn., 1961.

SPENCER, P. L., and M. BRYDEGAARD, *Building Mathematical Competence in the Elementary School,* Holt, Rinehart and Winston, Inc., New York, 1968, pp. 214–232.

SWENSON, E.: *Teaching Mathematics to Children,* Chapter 15, Crowell-Collier and Macmillan, Inc., New York, 1964.

Addition and Subtraction
of Fractional Numbers

INTRODUCTION

Adding and subtracting fractional numbers is based on adding and subtracting whole numbers. In adding and subtracting whole numbers students learned that in our number system only like units can be added or subtracted. This is why addends are usually placed in columns so that the ones are beneath ones, tens beneath tens, and hundreds beneath hundreds. It simplifies adding. In subtraction the addend is placed under the sum so that the ones are under ones, tens under tens, hundreds under hundreds, and so on. In fractional numbers the denominators play the same role as place value of the digits. Only like fractions can be added or subtracted. Like fractions are fractions with the same denominator. The denominator indicates the unit being used and the units are added and subtracted with the numbers in the numerator. This procedure leads directly to one of the main prerequisites of fractional numbers. Students who have difficulty adding and subtracting whole numbers will have difficulty adding and subtracting the numbers in the numerators. The other prerequisite is to understand the meaning of fractional numbers.

ADDING AND SUBTRACTING
FRACTIONAL NUMBERS IN THE
PRIMARY GRADES

After the middle of the second grade most pupils can begin to learn to add and subtract like fractions. The first activities should involve concrete experiences. A rectangular region such as a piece of paper should be divided into four congruent parts, first by folding, and then by cutting along the folds. The parts should each be labeled one fourth. Now have the pupils place two fourths on their desk, then place another one fourth on the desk beside the two fourths. How many fourths in all? The pupils will answer three fourths.

Now the teacher should write two equations on the chalkboard like the ones following:

$$\frac{2}{4} + \frac{1}{4} \overset{?}{=} \frac{3}{4} \qquad \frac{2}{4} + \frac{1}{4} \overset{?}{=} \frac{3}{8}$$

Which of these equations reflects the activity we just performed? If some pupils choose $2/4 + 1/4 = 3/8$, ask them to show how they can get the sum three eighths by using the congruent parts. Specifically point out that the parts are all fourths and the sum is in fourths. Never add the denominators, because they indicate the unit being used. Adding the denominators changes the unit.

Now pupils should take a rectangular or square piece of paper and divide it into 8 congruent parts by folding and then cutting along the folds. The fraction 1/8 should be written on each piece. Pupils should show five eighths by placing the parts on their desks. Now ask them to place two more parts on their desks. What is the sum? The response will be seven eighths. The teacher should write two equations on the chalkboard like the ones following:

$$\frac{5}{8}+\frac{2}{8}\overset{?}{=}\frac{7}{8} \qquad \frac{5}{8}+\frac{2}{8}\overset{?}{=}\frac{7}{16}$$

Which of these equations records the activity you just performed? Again, if some pupils say $5/8 + 2/8 = 7/16$, ask them to show this result with the parts they have made. Once again make the point that it is not possible to add denominators. The denominators tell the unit being used. It is the numerators that are added.

Many teachers make the mistake of using a flannel board in beginning the addition of fractional numbers. A flannel board is good for demonstration purposes, but the real learning occurs when pupils are involved in the activity themselves and are not merely spectators to a performance conducted by the teacher.

Similar activities on the number line should be practiced. This is a more abstract exercise than using the geometric shapes. With the number line pupils will apply what they learned in adding whole numbers to the addition of fractional numbers. Have them look at a number

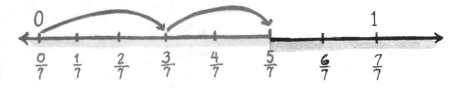

line like the one shown here and tell which addition exercise is being illustrated. The arrow going from 0 to 3/7 indicates the first addend. The arrow going from 3/7 to 5/7 indicates the other addend. The exercise is $3/7 + 2/7 = 5/7$. When pupils are able to read problems from the number line they should be given the addition problem to portray on the number line. For example, the problem might be $1/6 + 4/6 = \square$. On the number line only the points 0 and 1 should be labeled. Pupils should divide the unit into six congruent parts and label each of the parts.

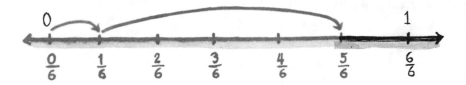

Then they should draw the arrows to represent the addends. Where the last arrow stops is the sum.

Subtraction of like fractions also should begin with concrete experiences. Pupils can take five of the eighths and place them on their desks. Now ask them to take away two of the parts. How many eighths are left? Record the activity on the chalkboard by writing $5/8 - 2/8 = 3/8$. Which of the fractions represents the sum? Is 2/8 a sum or an addend? How would you check to see if your answer is correct? Pupils should recall that they add the addends in whole numbers to check for the original sum. They check subtraction of fractional numerals in the same way.

The next stage is the more abstract method of seeing the subtraction of fractional numbers on a number line. Pupils have used the number line to subtract whole numbers. It is used in a similar fashion to represent subtraction of fractional numbers. First an arrow is drawn to the

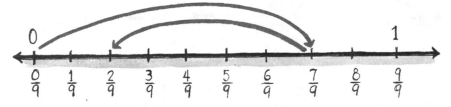

sum; then an arrow is drawn from the sum to the left the number of spaces indicated by the addend. The number line here shows the problem $7/9 - 5/9 = 2/9$. When they can read the problems from the number line they should be given exercises to represent on the number line by drawing the arrows.

$$\begin{array}{c} \dfrac{3}{7} \\[4pt] +\dfrac{2}{7} \\ \hline \end{array} \qquad \dfrac{9}{10} - \dfrac{6}{10} = \square \qquad \begin{array}{c} \dfrac{7}{9} \\[4pt] -\dfrac{2}{9} \\ \hline \end{array} \qquad \dfrac{11}{13} - \dfrac{5}{13} = \square \qquad \dfrac{8}{9} + \square = \dfrac{13}{9}$$

When assigning practice exercises in subtracting and adding like fractions, some problems should be set in vertical form and some in horizontal form. Pupils should be encouraged to look at the problems first to decide if they are finding a sum or an addend before they try to solve them.

In doing exercises, some of the fractions will represent numbers larger than 1. This means that the numerator will be larger than the denominator. In some cases pupils might be asked to write their answers as mixed numerals when the number is greater than 1, and as a whole number when the numerator is a multiple of the denominator. Slower students should be allowed to leave the answers in fraction form, waiting until the middle grades to learn to write the answers in mixed numerals.

$$\frac{9}{8} + \frac{7}{8} = \frac{16}{8} \text{ or } 2 \qquad \frac{7}{6} + \frac{4}{6} = \frac{11}{6} \text{ or } 1\frac{5}{6} \qquad \frac{9}{5} - \frac{4}{5} = \frac{5}{5} \text{ or } 1$$

The brighter students should be asked to look at the answer. If the numerator is greater than the denominator, determine if it is a multiple of the denominator. If it is not, determine how many ones there are and what part is left over. For example, the sum 16/8 can be named 2 and pupils should recognize that 16 is a multiple of 8. In the case of 5/5, the sum can be called 1.

Problems involving money are introduced in the primary grades. As pupils add $4.36 and $10.17, or subtract $5.29 from $10.79, they should be aware that they are working with tenths and hundredths. The fraction 36/100 can be added to 17/100 because the denominators are the same. It is possible to write 36/100 as 0.36 and it is possible to write 17/100 as 0.17 in the decimal system. Some of the fractions used in practice should have denominators that are powers of ten. Point out these problems and ask the pupils to write the fractions in decimal form and to find the answers in decimals as well as fractional numbers.

ADDING AND SUBTRACTING FRACTIONAL
NUMBERS IN THE MIDDLE GRADES

A review of adding and subtracting like fractions should be given in the middle grades to make sure students understand that they can add and subtract like units only. Students who have difficulty should work together in groups before they begin to add and subtract unlike fractions.

Before adding and subtracting unlike fractional numbers students must find the least common denominator. Tell them that they must find the least common denominator in order to arrive at an answer in the simplest form. Review with them how to find the least common multiple of two or more whole numbers. Now students must remember the subsets, primes, and composites. They must also remember how to perform prime factorization. They use the prime factorization of the numbers given to find the least common multiple of the numbers. First of all, be sure that all students understand the concept of multiples. Give them a few problems in which to write 5 multiples of 4, then 8, then 12. Ask them to list the multiples in set form. Ask them to list 10 multiples of 8, and of 12, as follows:

Multiples of 8   {8, 16, 24, 32, 40, 48, 56, 64, 72, 80}
Multiples of 12   {12, 24, 36, 48, 60, 72, 84, 96, 108, 120}

As they look at the two sets, ask them to list the common multiples: 24, 48, and 72. Now ask them which is the least common multiple of 8 and 12. Next, ask them to find the least common multiple of 8 and 12 by using prime factorization:

$$8 = 2 \times 2 \times 2$$
$$12 = 2 \times 2 \times 3$$
$$\text{L.C.M.} = 2 \times 2 \times 2 \times 3 \text{ or } 24$$

They should recall that the prime factorization method is much easier than listing the multiples of two or more numbers. Students who do not recall all these prerequisites should be given extra work and attention until they can find the least common multiple of two or more numbers. Those who have learned how to find the least common multiple of two or more numbers can begin by adding and subtracting unlike fractions.

ADDING UNLIKE FRACTIONAL NUMBERS

Write a problem such as 5/8 +1/12 on the chalkboard. Can you add these two numbers with the names they now have? In the discussion that follows point out that only fractional numbers with like denominators can be added. So these fractions should not be added in their present form. How can you find the smallest number of which the numbers 8 and 12 are factors? Lead students to use the method of finding the least common multiple. The numbers 8 and 12 are called what in the fractions? So the number that is the smallest multiple of 8 and 12 is called the least common denominator. This type of group work is needed to help students understand that finding the least common denominator in fractional numbers involves the same process as finding the least common multiple of two or more whole numbers. Now ask the students to find the least common denominator by explaining the prime factorization of 8, then of 12. Now what is the least common denominator? After they have established that 24 is the least common

$$\frac{5}{8} + \frac{1}{12} = ?$$

$$\left(\frac{5}{8} \times \frac{3}{3}\right) + \left(\frac{1}{12} \times \frac{2}{2}\right) = ?$$

$$\frac{15}{24} + \frac{2}{24} = \frac{7}{24}$$

$$8 = 2 \times 2 \times 2$$
$$12 = 2 \times 2 \times 3$$
$$\overline{\text{L.C.D.} = 2 \times 2 \times 2 \times 3 = 24}$$

denominator, they must find the equivalent fraction of 5/8 in the 24 family. Because of the property of one, they must multiply both numerator and denominator by 3 to get the equivalent fraction 15/24. Now find the equivalent fraction of 1/12 in the 24 family. This time, both numerator and denominator will be multiplied by 2. The result is 2/24. Now that the fractions have the same denominator they can be added.

Teachers should be careful to avoid saying that they *cannot* add the numbers 5/8 and 1/12. This would be a false statement, for the numbers can be added but the difficulty is that the fractions need other names before the adding can be done. Point out to the students that they can find the number to multiply both the numerator and denominator by for the equivalent fraction by looking at the prime factorizations. Look at 8 in prime factorization. It is $2 \times 2 \times 2$ and the L.C.D. is $2 \times 2 \times 2 \times 3$. So what factor does the L.C.D. have that is not in the factorization of 8? The response should be 3. Now tell them that this is the number they multiply both numerator and denominator by to get the equivalent fraction 5/8. In the case of 1/12, ask them to look at the factors of 12, then at the factors of the L.C.D. Which factor is in the L.C.D. that is not in the factors of 12? The response should be 2. Then this is the number you use to multiply both numerator and denominator to get the equivalent fraction 2/24. Students should follow this procedure to find equivalent fractions.

When students realize that 5/8 and 1/12 can be converted to the like fractions 15/24 and 2/24, whose sum is 17/24, explain to them what really is happening. All the equivalent fractions that name the same number as 5/8 form an equivalent class. Ask them to name some of the members of this equivalent class. All the equivalent fractions that name the same number as the fraction 1/12 form another equivalent class. Ask them to name some of the members of this equivalent class. Now ask them if 17/24 is in either of these two equivalent classes. The answer is "no." The sum is another equivalent class because it names a number different from either one of the addends.

The mistake most teachers make in introducing the unit on adding unlike fractions is starting with problems that are so easy students can find the least common denominator by inspection and they get the false impression that all least common denominators should be found in this way. For example, beginning with the exercise $1/2 + 1/4$ is too simple. Most students can supply the sum 3/4 without doing any written work. When asked how they found the correct answer, they will say they knew that 1/2 and 2/4 name the same number. This is good but it does not provide the technique needed to add 1/6 and 3/8. To find the least common denominator of 6 and 8 students need to find the prime factorizations of each number, then the least common denominator. So this is a far better example to start with than $1/2 + 1/4$.

SUBTRACTING UNLIKE FRACTIONAL NUMBERS

All the foregoing about addition of unlike fractions is true for the subtraction of unlike fractions. The identical technique is used to find the least common denominator. Fractions must be renamed so that their denominators are in the same family. The first example for subtraction should be one that requires students to go through the prime factorization method for finding the least common denominator, such as $5/9 - 1/6 = ?$ Most students will be unable to guess that 18 is the least common denominator and will have to find it. This is far better than beginning with $3/4 - 1/2$, for many students will know immediately that the answer is $1/4$ because they know that $1/2$ can be named as $2/4$.

The first practice exercises should contain problems of various sorts so that students can analyze procedures for different situations.

A. $\dfrac{5}{7} - \dfrac{1}{3} = \square$ B. $\dfrac{5}{8} + \dfrac{7}{12} = \square$

C. $\dfrac{3}{5} + \dfrac{7}{20} = \square$ D. $\dfrac{9}{11} - \dfrac{3}{4} = \square$

In exercise A students should see that both denominators are prime numbers. Therefore, the least common denominator is the product of the denominators. In exercise B both denominators are composite numbers. To find the least common denominator they must use the prime factorization method. In exercise C one of the denominators is prime (5) and the other denominator is composite (20). The prime denominator is a factor of the composite denominator. Therefore, the least common denominator is the composite number 20. In exercise D one of the denominators is a prime number (11) and the other denominator is a composite number but the composite number does not contain the prime number as a factor. So the least common denominator is the product of the two denominators. Once the four varieties of examples are explained, most students will realize that they should stop and analyze a problem before they begin to look for the least common denominator.

There is an alternative method of adding and subtracting unlike fractional numbers. It can be taught to students in the middle grades who have difficulty in finding the least common denominator. The main prerequisite of this method is being able to add whole numbers.

Practice is needed in making display fractions before the alternative method can be taught. A display fraction is where you are given

Display Fraction

$$\frac{3}{4} = \frac{3+3+3}{4+4+4}$$

a fraction and you write it several times. There are always as many numbers in the numerator as there are in the denominator. In some problems you fill in the numerator as shown with 2/7. There are two

$$\frac{2}{7} = \frac{+}{7+7} \qquad \frac{5}{8} = \frac{5+5+5}{+\ +}$$
$$\underline{} = \frac{4+4+4+4}{9+9+9+9}$$

one-sevenths in the denominator so two 2s must be written in the numerator. In other problems you fill in the denominator as shown with 5/8, where three 8s are needed in the denominator. The last type is where you fill in the fraction as shown by the display faction of four 4s and four 9s, so the fraction is 4/9. When students can complete problems like these they are ready to learn the new method of adding and subtracting unlike fractional numbers.

It is important, as the first example is worked, that the students write down each step on their paper. They need to be involved in doing each of the steps. The model is established by doing the work.

The first example will be add 3/4 and 2/3. The first step is write the denominator of each fraction. The next step is to "give to the

$$\begin{aligned}\frac{3}{4} &= \frac{}{4}\\[4pt]+\frac{2}{3} &= \frac{}{3}\end{aligned}$$

poor." A 3 is less than a 4, so a 3 is added to the denominator. Now

$$\begin{aligned}\frac{3}{4} &= \frac{}{4}\\[4pt]\frac{2}{3} &= \frac{}{3+3}\end{aligned}$$

4 is less than $3+3$, so you "give to the poor." A 4 is added to the denominator.

$$\begin{aligned}\frac{3}{4} &= \frac{}{4+4}\\[4pt]\frac{2}{3} &= \frac{}{3+3}\end{aligned}$$

Now $3+3$ is less than $4+4$, so you give to the poor again. This time add another 3 to the denominator. Now $3+3+3$ is greater than

$$\begin{aligned}\frac{3}{4} &= \frac{}{4+4}\\[4pt]\frac{2}{3} &= \frac{}{3+3+3}\end{aligned}$$

$4+4$, so a 4 is added to the poor. The denominator $4+4+4$ is

$$\begin{aligned}\frac{3}{4} &= \frac{}{4+4+4}\\[4pt]\frac{2}{3} &= \frac{}{3+3+3}\end{aligned}$$

greater than $3+3+3$, so another 3 is added to the poor.

$$\frac{3}{4} = \frac{}{4+4+4}$$
$$\frac{2}{3} = \frac{}{3+3+3+3}$$

Now the sum of each denominator is the same. Stop and make display fractions for both fractions. Every bottom has to have a top and every top has to have a bottom. No topless bottoms allowed.

$$\frac{3}{4} = \frac{3+3+3}{4+4+4} = \frac{9}{12}$$

$$\frac{2}{3} = \frac{2+2+2+2}{3+3+3+3} = \frac{8}{12}$$

$$\frac{17}{12} \text{ or } 1\frac{5}{12}$$

Next add the numerators and add the denominators. The last step is to add the like fractions and simplify the answer.

The method always works and the common denominator is always the least common denominator. Students who are mathematically inclined will figure out that the method being used is an additive multiple method. In other words, you get the least common multiple by adding instead of multiplying.

After practicing the method for several days the students will find they can add and subtract unlike fractional numbers. They have a method that works for them and they are successful. Really that is the name of the game—finding success.

ADDING AND SUBTRACTING MIXED NUMBERS

When students are successful in adding and subtracting unlike fractions they are ready to add and subtract numbers written in mixed form. At the very beginning, students should be told that problems written with mixed numerals are really two problems. They must work first with the fraction part, then with the whole number part. The hardest part of working with mixed numerals is the necessity to write out all the work. In exercise A students must see that the fraction part of the

$$
\text{A.} \quad
\begin{array}{r}
4\dfrac{2}{3} = 4\dfrac{8}{12} \\[2mm]
+\,6\dfrac{3}{4} = 6\dfrac{9}{12} \\[1mm]
\hline
10\dfrac{17}{12} \ \text{or}\ 11\dfrac{5}{12}
\end{array}
\qquad\qquad
\text{B.} \quad
\begin{array}{r}
8\dfrac{7}{10} = 8\dfrac{7}{10} \\[2mm]
-\,3\dfrac{2}{5} = 3\dfrac{4}{10} \\[1mm]
\hline
5\dfrac{3}{10}
\end{array}
$$

numerals are unlike fractions. They must find the least common denominator: 12. Then they must rewrite the mixed numeral in each case with the fractions named in the twelfth family. Now they add the fractional numbers and then the whole numbers. The numerator of the fraction in the sum is greater than the denominator. Therefore, the fraction can be named as a whole number and a fraction. The whole number is added to the other whole numbers. Students should do the work as the teacher explains each step and the approach to the particular type of problem. The same is true of exercise B. Students must know that 2/5 can be named as 4/10. The mixed numerals must be rewritten, then the fractional numbers subtracted, and finally the whole numbers subtracted. The form is important. Students must write the equal signs and keep the whole numbers and the fractional numbers beneath each other. It is a lot of work but it must be done correctly or many errors will occur. Teachers should not expect pupils to do more than 10 problems with mixed numerals. Each one requires lots of work. If the assignment is too long students become sloppy in following the form and try to find short-cuts. In this case the form is as important as getting the right answer.

In subtracting mixed numerals, two kinds of problems cause trouble. One involves the fraction in the sum being less than the fraction in the addend. The sum must be renamed in order to get a larger fraction in the sum. The other type of problem arises when the sum does not have a fraction part but the addend does. Once again, the sum must be re-named to get a fraction part in the sum. This means that pupils must learn and practice renaming before they are assigned such problems.

The only renaming required in subtraction of mixed numerals is renaming 1 as a fraction if the numerator and denominator are the same numbers. Filling-in exercises should be designed for the students. In Exercises A and B that follow students are asked to rename 1 as a fraction. They are first to use the fraction indicated by the given nu-

A. $1 = \dfrac{?}{4}$ B. $1 = \dfrac{7}{?}$ C. $\dfrac{5}{5} = ?$ D. $\dfrac{8}{8} = ?$ E. $4 = 3\dfrac{?}{5}$

F. $6 = \dfrac{?\,7}{7}$ G. $8 = 7\dfrac{13}{?}$ H. $\dfrac{?}{-} = 5\dfrac{24}{24}$

merator or denominator. In exercises C and D they rename a fraction with like numerator and denominator as the whole number 1. In exercise E they see that the whole number 4 is renamed as 3 plus 5/5. In exercise F they must fill in the whole number left after renaming 1 as 7/7. In exercise G they must complete the fraction. In exercise H they must write the whole number equal to the mixed numeral. It is important to stress that they should never rename more than the number 1 as a fraction equal to 1. For example, they would never rename 6 as $4\frac{6}{3}$ for subtraction purposes.

Explain to students how they use this renaming process they have practiced in both types of subtraction problems. In exercise A have them show that the fraction part of the numerals are unlike fractions.

A.
$$8\dfrac{1}{3} = 8\dfrac{8}{24} = 7\dfrac{32}{24}$$
$$-5\dfrac{5}{8} = -5\dfrac{15}{24} = -5\dfrac{15}{24}$$
$$\overline{\phantom{-5\dfrac{15}{24}}\,2\dfrac{17}{24}}$$

B.
$$6 = 5\dfrac{7}{7}$$
$$-2\dfrac{3}{7} = -2\dfrac{3}{7}$$
$$\overline{\phantom{-2\dfrac{3}{7}}\,3\dfrac{4}{7}}$$

The first step is to find the least common denominator. When the least common denominator, 24, is found, they must rewrite the mixed numerals with like fractions in the twenty-four family. Now they are faced with subtracting 15/24 from 8/24, which is impossible. So they must rename $8\frac{8}{24}$ as $7\frac{32}{24}$. One of the whole number ones in eight ones is renamed as 24/24 and added to the 8/24. The value of the number has not changed; only the name. Now students can subtract 15/24 from 32/24 to get a remainder, 17/24; then they subtract 5 from 7. This is difficult and each of the steps must be repeated through several problems. The slower students will need the individual help of the teacher or aid from another student who understands the procedure. In exercise B it is not possible to subtract 3/7 from nothing. The number must be renamed as $5\frac{7}{7}$. Ask the students why 6 was renamed as $5\frac{7}{7}$ instead of $5\frac{4}{4}$. They should respond that the denominator of the fraction in the addend determines how they rename the whole number 1 taken from the 6 ones. Again, this procedure is difficult and pupils should be given many practice problems until they understand each step. Another way to illustrate renaming is to draw pictures of geometric regions for the whole numbers and parts of regions for the fractions. For slower students money problems can be used, such as subtracting $3.25 from $5.00. The $5.00 is renamed as $4.00 and four quarters. The amount remains the same; only the name is changed. Now it is possible to subtract a quarter and 3 dollars. Remember that when abstract symbols fail to communicate, money is always a good substitute for slower students.

Keep in mind that this work is not confined to one grade level nor to one school year. The work on fractional numbers for the middle grades is spread over three or four years. Then all of it is reviewed and retaught in the seventh and eighth grades for those who need it. Brighter students can accomplish all the work in fractional numbers in a short time, and then should be allowed to go on to a new unit. Many students have a great capacity for self-learning, if we allow them to use it. Slower students need a slower pace and more repetition. They will take longer to progress but once they learn it they are not likely to forget.

ADDING AND SUBTRACTING DECIMAL FRACTIONS

Addition and subtraction of decimal fractions is far easier than the addition and subtraction of other fractional numbers because of place value in our decimal system. Students should be shown a problem written in fraction form, then the same problem written in decimal form, as follows. They will see how much easier the decimal form is by com-

$$+ \quad \begin{array}{l} \dfrac{3}{10} = \dfrac{30}{100} \\[2mm] \dfrac{7}{100} = \dfrac{7}{100} \\[2mm] \hline \dfrac{37}{100} \end{array} \qquad \text{or} \qquad + \begin{array}{r} 0.3 \\ 0.07 \\ \hline 0.37 \end{array}$$

parison. To add 3/10 and 7/100 in fractions it is necessary to rename 3/10 as 30/100, then add to get the sum of 37/100. The same problem in decimal form is $0.3 + 0.07 = 0.37$. Emphasize that the place value of the digits takes care of the least common denominator and so no renaming is necessary.

Give students a problem such as $567 + 89 + 1,039 + 692 = $? Ask how many would rewrite the problem, putting the addends in a column. Then ask why they would do this. The students will say that this is the way to get the ones in the one's place, tens in the ten's place, hundreds in the hundred's place, and thousands in the thousand's place. Then if you were to add a problem such as $3.79 + 0.007 + 0.578 + 13.809 = $?, what would you do first? Many students will say that they would put the addends in column form. Why would you go through all that work? The answer again is to get the one in the ones' place, the tenths in the tenth's place, the hundredths in the hundredth's place, and the thousandths in the thousandth's place. All this assumes that the students have practiced writing fractions with powers of ten as denominators in decimal form through thousandths.

Subtraction of decimal fractions is the same as the addition of decimal fractions in that the digits must be placed in the same column according to place value. The one difficulty that occurs in subtraction is the renaming. Sometimes it is necessary to rename one whole number as ten tenths; sometimes one tenth must be renamed as ten hundredths. This renaming should be practiced before students are assigned any problems that require renaming.

Some students may have been careless and omitted the decimal point in the answer. They should be asked what their answer is and when they say 345 instead of 3.45, ask them to show how it is possible to get such a large sum when the addends were such small numbers. A teacher who praises those who study the problem and analyze it as well as finding the correct answer will find more students will be encouraged to proceed in this fashion. Again, only a few problems should be assigned so that students will not feel the pressure of solving simply to get answers and have no time to analyze the problems. It is better if a student solves 10 problems correctly than if he attempts 35 problems and gets only 7 or 8 right, simply because he is in a hurry to finish.

A teacher must adopt a positive attitude toward mistakes. Instead of making a federal case out of mistakes, point out which problems contain errors and ask the pupils to correct the mistakes. If they cannot find the errors, tell them to ask for help. It is far better if a student finds his own errors than if a teacher points out the errors to him and gives him the correct solution. We all learn by making mistakes. We should not be made to feel guilty if we make mistakes. The main idea is to learn from the mistakes. This means that pupils must understand what is causing their errors.

SUGGESTIONS FOR DRILL AND PRACTICE

Students have used the squares for addition and subtraction of whole numbers. They also can be used for fractional numbers, as shown here:

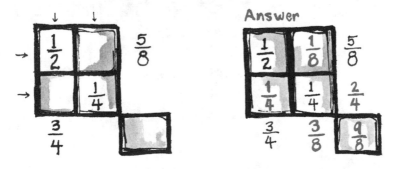

What do you add to 1/2 to get 5/8? What do you add to 1/2 to get 3/4? What is the sum of 1/4 and 1/4? What is the sum of 1/8 and 1/4? What is the sum of 5/8 and 2/4? What is the sum of 3/4 and 3/8? Does the grand sum check? To devise more problems like this, all that is needed is to put addends in the squares that contain the *x*s and two sums where

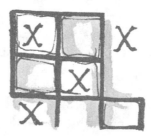

the outside *x*s are. Then have the students fill in the missing parts by adding and subtracting unlike fractional numbers.

Students enjoy filling in addition charts. Make them up with various fractions for which the sums must be found. One table can provide a great deal of practice. It is work, but it does not seem as difficult as nine problems assigned separately.

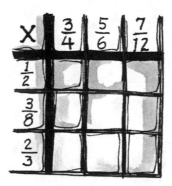

A table with sum, part, part, and difference can be made up, as shown.

Students are given two fractional numbers and are asked to find the other two missing numbers. This is fun for brighter students because it really makes them think. When the sum is 7/8 and the difference is 3/8 what are the two parts?

Another good exercise for brighter students is to tell them that for centuries man worked only with unit fractions. These fractions contain 1 in the numerator. For example, 1/2, 1/3, 1/4, 1/5, 1/6 are all unit fractions. Ask them to write the fractions 7/12, 5/18, 5/12, 4/9, 5/24 in terms of unit fractions. They will have to write 7/12 as $1/3 + 1/4$, 5/18 as $1/6 + 1/9$, and so on.

SUMMARY

Teaching addition and subtraction of fractional numbers is so much easier with the present mathematics curriculum. Students understand prime and composite numbers and they understand why they do certain things. For years students were forced to follow steps that were meaningless to them. Teachers must realize that success in learning to operate with fractional numbers depends on a pupil's knowing a great deal about the set of whole numbers. The more they know about how the number system works, the more they know about various sets of numbers and the more they can learn about another set of numbers. All mathematics relates, and students need to see the connecting links.

EXERCISES

1. How does a knowledge of prime and composite numbers help a student find the least common denominator of 3/7 and 5/8?
2. Show how the prime factorization method is used to find the least common denominator of the fractions 7/8 and 11/36.
3. What does a student have to know about renaming in order to find the answer to $6 - 3\frac{3}{5}$?
4. Why must form be stressed as much or more than the answer when students are adding and subtracting numbers expressed as mixed numerals?
5. Why isn't $1/4 + 1/2$ a good example to use as the first problem in learning to add unlike fractions?
6. What step comes before $4/7 = \dfrac{3 \times 4}{3 \times 7} = \dfrac{12}{21}$?
7. How is the role of the denominator in a fraction similar to the role of the digits in the place value of a number?

SELECTED READINGS

BANKS, J. H.: *Learning and Teaching Arithmetic,* Allyn and Bacon, Inc., Boston, 1964, pp. 291–306.

MARKS, J. L., C. R. PURDY, and LUCIEN B. KINNEY: *Teaching Elementary School Mathematics for Understanding,* Chapter 9, McGraw-Hill, Inc., New York, 1965.

Studies in Mathematics, Vol. IX, Stanford University Press, Palo Alto, California, 1963, pp. 219–256.

Topics in Mathematics for Elementary School Teachers, Twenty-Ninth Yearbook of the National Council of Teachers of Mathematics, The Council, Booklet No. 6, Washington, D.C., 1965.

Multiplication and Division
of Fractional Numbers

INTRODUCTION

Learning how to multiply and divide fractional numbers is easier than learning how to add and subtract unlike fractions. Two properties of fractional numbers explain the why of multiplication and division. The first is the *property of one* and the other is the *reciprocal property*. Once students understand these two properties and learn to apply them, they are on their way to understanding the operations of multiplication and division of fractional numbers. Perhaps some day the curriculum in elementary mathematics texts will be rearranged so that the easiest part will come first. There is a myth in education which claims that addition and subtraction must always be taught first. This really applies only to the first introduction to the operations in the set of whole numbers.

Fewer teachers today are saying, "Your's not to reason why; your's is only to invert and multiply." A generation of pupils who were taught that way are now adults and they no longer remember which fraction to invert and multiply. This shows we need to prove the "why" and give students a clear mental image of what is happening. The show-and-tell method of teaching produces no lasting results; one can recall only if he understands.

MULTIPLICATION OF FRACTIONAL
NUMBERS IN THE MIDDLE GRADES

Most students who know how to multiply with the set of whole numbers will give the correct answer to $3/5 \times 6/7$. They will automatically multiply numerator times numerator and denominator times denominator. The difficulty is that they do not *believe* the product or answer. They know a product of 18/35 is about 1/2 and they also know that 1/2 is less than 3/5 and less than 6/7. When multiplying whole numbers in the primary grades, the product was never less than the factors. Even if the product were 0, one of the factors was 0. Therefore, this is where the teaching must start.

What does 4×2 mean? The correct answer is $2 + 2 + 2 + 2$ or 4 sets of 2. It shows that in multiplication we should concentrate first on the second factor. We look at the 2 to see what the equal addend is before we decide how many times it will be added. The first factor tells how many times the second factor is used as an addend. Students need to review these facts before they begin multiplying fractional numbers. This is the same model used in fractional numbers.

FRACTION TIMES WHOLE NUMBER

The first step is to use an example in which the second factor is a fraction and the first factor is a whole number. Thus, $4 \times 1/2$ equals what? The second factor is 1/2 and is used 4 times. Then $4 \times 1/2$ means $1/2 + 1/2 + 1/2 + 1/2$, or 2. The next question is: How can you draw a picture of the multiplication problem $4 \times 1/2$? The first drawing must represent 1/2 of a whole region. So you need four of these drawings.

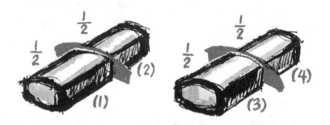

The same problem can be illustrated on the number line. First, the unit from 0 to 1 must be divided into 2 equal parts; then the unit from 1 to 2 must be divided into 2 equal parts. By drawing arrows we see that four 1/2s are 2. Many such exercises involving first factors as whole numbers and second factors as fractions should be worked through in class.

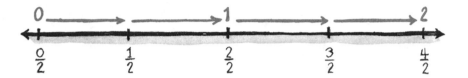

The next step is to use an example in which the first factor is a fraction and the second factor is a whole number. Thus, $1/2 \times 8 = ?$ The second factor states that we are considering 8 ones; the first factor, that we want to find one half of them. Students will quickly see that the product is 4. The following drawing shows that 4 is the correct product:

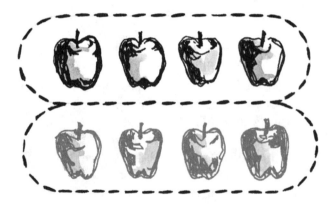

Now try an example such as $2/3 \times 18 = ?$ This time have your students draw 18 units then find two-thirds of them. After they make the drawings ask them to analyze what they did first, what they did next, and then what they did last. The first step was to draw the 18 units. The next was to divide the set of 18 into 3 equal subsets. The last was to consider two of the subsets. In mathematics this means to divide 18 by 3, then multiply that number by 2. By analyzing the steps involved in making the drawing, students will see that when multiplying a fraction times a whole number, they always divide by the divisor, then multiply that answer by the numerator of the fraction.

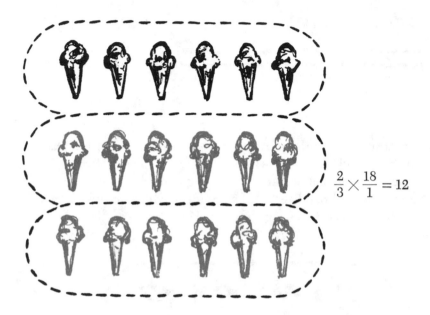

$$\frac{2}{3} \times \frac{18}{1} = 12$$

Teachers will be amazed at the success they get by using the terms *shrinkers* and *stretchers* to help slow students. This vocabulary was invented at the University of Illinois in a project concerned with writing materials for slow learners. Begin by saying, "Shrink 10 two times." The response will be 5. Then say, "Shrink 12 three times." The response will be 4. There is no reason why students should respond correctly, because what you are saying really does not make sense. But they do answer correctly. Now ask them to stretch 2 three times. The answer will be 6. Stretch 5 four times. The response will be 20. Now tell them *shrinkers* always have a bar over them; stretchers do not. For example, in the fraction 3/4, the 4 is the shrinker and the 3 is the stretcher. Now 2/9 × 27 means that you first shrink 27 nine times. When they answer 3, tell them to stretch 3 two times, and the response will be 6. After students are successful in finding products with shrinkers and stretchers, tell them shrinkers mean divide and stretchers mean to multiply. The amazing part of it all is that students will now remember and will be able to multiply fractions times whole numbers quickly and successfully. The only students who will still have difficulty are the very slow ones who do not know their multiplication and division facts. Those students should not yet try to multiply and divide with fractional numbers.

Multiplication in which one factor only is a fraction is usually learned in fourth or fifth grade. This first exposure should come a year before attempting problems in which both factors are fractions. To test the brighter students, give them a problem such as $9/2 \times 10 = ?$ If they know they must first divide by the divisor, then multiply by the numerator, they will have no difficulty with fractions in which the numerator is larger than the denominator. Try another problem such as $2/3 \times 0 = ?$ Those who understand will say they must divide 0 by 3, which is 0, then multiply by 2, which is 0. Would you expect the product to be 0? The answer is "yes," because in the set of whole numbers, when 0 is one of the factors, the product is 0. Now students have discovered that the property of zero is true in the set of fractional numbers for the operation of multiplication.

PROPERTIES OF MULTIPLICATION

While students are learning how to multiply with one factor as a fraction, they should consider products of $2/3 \times 12$ and $12 \times 2/3$. In both cases the product is 8. Would you expect this to be true? Again, the response should be "yes," because the *commutative property of multiplication* is true for whole numbers and they would expect it to be true for fractional numbers.

How would you solve the problem $1/2 \times 5 \times 6$? Allow several students to tell how they would solve the problem. Some will find $1/2 \times 5$, which is $5/2$, then multiply by 6. Others will multiply 5×6 then multiply by $1/2$. A few mathematically inclined students may multiply $1/2 \times 6$ then multiply by 5. A discussion should follow explaining why each solution yields the same product. Bring out the associative and commutative properties of multiplication. A student who multiplied $1/2 \times 6$

then multiplied by 5 used which property first? He changed the order of the factors, using the commutative property of multiplication. Those who decided to multiply $1/2 \times 6$ used the *grouping* or *associative property of multiplication*. During the discussion students will discover that the properties of multiplication in whole numbers are all true in the set of fractional numbers.

Give another example to include all the properties, such as $3/4 \times 1 = ?$ The response will be $3/4$. What role does 1 or $1/1$ play in fractional numbers? Students should remember that 1 was the *identity element in multiplication* of whole numbers and is still an identity element in multiplication for the set of fractional numbers.

Give students exercises in which they must apply these properties.

$$\frac{1}{5} \times 4 = \boxed{} \times \frac{1}{5} \qquad \frac{7}{3} \times \boxed{} = 0 \qquad \boxed{} \times \frac{7}{11} = \frac{7}{11}$$

$$\left(\frac{1}{8} \times 4\right) \times 2 = \boxed{} \times (4 \times 2)$$

Do not ask them to compute the answer but merely to tell how they would go about doing them from their knowledge of the properties involved,

Review multiplication of fractional numbers with one factor as a fraction in the grade following the one in which this kind of multiplication is first introduced. Before going on with multiplication of two fractional factors, students must be able to multiply with one factor and one whole number. Slower students may need another year to reinforce this skill. If so, give them the extra time while the other students go on.

FRACTION TIMES FRACTION

Before attempting multiplication of two or more fractional numbers, make a drawing like the one shown here for multiplying whole numbers to illustrate the array 3×3. What are the dimensions of each of the small squares in the array? The answer should be 1 unit by 1 unit. Then the area of each square is 1 square unit. Students should have had experience with area and perimeter before they start to multiply fractional numbers. The array is made up of how many 1 square units? (9) Does this array show that $3 \times 3 = 9$? (Yes it does.)

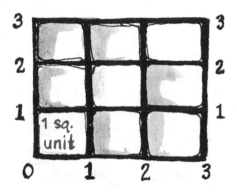

In our next array the horizontal unit from 0 to 1 has been divided into 2 congruent pieces. Each of these units or pieces represents what fractional number? The response should be 1/2. The unit from 0 to 1 in vertical form is divided into 3 congruent parts or pieces. Each of these pieces represents what fractional number? The response this time

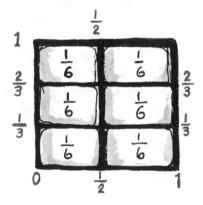

should be 1/3. What are the dimensions of each of the small rectangles in the array? The answer is $1/3 \times 1/2$. Each of the rectangles is one half of a unit long and one third of a unit high, or wide. What is the area of each of the small rectangular regions? The answer is $1/3 \times 1/2$, or 1/6 square unit. It is very important that students see that each rec-

tangular region in the array represents the fractional number 1/6. There
are 6 of the rectangular regions and $1/6 + 1/6 + 1/6 + 1/6 + 1/6 +$
$1/6 = 1$. What is the area of the large rectangular region? The answer
should be 1×1, or 1 square unit. Have the students make the array by
drawing a line segment horizontally 6 inches long. Divide the line segment into 2 congruent parts and label the midpoint 1/2. Now draw a
vertical line 6 inches long and divide this line segment into 3 congruent
parts and label the division points 1/3 and 2/3. Now extend the line
segments from each division on the lines to make the array. Ask them
to shade the rectangular region whose length is 1/2 and whose height
is 2/3.

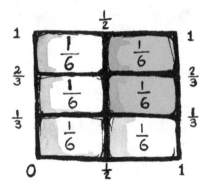

What is the area of this rectangular region? The answer is $2/3 \times$
$1/2$, or 2/6. Does the shaded region cover two of the small rectangles?
(Yes it does.) Does each of the small rectangular regions represent 1/6
of the whole? (Yes it does.) Then is $2/3 \times 1/2$ equal to 2/6? Can you
simplify the fractional number 2/6? The answer should be "yes," to
1/3. Is the shaded region 1/3 of the whole region? By drawing an array
and dividing the basic unit into fractional parts, students can see the
picture of the product of two fractional numbers. Using the same array,
have the students analyze the problem $2/3 \times 1/2 = ?$ First, show 1/2
of the whole region. But the problem asks for only 2/3 of the 1/2.
Where is that shown in the array? Students should use their fingers to
show that the line segment at 2/3 cuts off part of the 1/2 of the whole
unit. The cut-off is at the shaded area illustrating the two 1/6 regions.
They can see that $2/3 \times 1/2$ is less than 1/2 and is also less than 2/3 of

the original whole unit. Therefore, the product must be less than either of the fractional numbers in the factors of the multiplication problem.

Give the students another exercise and let them perform all the steps involved in drawing the picture to reinforce their mental image of multiplication of fractional numbers. Let them try $2/3 \times 3/4 = ?$ Look first at the second factor, 3/4. Represent the basic unit by drawing a rectangle and divide it into four equal parts. Then shade three fourths of

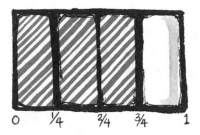

the rectangle by using diagonal lines to the right. The first factor is two thirds, so the students should next divide the rectangle into thirds horizontally. Then have them shade two thirds of the whole region with diagonal lines going to the left.

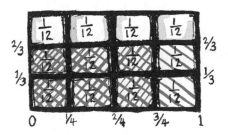

How many small rectangular regions are there? (12) How many of these regions are double shaded? (6) Does the region with double shading show $2/3 \times 3/4$? (Yes it does.) They can see that $2/3 \times 3/4$ is less than $1 \times 3/4$. Impress upon the students that 2/3 implies 2/3 of a whole unit and 3/4 implies 3/4 of a whole unit. That is why the whole region has to be divided first into fourths, then into thirds. The product of $2/3 \times 3/4$ is equal to 6/12, or 1/2.

The number line also can be used to convey the same idea. Divide a unit from 0 to 1 into fourths. Have the students put their fingers on

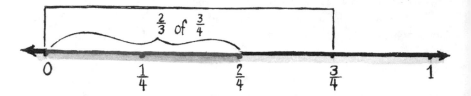

the dot that represents 3/4. How many small units are there between 0 and 3/4? (3) Then 2/3 × 3/4 means that they are to find the point two-thirds of the distance between 0 and 3/4 on the number line. What is the name of that dot? (2/4) Does this exercise show that 2/3 × 3/4 = 2/4, or 1/2?

Another way to illustrate multiplication of fractional numbers is by transparencies shown on an overhead projector. The transparencies can be put together to show each step in the process and shading or coloring can be used to highlight the divisions and intersections. Accurately prepared transparencies provide a very precise and vivid model for students.

Still another way to teach multiplication of fractional numbers is to work with the symbols and omit drawings. Start out with the symbols of whole numbers in multiplication to show the model and then use the model to transfer to the fractional numbers. A sample problem might be 30 × 40 = 1200.

$30 \times 40 = (3 \times 10) \times (4 \times 10)$	expanded form
$= 3 \times 10 \times 4 \times 10$	remove parentheses
$= 3 \times 4 \times 10 \times 10$	commutative property of multiplication
$= (3 \times 4) \times (10 \times 10)$	associative property of multiplication
$= \quad 12 \quad \times \quad 100$	binary operation
$= 1200$	binary operation

This sample shows all the steps. Students see that 30 can be written as 3×10 and 40 as 4×10. The factors 10 and 4 can change order because of the commutative property of multiplication. Only two factors can be multiplied at one time so the factors must be grouped. They are grouped as 3×4 and 10×10, in line with the associative property of multiplication. Next, two factors are multiplied—the binary operation of multiplication—which shows that when multiplying the unit *ten* by the unit *ten* a new unit called *hundreds* is obtained. Now multiply by the number of *ten* units (3×4), which is 12. In 3 tens and 4 tens, the 3 and the 4 are the face values of the numbers which together (3×4) answer the question, How many? The ten is the place value and answers the question, How many what? The place values are multiplied together (10×10) to find the answer to that question. This concept of forming a new unit when multiplying units is very important.

In a multiplication problem such as $3/5 \times 2/7$, the fractional numbers must be expanded to illustrate the meaning of the denominators and the numerators.

$$\frac{3}{5} \times \frac{2}{7} = \left(3 \times \frac{1}{5}\right) \times \left(2 \times \frac{1}{7}\right) \qquad \text{expanded form}$$

$$= 3 \times \frac{1}{5} \times 2 \times \frac{1}{7} \qquad \text{remove parentheses}$$

$$= 3 \times 2 \times \frac{1}{5} \times \frac{1}{7} \qquad \begin{array}{l}\text{commutative property} \\ \text{of multiplication}\end{array}$$

$$= (3 \times 2) \times \left(\frac{1}{5} \times \frac{1}{7}\right) \qquad \begin{array}{l}\text{associative property} \\ \text{of multiplication}\end{array}$$

$$= 6 \times \frac{1}{35} \qquad \text{binary operation}$$

$$= \frac{6}{35}$$

Three fifths means $3 \times 1/5$, and $2/7$ means $2 \times 1/7$. Students must understand this point before they can operate with the fractional numbers. The factors $1/5$ and 2 can change order because of the commutative property of multiplication. Since only two numbers can be multiplied at one time and since there are four factors, the factors must be grouped in twos. The new grouping is 3×2 and $1/5 \times 1/7$, which is possible because of the associative property of multiplication. Now the two sets of two factors are multiplied because of the binary operation of multiplication, and the resulting factors 6 and 1/35 are multiplied, again because of the binary operation of multiplication. When the unit 1/5 and the unit 1/7 are multiplied, a new unit is formed called thirty fifth. The factors 3 and 2 told how many of the units 1/5 and 1/7 there were; when they are multiplied (3), they tell how many thirty fifths (1/5 $\times$ 1/7 = 1/35) there are. Point out to students that just as in whole numbers, tens times tens yield a new unit called hundreds, so in fractional numbers a unit such as 1/5 and a unit such as 1/7, multiplied together, yield a new unit, 1/35. The denominators are multiplied to form a new unit and the numerators are multiplied to find out how many of the new unit exist.

SIMPLIFYING FRACTIONS

Tell the students to look for short-cuts when they are practicing multiplication of fractional numbers. Often a common factor occurs both in the numerator and the denominator and can be renamed as 1 because of the property of one. This will eliminate simplifying the product. In the example shown here, students can see that the factors 3 and 5 are in both the numerator and the denominator. The fractions

$$\frac{3}{5} \times \frac{5}{6} = \frac{\overset{1 \times 1}{\cancel{3} \times \cancel{5}}}{\cancel{5} \times \cancel{3} \times 2} = \frac{1}{2}$$

3/3 and 5/5 are other names for 1, because if any number is divided by itself, except for zero, it names 1 (the property of one). The only factor now left in the numerator is 1 $\times$ 1, and the only factor left in the denominator is 2. Therefore, the product is 1/2. If students fail to eliminate the common factors before multiplying, their product will be 15/30, which must then be simplified to 1/2. Tell them to look at each numerator and at each denominator before they start to multiply to see if there are any common factors. If there are common factors, they should be renamed as 1 and then the multiplication can be carried out. Point out that the numbers being renamed must be factors. For example, in $3 + 5/6$, it is not possible to rename the 3 in the numerator and the 3 in the denominator because the 3 in the numerator is an addend, not a factor. A problem like this should be written on the chalkboard for all the students to see and they should be told why the 3 in the numerator cannot be renamed. They must understand that a number can be renamed only if it is a factor.

The bright students will find the short-cuts themselves. The others must have them pointed out to them. Short-cuts usually make for more accurate work. The smaller the numbers used in multiplying, the greater the chance of finding the right answer.

MULTIPLICATION OF NUMBERS IN MIXED FORM

Multiplying numbers in mixed form requires the ability to write a number in mixed form as the same number in fraction form. Here a review in writing $4\frac{1}{2}$ as 9/2 should be given. To begin, ask how many halves there are in the whole number 1. How many halves are there in four whole numbers? Then how many halves are in $4\frac{1}{2}$? Remind students that the symbol $4\frac{1}{2}$ is a short way of writing $4 + 1/2$. In writing $5\frac{2}{3}$ as 17/3, why do we multiply 3×5? Here we hope students will say that there are 3 thirds in 1 so there are 3×5 thirds in 5. After students are successful at writing numbers in mixed form as fractions, they should try to multiply fractions. Once again they should be reminded to look for common factors before they multiply. For example, in multiplying $4\frac{1}{2} \times 3\frac{2}{3}$ they will write $9/2 \times 11/3$ and should see that 3 is a common factor in both the numerator and the denominator and can be renamed 1. Then the product is 33/2, which can be renamed $16\frac{1}{2}$.

$$4\frac{1}{2} \times 3\frac{2}{3}$$

$$\overset{3}{\cancel{9}} \times \frac{11}{\underset{1}{\cancel{3}}} = \frac{33}{2}, \text{ or } 16\frac{1}{2}$$

When a whole number is one of the factors in a multiplication problem in which the other factors are fractions, the whole number should be rewritten as a fraction with a denominator of 1. In the example $4\frac{1}{2} \times 6 \times 7/9$, students should rewrite the problem as $9/2 \times 6/1$

$$4\frac{1}{2} \times 6 \times \frac{7}{9}$$

$$\frac{\overset{1}{\cancel{9}}}{\underset{1}{\cancel{2}}} \times \frac{\overset{3}{\cancel{6}}}{1} \times \frac{7}{\underset{1}{\cancel{9}}} = \frac{21}{1} \text{ or } 21$$

$\times 7/9$. By looking at the numerators and the denominators, it is apparent that 2 is a common factor of 2 and 6, and that 9 is common factor of 9 and 9. These common factors can be renamed as 1. The product becomes 3×7 in the numerator and 1×1 in the denominator, which is 21/1, or 21. It is important for students to realize that all whole numbers can be written with a denominator of 1. Whole numbers are a subset of the fractional numbers and can be written in fraction form.

MULTIPLYING DECIMAL FRACTIONS

Fractions with powers of ten for denominators can be multiplied another way because of our decimal system. First, students should multiply the fractions to see what happens to the product. For example, consider $3/10 \times 17/100 = 51/1000$. This problem shows that tenths times hundredths yields a product of thousandths. There is a pattern in the number of zeros in the denominators. If one factor has one zero and the other factor has two zeros, the product has three zeros. The problem should be illustrated both in fraction form and in decimal form so that the relationships can be pointed out. Decimal places are the places to

$$\frac{3}{10} \times \frac{17}{100} = \frac{17}{1000} \qquad \begin{array}{r} 0.3 \quad (1) \\ \underline{\times 0.17} \quad (2) \\ 0.051 \quad (3) \end{array}$$

the right of the one's place. The sum of the number of decimal places in the factors of the decimals is the number of decimal places in the product. Multiply the same way as you would with whole numbers. Then place the decimal point in the proper position according to the value of the number in the product. Call to the students' attention that when the problem is in fraction form, the sum of the number of zeros in the denominators of the factors determines the number of zeros in the denominator of the product. This explains why it is possible to add the number of decimal places when the problem is written in decimal form. In counting the decimal places in the product, start with the digit at the extreme right. Illustrate this point with a set of problems in which the digits are the same but the value is different because of the location of the decimal point. This drill will not only help students see the pat-

$$
\begin{array}{cccccccc}
24 & 2.4 & (1) & 2.4 & (1) & 0.24 & (2) & 0.24 & (2) \\
\underline{13} & \underline{\times 13} & (0) & \underline{\times 1.3} & (1) & \underline{\times 1.3} & (1) & \underline{\times 0.13} & (2) \\
72 & 72 & & 72 & & 72 & & 72 & \\
\underline{24} & \underline{24} & & \underline{24} & & \underline{24} & & \underline{24} & \\
312 & 31.2 & (1) & 3.12 & (2) & 0.312 & (3) & 0.0312 & (4)
\end{array}
$$

tern of counting decimal places, but also will point out to them that as the factors become smaller, the product becomes smaller. Also point out that as long as the digits in the factors remain the same, the digits in the product remain the same but the value changes because of the place value of the digits.

RECIPROCAL PROPERTY

Before completing the unit on multiplication of fractional numbers students need to learn the reciprocal property or multiplicative inverse.

$$\frac{1}{4} \times \overset{?}{-} = 1$$

$$\frac{6}{1} \times \overset{?}{-} = 1$$

$$\frac{2}{3} \times \overset{?}{-} = 1$$

What number times 1/4 equals 1? What number times 6 equals 1? What number times 2/3 equals 1? After the students have volunteered the answers, tell them to look at the three examples and tell what they notice about the products in all three. Is 1 a special number in multiplication? Do you think that you could complete $3/7 \times ? = 1$? (7/3) by looking at the factors in these three examples. Two numbers whose product is 1 are each the reciprocal of the other. Two thirds is the reciprocal of three halves and three halves is the reciprocal of two thirds. Another name for the numbers whose product is 1 is *multiplicative inverse*. You cannot have an inverse until you first have an identity element. In multiplication the identity element is 1. Therefore, the inverses are numbers that make the product 1. The word "reciprocal" is usually used in the upper middle grades and the words "multiplicative inverse" in junior high and secondary mathematics. The reciprocal or multiplicative inverse is another property of our number system and is found in the set of fractional numbers with the operation of multiplication. It is important for students to understand the property because it is used to explain division of fractional numbers. In providing exercises to practice finding the reciprocal, all kinds of numbers should be included, such as whole numbers, fractional numbers, and decimals.

$$\frac{4}{3} \times ? = 1 \qquad ? \times .6 = 1 \qquad 4\frac{2}{3} \times ? = 1 \qquad ? \times 8 = 1$$

When a number is written in mixed form, such as $4\frac{2}{3}$, students must think of the number in fractional form in order to name the reciprocal.

DIVISION OF FRACTIONS

Teaching division of fractions has always caused difficulty for teachers and students. At one time writers concerned mostly with the social utility of arithmetic topics suggested that division of fractions might be deleted from the arithmetic curriculum. In recent years most authorities on the teaching of elementary school mathematics have agreed that the study of division is valuable because the process is often used in scientific fields and is essential to the study of algebra.

As recently as 1945 many writers maintained that pupils in the upper grades could not be taught to understand "why" and therefore should be taught the rule of "invert and multiply." Research and classroom experience since 1945 indicate that pupils can learn why division of fractions is the same as multiplying by the reciprocal of the divisor.

There are two major methods of teaching the meaning of division of fractions, the common denominator approach and the reciprocal approach. Each has its advocates and valid reasons to support it.

The common denominator method can be developed from the division of whole numbers. Thus,

$$8 \div 2 = n \text{ can be written } 2\overline{)8}^{\,4} \quad \text{check: } 2 \times 4 = 8$$
$$\underline{8}$$
$$0$$

Eight divided by 2 means, How many 2s make 8?

$$\frac{7}{12} \div \frac{1}{12} = n \text{ can be written } \frac{1}{12}\overline{)\frac{7}{12}}^{\,7} \quad \text{check: } 7 \times \frac{1}{12} = \frac{7}{12}$$
$$\underline{\frac{7}{12}}$$
$$0$$

Seven twelfths divided by one twelfth means, How many twelfths make seven twelfths?

$$\frac{7}{12} \div \frac{1}{12} = \frac{7 \div 1}{12 \div 12} = \frac{7 \div 1}{1} = \frac{7}{1} \text{ or } 7$$

If the fractions have a common denominator, the denominators, when divided, equal 1 because of the property of one. In the example above, $12 \div 12$ equals 1. Thus the answer is the division of the numerators. This result leads pupils to conclude that when fractions have common denominators and the indicated procedure is divided, it is necessary to divide only the numerators to obtain the answers.

In the example $2/3 \div 3/4$, the fractions must be renamed to get a common denominator.

$$\frac{2}{3} \div \frac{3}{4} = \frac{8}{12} \div \frac{9}{12} = 8 \div 9 \text{ or } \frac{8}{9}$$

$$\frac{3}{5} \div \frac{6}{7} = \frac{21}{35} \div \frac{30}{35} = 21 \div 30 \text{ or } \frac{21}{30}$$

After a few examples like the ones above, pupils will see that if they do cross-products of the number pairs they will get the answer. In the case of $2/3 \div 3/4$, they multiply 2×4 and 3×3 to find the answer, 8/9. Thus, division of fractions can be performed with little work beyond multiplication.

The inversion method is based on the identity property of multiplication, the property of one, and the reciprocal property. The division must be written in complex fraction form. The first step is to remove the denominator.

$$\frac{2}{3} \div \frac{5}{7} = \frac{\dfrac{2}{3} \times \left(\dfrac{7}{5}\right)}{\dfrac{5}{7} \times \left(\dfrac{7}{5}\right)} = \frac{\dfrac{14}{15}}{1}, \text{ or } \frac{14}{15}$$

The next step is to rename the denominator as 1. Any whole number can be written with a denominator of 1 without changing the number. The reciprocal of five sevenths is seven fifths, so multiply by seven fifths to rename the denominator 1. Then the numerator must be multiplied by seven fifths because of the property of one. Students must understand that 7/5 divided by 7/5 is the same as 1 because of the property of one. Now multiply and the answer is 14/15. When multiplying, you are simply multiplying by another number that is the same as 1, which does not change the original fraction because 1 is the identity element of multiplication. Therefore, 14/15 is another name for the division problem originally stated, because all that was done was to multiply by a form of 1. Draw attention to the numerator so that students can see that it is being multiplied by the denominator of the fraction in reciprocal form. So again they see that they can divide fractions by multiplying by the reciprocal of the divisor. Now the old saying, "invert and multiply" has some meaning because *invert* means using the reciprocal property. After students have formed a clear mental image of what is happening when they divide fractions, assign them practice problems.

Another approach to the use of the reciprocal in the division of fractional numbers is to relate division to multiplication. For example $9 \div 3 = n$ can be restated as $3 \times n = 9$. This means that $2/3 \div 3/4 = n$ can be restated as $3/4 \times n = 2/3$. What can you multiply $3/4$ by to get the product of 1? The answer is the reciprocal $4/3$. If you multiply one side of an equation by $4/3$ you must multiply the other side of the equation by the same number or you change the value of the equation, as the following exercise indicates:

$$\frac{2}{3} \div \frac{3}{4} = n$$

$$\frac{3}{4} \times n = \frac{2}{3}$$

$$\left(\frac{4}{3} \times \frac{3}{4} \right) \times n = \frac{2}{3} \times \frac{4}{3}$$

$$1 \times n = \frac{8}{9}$$

To find the value of n or of the missing factor you multiply the first fraction or dividend by the reciprocal of the divisor. The divisor is always the fraction to the right of the division sign.

DIVISION OF DECIMAL FRACTIONS

Division with numbers written in decimal form should be shown first in fraction form so that students can see how the property of one is used in creating an equivalent problem that has the same solution.

$$\frac{4.5}{0.05} \times \left(\frac{100}{100} \right) = \frac{450}{5} \text{ or } 90$$

The problem 4.5 divided by 0.05 can be changed to 450 divided by 5 by multiplying both numerator and denominator by 100. The fraction 100 divided by 100 is another way of stating the number 1 according to the property of one. This means that the original fraction has been multiplied by 1, which does not change the product because of the identity element of multiplication. Students should be able to divide 450 by 5 and come up with 90 as the quotient. It is easier to divide by a whole number than by a decimal so the problem is changed into an equivalent problem with the same quotient. The denominator determines what number is used to multiply both the numerator and denominator. In the example used here, the denominator is in hundredths so it is necessary to multiply by 100 to get a whole number, 5. After students appear to understand how to write decimals in fraction form, have them try to solve the division problem in the conventional form of division. Five hundredths is the divisor. Multiplying it by 100, the divisor becomes 5. You must also multiply the dividend, 4.5, by 100 because of the property of one. The phrase, "move the decimal point"

$$\frac{4.5}{0.05} \quad \text{or} \quad 0.05.\overline{)4.50.}^{\,90.}$$

simply means that you are multiplying by a power of 10. The decimal point does not move; the digits do. For example, when multiplying 4 by 10, the product is 40. The digit 4 has moved one place to the left. The same is true when multiplying 0.05 by 100. The product is 5. The digit 5 has moved 2 places to the left. Because of the decimal system our place value is based on powers of 10. All this means is that one can say, "Move the decimal point two places to the right or to the left" so long as the students know that this really indicates a change in place value of the digits.

Careless students have trouble placing the decimal point in the proper position in the quotient. Have them check their answers by multiplying. Point out that they must look to see if the quotient they get is sensible. Relationships should be pointed out. If the denominator or divisor is a very small number, such as five hundredths, the quotient will be greater than the dividend. If the denominator or divisor is a large number, the quotient will be smaller than the dividend. Exercises

$$.05\overline{)1.25} \qquad 4\overline{).08} \qquad .3\overline{)0.27} \qquad 18\overline{)3.6}$$

should be used that will require students to state only whether the quotient is larger or smaller than the dividend. Teachers must remember that in order to impress an idea on the minds of students they must do more than simply tell them about it. Involve them in activities and exercises which require practical use of the idea.

Needless to say, students who are not successful in dividing with whole numbers will not be successful in dividing with decimals. Do not force students to complete a unit before they possess the necessary tools or skills to accomplish the task. Slower students will have to work longer on division with whole numbers than brighter students who meanwhile can go on to division with decimals.

SUMMARY

Children will not learn how to multiply and divide fractional numbers just by being told how these processes are performed. Students need to understand why the answers they get are correct, which means they must be shown by diagrams and pictures just what is happening. They must draw pictures in addition to seeing them being drawn. This phase cannot be rushed. Preparation is more important than practice. The properties of multiplication must be understood, then used, so that students will understand what is happening when they divide fractional numbers. Once they understand the operation, they will have a basis for relearning the process if and when they forget it. Many aids should be used, such as transparencies, drawings, film strips, and the number line. The more methods used, the more chance a teacher has of reaching all his students.

EXERCISES

1. Make a diagram to prove that $3/4 \times 5/6$ is $5/8$.
2. What property explains what is usually called cancellation?
3. Instead of saying "invert and multiply" when dividing $3/5$ by $2/7$, say "You multiply by $\underline{\ ?\ }$."

4. What problem is involved in learning how to multiply fractional numbers?
5. How is the property of one used in the division of numbers expressed as decimal fractions?
6. How is the property of one used in some problems involving multiplication of fractional numbers?

SELECTED READINGS

COPELAND, R. W., *Mathematics and the Elementary Teacher*, 2d ed., W. B. Saunders Company, Philadelphia, 1972, pp. 295–312.

GROSSNICKLE, F. E., L. J. BRUECKNER, J. RECHZEH: *Teaching Elementary School Mathematics*, Chapter 14, Holt, Rinehart and Winston, Inc., New York, 1968.

MARKS, J. L., C. R. PURDY, and L. B. KINNEY: *Teaching Elementary School Mathematics for Understanding*, McGraw-Hill, Inc., New York, 1965, pp. 281–295.

PETERSON, J. A., and J. HASHISAKI, *Theory of Arithmetic*, 3d ed., John Wiley & Sons, Inc., New York, 1971, pp. 10–18.

Studies in Mathematics, Vol. IX: Stanford University Press, Palo Alto, California, 1963, pp. 257–291.

Topics in Mathematics for Elementary School Teachers, Twenty-Ninth Yearbook of the National Council of Teachers of Mathematics, The Council, Washington, D.C., 1964, pp. 254–286.

Informal Geometry

INTRODUCTION

Geometry is a part of elementary mathematics and of our everyday lives. Geometric shapes are all around us. Geometric terms like *points, lines, planes,* and *space* are part of the space age vocabulary. Man has studied geometry for over 1000 years in an effort to improve his understanding of the world in which he lives.

Geometry is divided into two parts, the non-metric and the metric. Non-metric geometry is concerned with the geometric properties of familiar objects and is taught intuitively. The formal, deductive method of instruction is reserved for high school. Metric geometry involves measuring the perimeters, areas, and volumes of geometric shapes. Mathematical patterns often are found in geometric shapes and can then be related to number patterns. Students should be conscious of these relationships and be alerted to look for them.

Elementary teachers should not hesitate to introduce informal geometry in the elementary grades simply because they themselves may have had difficulty with geometry in high school. In the elementary grades only the correct names of geometric shapes and their properties should be taught. Logical proof of method is not required, although students should be encouraged to think logically about what they are studying because logical thinking is important in understanding mathematics at any level.

INFORMAL GEOMETRY IN THE
PRIMARY GRADES

Students should not be required to learn the definitions of the basic geometrical terms, such as points, lines, line segments, and planes.

As we have indicated, these basic elements should be described in terms of their properties. There are two approaches to teaching these basic ideas. One approach is set point geometry, which we will describe first. The other approach is called three-dimensional geometry.

SET POINT GEOMETRY

Set point geometry starts with the idea of a point as suggested by the tip of a pencil or a dot on a piece of paper. The tip of the pencil and the dot are thought of as being so small that they really have no size. They merely represent a point which is a fixed location in space. Notice that even in this description involving point we use the word "space," because to describe what we mean by space we must do it in terms of "point." Our aim is to help pupils understand that a point is an exact location but does not have size. They cannot "see" a geometric point, only the very small dot that represents it. A point is a fixed location. The dot that represents a point can be erased, but the point will still be there because the location indicated by the dot is still there after the dot disappears. Pupils should make dots on a piece of paper. The smaller the dots, the better their representation of a point. A big fat dot covers many, many points. In helping pupils understand location, have them look at a corner of the room where the two walls and the ceiling meet and tell them that this is a location.

Now ask the pupils to draw a dot to represent a point and label it with a capital letter. We use capital letters to designate points.

.A   .B

The points shown here are called "point A" and "point B." Pupils should make several dots on their paper and label the dots with letters.

Once students understand the geometrical meaning of "point," describe a geometrical space, or simply "space," as the set of all points. Since points are thought of as locations, space may be thought of as all possible locations in the universe.

Two points in space are indicated by dots on a piece of paper.

Pupils should take their pencils and draw paths from point *A* to point *B*. All these paths from point *A* to point *B* are called *curves* in geom-

etry. One of the paths is straight and is the shortest distance from point *A* to point *B*. This curve has a special name called "line segment." Emphasize that a curve is a set of points. The line segment is a curve because it is a path made up of a set of points, but a special path nevertheless.

In drawing line segments pupils should use a ruler so that the line segment will be straight. The line segment is all the points between the two given points and includes the endpoints. For example, pictured here is line segment *CD*. The endpoints are points *C* and *D*. The line

segment *CD* is made up of all the points between *C* and *D* and includes the points *C* and *D*. A line segment is named by its endpoints. Line segment *CD* and line segment *DC* are the same line segment. The symbol for line segment is an overbar; thus, $\overline{DC}$ means line segment $\overline{DC}$.

If we think of a line segment as extending in both directions, we develop the idea of a line. A line is a set of points that extend in two directions without ending. Arrowheads are drawn on the ends to indi-

cate that the line is endless. Pupils must use their imaginations to conceive the unlimited nature of the line. Pictured here is line EF. We name a line by any two points on the line. A real geometric line or line segment cannot be seen because it has only one dimension, length. The pictures we draw must represent lines or line segments. The symbol for line is $\leftrightarrow$ and $\overleftrightarrow{EF}$ means line EF. Once again, notice that line EF and line FE are the same line.

One of the first activities pupils should practice after they learn the difference between line and line segment is to draw many lines through one given point. Have pupils mark a dot on a piece of paper and label it A. Then have them take their rulers and draw three lines through

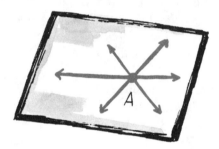

point A. They must remember to draw arrowheads on the ends of the lines to show that they are drawing lines. Now ask them if they could draw more lines through point A. The answer is "yes." Ask them how many lines do they think could pass through point A if point A were a real geometric point and the lines were real geometric lines. They will answer many lines, or lots of lines. They are right. The answer is lots of lines or an infinite number. Immediately following this activity, on the same day, ask the pupils to mark two dots on a piece of paper and ask them to draw a line that passes through both points. For some pupils in the second and third grades it is difficult at first to get the

ruler lined up with both dots and they will need help. After they draw one line through both points, ask them to draw another line that passes through both points. They must use the ruler. Now they begin to encounter some difficulty, and finally some child will say something like "The other line is on top of the first line." Thus they see that one, and only one, line passes through two given points. This is an important concept and each child must discover it for himself by seeing that a second line drawn through the points would fall atop the first line.

A *closed curve* in geometry is the path followed from the starting point back to the same starting point. In drawing this path, it may cross itself or it may not. All the figures below are closed curves. Some of

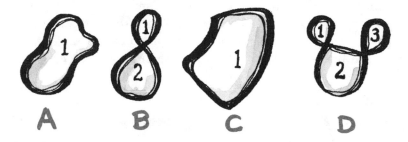

the curves have only one interior. Figures *A* and *C* have one interior. Figure *B* has two interiors and Figure *D* has three interiors. Pupils should draw closed curves with one interior and with more than one interior. Figures with one interior have a special name. They are called *simple closed curves,* the word *simple* meaning one interior. Pupils must understand simple closed curves before they are introduced to polygons. Have them look at figures like the five depicted here. Are

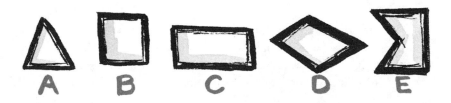

they all simple closed figures? (Yes they are.) Why? Because they have only one interior and they are all closed. What do you notice about all the figures? They are all made up of line segments. Simple closed figures made up of more than two line segments are called *polygons*. Try to draw a closed curve with two line segments. Students will find this task impossible. Therefore, a polygon must have more than two line segments. Can you name any of the polygons shown in the pictures? (Yes) Name some of them. Figure *A* is a triangle; Figure *B* is a square; Figure *C* is a rectangle. In naming these figures pupils realize that they already are familiar with many polygons. The idea behind teaching closed curves first, then simple closed curves, is to prepare students for the definition of a polygon, which they will use over and over as they study geometric shapes.

Activities must be designed in which pupils draw closed curves, simple closed curves, and then polygons. They should also be shown many different figures and he asked to pick out the simple closed curves and then the polygons. In performing this activity, many types

of shapes can be used. It is important that the pupils recognize that the circle is a simple closed curve but not a polygon, because the circle is not made up of line segments.

POLYGONS

Now ask the pupils to draw three dots on a piece of paper, not all in a straight line. Have them label the dots *A*, *B*, and *C*. Then ask them to draw a line segment from point *A* to point *B*, a line segment from point *B* to point *C*, and last, a line segment from point *C* to point *A*.

They should be reminded that line segments are pieces of line extending from one point to another. What is the figure called that you have just drawn? (It is called a triangle.) How many line segments did you draw? (3) How many sides does a triangle have? (3) Now write a numeral 3 within the triangle. By performing this exercise pupils are learning that a triangle has three line segments and there is an inside to the triangle and an outside. The triangle does not include the inside. Also, pupils are learning to follow directions. Teaching geometry in the primary grades is a good way to get pupils to learn to follow directions. All pupils are doing something they have never tried before and therefore they cannot "tune out the teacher."

Now instruct the pupils to make four dots on a piece of paper. These dots are placed so that none of them is in a straight line. Instruct

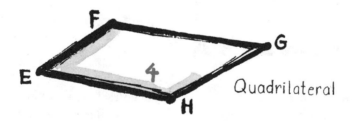

Quadrilateral

them to draw four line segments connecting the four dots. When they have finished they should be asked how many line segments they drew. (4) Ask them to write the numeral four inside the figure. Is this figure a square? (no) Is this figure a rectangle? (no) A closed curve with four line segments is called a quadrilateral, in this case quadrilateral *EFGH*. Pupils should learn the word "quadrilateral" and use it when they refer to four-sided figures with line segments.

Next, have the pupils mark four dots on a piece of paper so arranged that they will form a square when joined by line segments. Is a square a quadrilateral? (Yes) Is a square a special quadrilateral? (Yes) What do you notice about the sides of the square? (They are

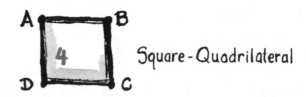

Square - Quadrilateral

all the same length.) At this time one can observe that the square also has 4 corners.

After finishing with the square, pass out more paper and direct the pupils to draw four dots so that they will form a rectangle after they are joined by four line segments. Is a rectangle a quadrilateral? (Yes)

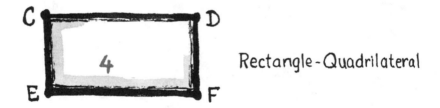

Rectangle - Quadrilateral

What do you notice about the sides of the rectangle? (The two opposite sides are the same length.) Then square and rectangle are special quadrilaterals. Mention that the opposite sides of a square are the same length. Therefore, a square is a special rectangle. From quadrilaterals go on to five-sided polygons, or pentagons. Have students draw five dots on a piece of paper and connect them with line segments. Then, following this same procedure, take up six-sided polygons, or hexagons.

For variety, have students make the various geometric figures out of straws, pipe cleaners, plastic tubes, or other materials. Making geometric figures out of various materials enables pupils to discover that many geometric figures such as quadrilaterals are "moveable." For example, you can start with a square and by moving the sides convert

the square into a quadrilateral (see diagram). The same is true of a rectangle. As you move the sides, the figure changes from a rectangle to a quadrilateral. Quadrilaterals are movable shapes, not static. You can make a triangle with any length sides, yet the sides will not move and the angles will not change. A triangle is a static shape. This exercise alerts pupils to some of the properties of various geometric figures.

CONSTRUCTIONS

By the third grade pupils should be learning to use the compass. With the compass they can construct a circle. On paper, ask them to draw a line segment such as *AB* in the figure. They measure the line

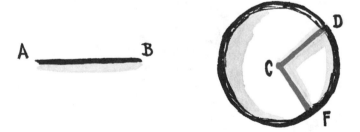

segment with the compass by placing the metal point on point *A* and the pencil point on point *B*. Then, without squeezing the compass, they lift it and place the metal point on point *C* and construct a circle. The circle is a set of points all of which are the same distance from a point at the center. Point C is the center point so this circle is called circle C. Next, have the pupils draw a dot on the circle and label it D. Then with a ruler, have them draw a line segment from point C to point D. Next, they measure line segment CD with the compass, lift the compass, and place it on line segment AB. Line segment AB and CD are congruent because they are the same size and shape. Line segment CD is a special line segment called the radius. Now instruct them to draw another dot on the circle and label it F. With a ruler have them draw a line segment from point C to point F. The plural of radius is radii. CD and CF are radii of circle C.

Pupils should be given different length line segments to use as radii of circles and then be directed to construct the circles. By looking at different circles pupils will see that the larger the radius, the larger the circle. Emphasize the points inside the circle, points on the circle, and points outside the circle. By drawing many dots on a circle, then drawing the radii of the circle, pupils will again see that a circle has many radii and all the radii of the same or congruent circles are the same length.

A line segment drawn from two points on a circle is called a chord. Pupils should construct a circle, draw some dots on the circle, and then use a ruler to draw the chords. A special chord of a circle is a chord that passes through the center of the circle. This chord is called

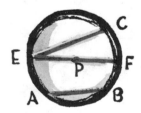

the diameter of the circle. Notice that a diameter of a circle is made up of two radii of the circle. A circle has many diameters and they are all the same length. Chords are line segments and therefore are named by their endpoints. Diameter EF is the same as diameter FE.

Dividing a line segment into two equal parts is a good way to afford students practice in making circles. You start with a given line segment, such as line segment *AB*. Then measure the line segment with a com-

pass and use point *A* as the center of a circle. After circle *A* is drawn, use the same measurement and draw a circle with point *B* as its center.

Circles *A* and *B* intersect in two places. At the intersections dots are

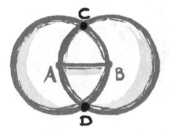

drawn and labeled *C* and *D*. Then with a ruler the line segment *CD* is drawn. This line segment intersects the given line segment *AB*. At the intersection of the two line segments a dot is drawn and labeled *E*. Now students can take their compasses and measure line segment *AE* and *EB*. They will find that they are the same length. Point *E* is the bisector of line segment *AB*. During the discussion that should be going on, try to get the pupils to point out that *C* and *D* are points on both

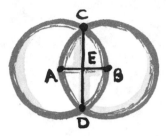

circles. This means that C and D are the same distance from AB. Every point on line segment CD is the same distance from line segment AB. The circles are the same, or congruent, because the radii are the same length.

After they have bisected a line segment, pupils can construct an equilateral triangle. An equilateral triangle is a triangle whose three sides are the same length. Begin the construction with a given line segment, say AB, which will be one side of the triangle. Construct circles with the line segment as the radius of each. Where the two circles intersect at the top draw a dot and label it C. Now draw line segments AC and CB with a ruler. The triangle ACB is an equilateral

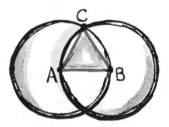

triangle because C is on both circles and AC and AB are radii of two congruent circles. Therefore, all three sides are radii of congruent circles and are equal in length.

This exercise can be shortened by having the pupils draw only a part of the circles. A part of a circle is called an arc. Pupils start with a line segment such as AB and measure it with their compasses. Then with the metal point on point A, they draw an arc upward until the arc is precisely over point A. Then with metal point on point B, they draw an arc starting at A and going upward until the arc is exactly over B. Where the two arcs intersect, a dot is drawn and labeled C.

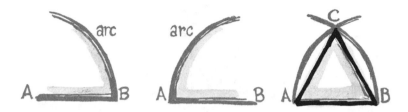

With a ruler, line segments AC and BC are drawn. The triangle ABC is an equilateral triangle because all three sides are radii of the congruent circles.

TETRAHEDRON AND OCTAHEDRON

After pupils have practiced making several equilateral triangles they are ready to construct a model of a tetrahedron. A tetrahedron is composed of four equilateral triangles. The first step is to have a line segment that is divided into two equal parts. Using each line segment a equilateral triangle is constructed. The intersections are labeled. In

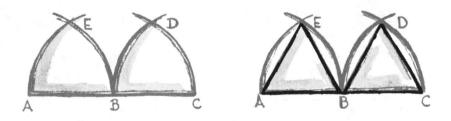

the example shown the intersections are E and D. Line segments AE, EB, BD, DC are drawn with a ruler. Using line segment ED another equilateral triangle is constructed with the compass and the intersection is labeled F. Line segments EF and ED are drawn. The large

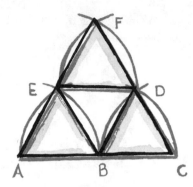

triangle AFC is cut out and each of the line segments EB, ED, BD are folded the same direction. Last, the same triangles are folded up so the vertices A, C, and F meet at a point, and the sides are taped. The three dimensional model is a regular tetrahedron. The points are called vertices, the line segments are called edges, and the triangles are called faces. The tetrahedron has four faces, six edges, and four vertices. Pupils should count the faces, the edges, and the vertices.

An octahedron can be made with eight equilateral triangles. The construction involves two models of a tetrahedron, one constructed upward and the other fashioned downward. When the pupils cut out the model, they should be warned not to cut line segment BC. Instruct them to cut along AF, then FC, then CD, down to J, up to B, and then along AB. Then they fold on all the line segments EB, BD, CH, and

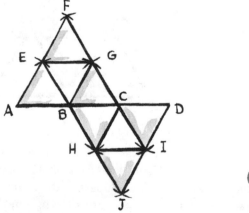

Octahedron

CI. The model should be put together like a top, with all faces on the outside. No two should be folded inside. The three-dimensional model is a regular octahedron composed of eight equilateral triangles. Have the pupils count the number of faces, edges, and vertices. After they have constructed the regular tetrahedron and the regular octahedron, they should make the models with straws, pipe cleaners, or plastic tubes.

Upper primary students enjoy constructions and in doing them they are gaining experiences that they cannot get simply by looking at pictures of models. They can see the properties in a model they have made far better than by studying a model made by someone else.

INFORMAL GEOMETRY IN THE
MIDDLE GRADES

Teachers in the middle grades should review the meanings of point, line segment, and line with their students as well as closed curves, simple closed curves, and polygons. These elements are basic to further study in geometry.

RAYS AND ANGLES

Ask students to draw a line segment from point *A* to point *B*, then take their rulers and extend the line segment beyond point *B*. The figure they have drawn is ray *AB*. A ray has one endpoint and continues on indefinitely in one direction. A ray is named by its endpoint and one other point on the ray. The name of the endpoint is always stated first. Ray *AB* is different from ray *BA*. In ray *AB* the endpoint is *A* and

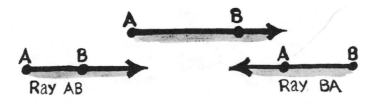

Ray AB   Ray BA

the ray continues through point *B*. In ray *BA* the endpoint is *B* and the ray continues through point *A*. The symbol for a ray is →. There fore, $\overrightarrow{AB}$ means ray *AB*. The length of a ray, like the length of a line, cannot be measured. A line segment can be measured because it has two endpoints. Students should practice drawing rays in many directions so that they will not think that all rays are vertical or horizontal.

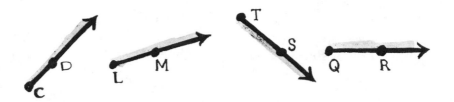

Two rays that have the same endpoint form an angle. An angle in the elementary grades is named with three capital letters. The common endpoint is called the vertex of the angle. The name of the vertex is always written in the middle. Shown here is angle *ABC* or angle *CBA*.

The symbol for an angle is ∠. Therefore, ∠*ABC* means angle *ABC*.

The measure of an angle is the interior of an angle which is the set of points between the rays. Angles are measured with angles. A circle can be divided into 360 small sectors or angles and one of the sectors

is called one degree. A protractor is used to measure angles. A protractor is one half of a circle, or a semi-circle. The markings on a protractor run from 0 to 180 degrees. An angle that measures 90 degrees is called a right angle. Angles that measure less than 90 degrees or more than

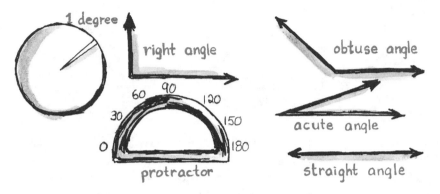

zero degrees are called acute angles. Angles that measure more than 90 degrees and less than 180 degrees are called obtuse angles. A straight angle is the same as a straight line and measures 180 degrees. Students should learn to measure angles and should learn the names of the various types of angles.

When they have learned to measure angles, students should examine some polygons and observe some of their properties. Ask them

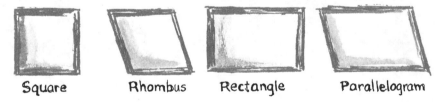

Square   Rhombus   Rectangle   Parallelogram

what they notice about the angles of a square and of a rectangle. Can a figure have four equal sides and not be a square? (Yes it can.) A figure that has four equal sides and whose angles are not right angles is called a rhombus. Can the opposite sides of a figure be parallel and of the same length and yet the figure not be a rectangle? (Yes.) A parallelogram is a quadrilateral whose opposite sides are parallel and of the same length, but the angles are not right angles. The rhombus and parallelogram can be illustrated by having students cut four strips of paper of equal length. With paper fasteners to hold the corners, have them form a square. Then ask them to move the sides, as shown in the figure. They see that the angles are no longer right angles once

Square   Rhombus   Rhombus

they move the sides of the paper. The square has become a rhombus. The same activity can be performed with four strips of paper, one pair of which is one length and the other pair a different length. Start out with a rectangle. As the students move the sides, the figure becomes a parallelogram because the angles are no longer right angles.

Rectangle   Parallelogram   Parallelogram

A good way to study triangles is to have students measure the degrees in the angles of a triangle. Students can construct an equilateral triangle, then measure the number of degrees in each angle. They will find that the angles are equal and measure 60 degrees. Therefore, all three sides of an equilateral triangle are the same length and the three

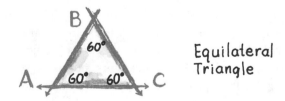

Equilateral Triangle

angles are all the same measure. Some triangles have two equal sides. Students can measure the angles opposite the equal sides. They will find that these angles have the same measure. These triangles are called isosceles triangles. The angles of a triangle whose sides are all

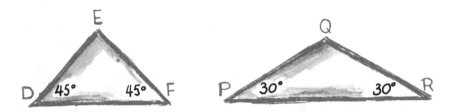

unequal will contain a different number of degrees. These triangles are called scalene triangles. After measuring the angles of many triangles,

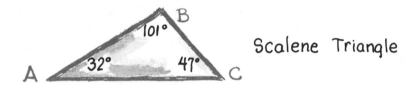

Scalene Triangle

students should discover that the three angles of a triangle in a plane measure 180 degrees.

Polygons can be inscribed within a circle. Keeping their compasses set at the same length as the radius of the circle and starting at a dot on the circle near the top, labeled A, instruct them to draw arcs around the inside of the circle. Where the first arc is drawn, they place a dot

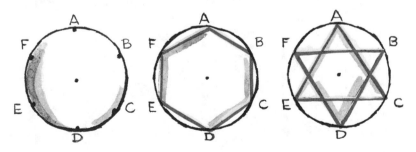

and label it *B*. Next, they place the point of the compass on *B* and make the next arc. Again they draw a dot and label this point *C*. Have them continue to draw arcs until the last arc falls on point *A*. The circle now is divided into six equal parts. Then, to inscribe a regular hexagon within the circle, instruct the students to draw line segments from *A* to *B*, *B* to *C*, *C* to *D*, *D* to *E*, *E* to *F*, and *F* to *A*. All six sides will be of the same length. As a bonus, have the students make a six-pointed star by drawing line segments from *A* to *C*, *C* to *E*, *E* to *A*, *B* to *D*, *D* to *F* and finally *F* to *B*.

In junior high school students will learn to construct perpendicular lines. They can then inscribe squares in a circle. They will also learn to make many other constructions, such as parallel lines. The background they receive in the elementary grades, however, should be firm so that the constructions they encounter in the junior high grades will not be too difficult for them and they can build on the knowledge they already have learned.

The word *plane* is used in elementary geometry but the idea is difficult to teach. A plane is a flat surface and extends indefinitely in all directions. The best way to describe a plane is by using a piece of paper, the top of a desk, or the surface of a chalkboard as models. A plane cannot be seen because it does not have depth, but it does have length. All the geometric figures discussed in elementary geometry are plane figures because they lie in a plane. Teachers in the elementary grades should not spend too much time working with the concept of a plane. Planes are taken up in junior high school, not only planes but also parallel planes and intersecting planes.

Polyhedrons are solid figures formed by portions of plane surfaces called faces. Prisms are polyhedrons with two congruent and parallel faces called bases. A familiar example of a rectangular prism is a

Prism

cracker box. The shape of its base gives a prism its name. Thus there are triangular prisms, hexagonal prisms, pentagonal prisms, and so on.

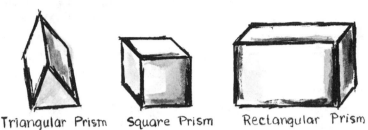

Triangular Prism   Square Prism   Rectangular Prism

After examining many kinds of prisms, students will see that although the shape of the base may be different, the sides are always rectangles. They should count the number of faces, edges, and vertices of the different types of prisms.

Pyramids are polyhedrons whose sides are triangles and whose bases are squares, rectangles, or triangles. Because the sides are tri-

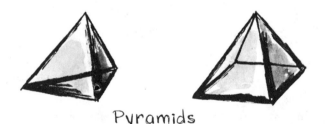

Pyramids

angles, all pyramids have a top vertex. The students learned to construct pyramids while they were working with tetrahedrons and octahedrons.

More is done with solid shapes in junior high school mathematics, but students in the middle grades should learn the names of some of the solid figures and something about their properties.

METRIC GEOMETRY

Metric geometry involves learning to measure the distance around plane figures, the surface of plane figures, and the volume of the interior of solid figures. One of the trouble spots in the middle grades is to teach students to make a distinction between finding the perimeter of a figure and finding the area of a figure. The reason for the trouble spot is that not enough time is spent involving the students themselves in finding perimeter and area before they are introduced to formulas.

A geoboard can be used to introduce the concept of measurement. A geoboard is a wooden or plastic board with an array of nails and is a particularly good device to use to show students that plane figures are the line segments that make them up, not their interiors. Students

Geoboard

use rubber bands to form geometric figures on the board, such as triangles, squares, rectangles, and other quadrilaterals. The distance between nails is called a unit.

To acquaint your students with the idea of perimeter, have them make a rectangle on the geoboard, then count the number of units

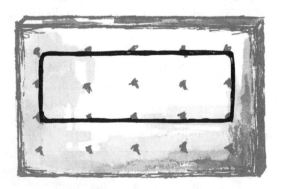

1 unit

around the rectangle and the number of nails touched by the rubber band. In the figure shown here the number of units around is 12 and the rubber band touches 12 nails. The distance around a plane figure is called its perimeter. Perimeter is measured in linear units. If the units are standard units such as inches, feet, yards, centimeters, or meters, the distance is written in terms of the number of standard units. When measuring line segments, use standard size line segment for the unit. This is an important concept.

After measuring many rectangles and squares of different sizes, students are ready to try to generalize a rule for all rectangles and all squares. The terms *length* and *width* are generally used in speaking of the sides of a rectangle or a square. When speaking of triangles the words *base* and *height* are used. Some confusion could be eliminated if the words *base* and *height* also were used in speaking of rectangles and squares. The rules or formulas the students use will be $P = (2 \times l) + (2 \times w)$, where l stands for length and w stands for width if the figure is a rectangle. The formula could also be $P = (2 \times b) + (2 \times h)$, where the letter h stands for height and the letter b stands for base. The square is a special rectangle and the formula for squares is $P = 4 \times s$, where s stands for the side. This formula also could be expressed as $P = 4 \times b$, where b stands for base. The important idea is that the formulas must be suggested by the students, not volunteered by the teacher. Students must understand that they can write the addition $8 + 2 + 8 + 2$ as $(2 \times 8) + (2 \times 2)$.

After the formulas are established, students should be asked to find the perimeter of many different figures, including some that are not regular. For a triangle they must add the number of units on all three sides. They can use a shorter method only when they are dealing with an equilateral triangle, whose sides are the same length. In this case they multiply the length of the base by 3.

AREA

The geoboard also can be used to introduce the concept of area of plane figures. Make a small square on the geoboard and call it a square

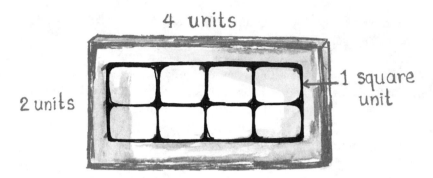

4 units

2 units

1 square unit

unit. Then the students should make a large rectangle, using rubber bands to divide the interior of the rectangle into square units. Now they can see that the interior of the rectangle has eight square units. The picture on the geoboard will look like the rectangular arrays they used as models of multiplication facts. After finding the area of several rectangles on the geoboard, ask them if they can find the areas without counting each square unit. The correct procedure is to multiply the number of units in the length by the number of units in the width or the number of units in the base by the number of units in the height. So $A = l \times w$ or $A = b \times h$ is the formula for finding the area of a rectangle. Area involves measuring surface and a standard unit to measure surface must be used. Some of the units are square inches, square feet, square yards, square centimeters, and square meters. Squares are special rectangles and the formula for the area of a square is $A = s \times s$ or $A = b \times b$.

Before students start to find the area of triangles they should be given considerable practice finding the perimeter and area of many different sizes of rectangles and squares. They should draw as many rectangles as they can with a perimeter of 16 units. They should then find the area of each of the rectangles. They will see that the areas are not the same. The rectangle with the largest area, using a perimeter of 16 units, is the square. Give the students the perimeter and the length of a rectangle and ask them to find its width. The more they become involved in different approaches to finding the perimeter and area, the more understanding they will acquire.

To find the area of a triangle, students should start with a rectangle.

Let them make a rectangle on the geoboard, then use another rubber band to divide the rectangle into two congruent triangles. They can

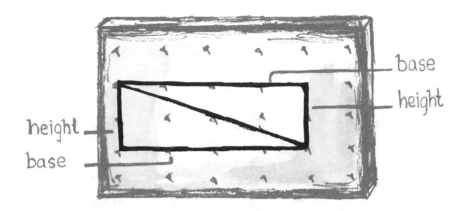

find the area of the rectangle by multiplying the number of units in the base by the number of units in the height. And they can see that the area of each of the triangles is one half the area of the rectangle. Ask them, "What is the length of the base of the triangle and what is the height of the triangle?" The height of the triangle is the same as the height of the rectangle, and the base of the triangle is the same as the base of the rectangle.

Now, dismantling the rectangle divided into triangles, make a tri-

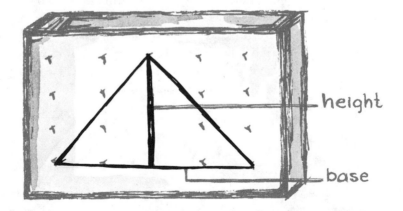

angle on the geoboard. Tell the students the height of a triangle is the perpendicular distance from the top vertex to the base. Have them first count the units from the top to the base then the units in the base. Rubber bands can be placed on the geoboard to make two rectangles, one on each side of the height of the triangle. The base of the rectangle

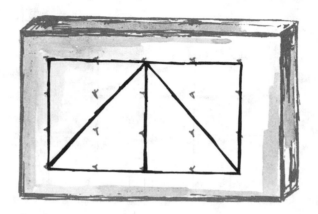

is one half of the base of the triangle. Each of the smaller triangles is one half of the area of the area of the rectangles divided by the height. So students can see that the area of a triangle is one half times the height times the base of the triangle.

Some introductory work with the volume of a prism is performed in the upper middle grades. Students should understand that in order to find the volume of the inside of a rectangular prism or box they can fill in the prism with cubes. Then, to find the volume, they multiply the length times the height times the width. This kind of exposure will help students when they begin more advanced work with volume in junior high school. It is not necessary to develop formulas for volume at this stage.

SUMMARY

Geometry can be meaningful to students if they are given plenty of opportunity to see and feel the shapes they are dealing with. They need time to draw conclusions and to look for properties. Students will find it relatively easy to learn the names of figures if they are given an opportunity to become acquainted with the figures. Generalizations such as formulas should not be introduced, or required until students have had enough exposure to geometric shapes to draw their own generalizations.

Teachers must be creative in developing exercises that will actively involve their students. Teach them to observe and help them build their own models. The easiest way to proceed is simply to tell them what they should know, but they will never retain merely what they are told. We must remember constantly that what we do, we know. This fact is very important in geometry.

EXERCISES

1. Why do students have to understand what line segments, closed curves, and simple closed curves are before they can understand the definition of a polygon?
2. How do you name a line segment? a line? a ray?
3. How do pyramids and prisms differ?
4. Why can't you measure the length of a line or a ray?
5. How do you find the perimeter of a regular hexagon?
6. How are the square and the rhombus related? How are they different?
7. Why do primary teachers use wire frames to illustrate geometric shapes?

SELECTED READINGS

BRYDEGAARD, M., and J. E. INKEEP, JR., eds., *Readings in Geometry from the Arithmetic Teacher*, National Council of Teachers of Mathematics, Washington, D.C. 1970.

FEHR, H. F. and T. J. HILL: *Contemporary Mathematics for Elementary Teachers*, Chapter 6, D.C. Heath and Company, Boston, 1966.

ROPER, S., *Paper and Pencil Geometry*, Franklin Mathematics Series, Lyons and Carnaham, Chicago, 1970.

SCHAAF, W. L.: *Basic Concepts of Elementary Mathematics*, Chapter 3, John Wiley & Sons, Inc., New York, 1966.

WHEELER, R. E.: *Modern Mathematics, An Elementary Approach*, Chapters 10 and 11, Brooks-Cole, Division of Wadsworth Publishing Company, Belmont, California, 1966.

Problem-Solving

INTRODUCTION

Problem-solving is a complex mental process involving visualization, imagination, manipulation, abstraction, and the association of ideas. This is why there is no easy or quick way to learn the technique. Do not lead students to believe that one pattern that successfully solves one particular problem will solve all problems. Problem-solving requires unique and original responses; the best problem-solvers are nonconforming and creative people. Problem-solving also requires skill in reading and computing. Students who have difficulty in either or both of these areas will be severely handicapped in solving problems.

Learning to solve problems is the most significant learning that occurs in any mathematics class—and the most difficult. In teaching problem-solving teachers must analyze closely all the steps required in the process so that they can reach all students, and the students themselves must recognize the steps if they are to solve problems successfully.

PROBLEM-SOLVING IN THE
PRIMARY GRADES

In solving word problems, start by teaching pupils to observe and judge the important details in a problem. In the first and second grades pupils should be given pictures and asked to explain the theme of each picture. For example, if a picture shows three girls and five boys playing with a ball, ask the pupils to tell what they see in the picture. Some may say that they see a blue sky, a yellow sun, a big tree, and so on. These are unimportant items in the picture, and pupils should be encouraged to look for the important details, in this case, the children playing with the ball. Require only oral responses at first. The next stage is to have some pupil recite a story in a few sentences while the other pupils draw a picture of the story. Again, it is important for the pupils to draw the important details in the story. The incidental part of the story may be included but only as long as the important theme is not forgotten.

Next, present a picture and ask the pupils to write a few sentences about it. Do not emphasize grammar or spelling. Concentrate on the pupils' expressing the main theme. Divide the class into several separate groups or teams and use different pictures if you wish. Members of each group can pool their responses and write down what represents a summation of all their ideas. Now ask a student in class or a group to write a story in a few sentences and have the other pupils draw a picture that represents the story. Allow the pupil or pupils who write the story to judge which picture best describes the story.

Finally, show the pupils a picture and ask them to write a story about the picture and then a mathematical sentence to describe the story. Before they begin tell them that they must learn the translations before going from written words to mathematical symbols. The word "is" always translates to the mathematical symbol $=$. The words "and," "more," and "increase" translate to the mathematical symbol $+$. The words "less," "not as many," and "decrease" are translated to the mathematical symbol $-$. The word "of" is usually translated as the mathematical symbol $\times$. The unknown or the answer is translated as the letter n, or a frame. Often, more than one mathematical sentence will describe a story correctly. Teachers should avoid creating the impression that all pupils must write the same mathematical sentence. For example, one story might be: Tom has twenty-five cents and he spends 15 cents for candy. How much money does he have left? The mathematical sentence could be $25 - 15 = n$ or it could be $n + 15 = 25$, or $15 + n = 25$. All the sentences are correct. Some pupils will see the problem as additive subtraction; others, as straight subtraction.

Pupils should be given short written stories and asked to write the mathematical sentences that go with the stories. Do not require, or even ask for, answers at this time. Students who are able should help the teacher write the short stories and the other pupils should write the mathematical sentences. Then reverse the activity; give the pupils a simple mathematical sentence and ask them to write a story that fits the sentence.

After students are successful at writing mathematical sentences for simple word problems, and can write word problems for simple mathematical sentences, they are ready for the next step. Now the teacher should compose stories that are longer and include details that are not essential to solving the main part of the problem. Ask the pupils to tell which part of the story might be eliminated without damaging the word problem. For example: Johnny has 5 baseball cards. He bought two of them and his brother gave him the other three. Jimmy has 8 baseball cards. How many more baseball cards does Jimmy have than Johnny? Pupils should reply that the sentence about Johnny buying two cards and his brother giving him three cards has nothing to do with the problem. Ask some pupils to supply word problems and have the rest of the class select what are the unnecessary details in the stories.

All these exercises in solving word problems should be conducted as a class activity, under the guidance of the teacher, and should not be assigned individually or as homework. The teacher must be the guide, must make judgments about correct and incorrect responses and ask questions to guide students who are having difficulty. Again, notice that up to this point pupils are never asked to find an answer to the problems. They are simply stating the problem and translating it into a mathematical sentence.

Teachers should be careful not to use all the word problems found in commercial primary books and workbooks. Often the problems are written with words that are too difficult for most pupils at that level. If the word problems in the second-grade workbook are written at a reading level of 3.4 and most of the pupils in the class cannot read at that level, then they will be unable to handle the problems. The teacher should make up word problems that she knows her pupils can read.

Word problems in mathematics should be centered around major curriculum studies or projects. If the third grade is studying about pioneers, many of the word problems in mathematics should have pioneer life as their theme. If the theme for the year is Indians, the word problems should center around the material the pupils are learning about Indians. Also, many of the problems can be made up to go along with the books being read at a certain grade level. If many of the girls in the third grade have read a book on the life of Helen Keller, some of the word problems can be written to include some of the facts about the life of Helen Keller. The same can be true of the boys who have read, say, a book on the life of John Glenn. Problems should contain materials of interest to boys as well as to girls. They should be timely and include facts and details of the space age we are living in. Some of the problems should be light and humorous, like comparing the weights of elephants and monkeys or the difference between travel by stage coach and by jet. Variety is the spice of word problems as well as of life. For too long pupils have had to read and solve problems that are uninteresting. Part of the motivation for solving word problems is having problems that are interesting enough to solve.

When pupils reach the stage where they can solve word problems, it is important that they learn to write a mathematical sentence that describes the word problem. It is also important that they learn to label their answers to all problems. Pupils should be encouraged to check their work. Is the answer reasonable? Ask this question constantly.

Do not require that all pupils solve the same word problems. Those who are good readers and good at math can do more complicated problems and should be encouraged to try them. Allow ample time for students to think, analyze and experiment. Encourage them to ask questions. Be patient with pupils who are having difficulty. Pupils must be successful at their own level if they are going to continue to try. Encourage them to draw a picture of the problem, then translate it into a mathematical sentence. Too often teachers in the primary grades create fear of word problems in the minds of pupils because they become impatient and try to push pupils into doing problems that they are not yet ready to solve. The attitude, "It is simple and I cannot understand how you can be so slow to understand," does not help and actually creates a block in students' minds.

We repeat, never assign word problems as homework. All this work should be performed in class where the teacher can control the situation. Parents are not teachers and should not try to teach. Teachers themselves cannot teach their own children, because they get emotionally involved in the situation. The setting for word problems should be leisurely; pupils should concentrate on only a few problems at a time. Give pupils an opportunity to explain various ways of solving the problems. Instead of emphasizing one preferred method, encourage creative thinking.

For pupils who are having difficulty, place the problems on a tape recorder so that the children can listen to the problems as they read them. Then they should try to solve them.

Film strips can be used to present problems. The teacher might show a film strip to the class and ask them to write a story about it, then solve it. The more pupils become involved in writing the stories as well as solving them, the more they will understand about problem-solving.

FINDING RULES

Pupils must learn how to write rules or formulas in mathematics to help them with problem-solving. A game called "What is my Rule?" is helpful. The teacher decides on a rule and writes some numbers on the chalkboard. In the example shown here the first number is 2 and

FIRST NUMBER	SECOND NUMBER
2	5
4	9
5	11
7	?
?	19
n	?

the second number is 5. Pupils try to think what they can do to 2 to get 5. They may decide to add 3. They test this on the second pair of numbers, 4 and 9. It does not work because $4 + 3$ is 7, not 9. Now they must go back to 2 and 5 and think of something else to do to 2 to get 5. This time perhaps they think they might add 2 twice, then add 1, or $2 + 2 + 1$. They test this approach on 4 and 9. Thus, $4 + 4 + 1$ equals 9, so this solution appears to be correct. They then try it on the third set of numbers, 5 and 11, and see that $5+5+1$ is 11. Now they have the rule. If the first number is 7, add 7, then add 1 and the sum is 15. When the second number is given, they must work the opposite of the rule. Subtract 1 to get 18. What number can be added twice to get 18? The answer is 9. If the first number is n, which stands for any number, how do they find the second number? The rule is $n+n+1$, or $2 \times n +1$. In the beginning the rules may be easy, such as add 7 or subtract 5. Then let the rules become more complicated, like the example. Students should be encouraged to try their hunches until they are sure they have the correct rule. When they can discover the rules supplied by the teacher, let them make up problems for the other pupils to solve. The thinking required to work problems like these helps pupils to solve word problems.

EDUCATED GUESSING

Another aid to problem-solving is "educated guessing." The famous problemist, George Polya, says: "We must teach guessing. Too many teachers encourage students not to guess. Such teachers fail to realize the trial and error approach sometimes yields adequate answers." A problem such as $2 \times (n+10) - 7 = 23$ might be written on the chalkboard. Pupils are told to guess what number the letter n stands for in the sentence. If the first pupil guesses 10 the sentence should be written on the board with 10 replacing the letter n. Now let the pupils

$$2 + (n + 10) - 7 = 23$$
$$2 \times (10 + 10) - 7 = 33$$

solve the sentence by adding 10 and 10, then multiplying by 2 and subtracting 7. The result is 33. What should the next guess be, larger or smaller than 10? Most pupils will say smaller than 10 because they can see that 33 is larger than 23. The next guess may be 8. Now the sentence is written with 8 replacing the letter n. The pupils add 8 to 10 and multiply by 2, then subtract 7 and the result is 29. Will the next

$$2 + (8 + 10) - 7 = 29$$

guess be larger or smaller than 8? Again, most of the pupils will say smaller because 29 is greater than 23. One pupil may guess 5, and 5 becomes the replacement for the letter n. Student will now see that 5 is the right answer. Through exercises such as these pupils are learning to guess with a purpose. When a guessed number turns out to be too large, they know that the next guess should be smaller. With each guess they should come closer to the answer. The same technique is used in problem-solving. If the wrong approach is used the first time, at least it provides some clues about the next approach. Much of mathematics can be solved by trial and error if pupils are taught how to use educated guessing.

CLUES

A game called clues is good practice for problem-solving because it helps develop game strategy. Pupils should be encouraged to find

1. There are 4 numbers.
2. All the numbers are odd numbers.
3. The sum of the 4 numbers is 32.

as many answers to the problem as they can, being sure they satisfy all the steps. Some of the answers are shown but there are many

$$11 + 11 + 7 + 3$$
$$17 + 5 + 5 + 5$$
$$21 + 7 + 3 + 1$$
$$29 + 1 + 1 + 1$$

more. The clues can be made more difficult, depending on the ability of the pupils. Given both "even" and "multiples of 3" makes the prob-

1. There are 5 numbers.
2. All the numbers are even numbers.
3. All the numbers are multiples of 3.
4. The sum of the 5 numbers is 132.

lem more difficult. Some of the answers are shown; but again, there

$$24 + 48 + 24 + 12 + 24$$
$$60 + 30 + 12 + 12 + 18$$

are many more. Once a teacher tries several clues with a group of pupils, the pupils should be encouraged to make up clues of their own. The only requirement is that you must have one answer to the clue you make up. Anyone can make up a clue that does not work. Teachers are always amazed how difficult some of the clues will become and how much mathematics the pupils really know. For example, if a pupil says in a clue that there are five numbers and all the numbers are odd and that the sum is 142, many children will know immediately the clue does not work because the sum of five odd numbers must be an odd number.

The real value of the game called clues is that all pupils will have to work to get the answer. No one should call out an answer immediately. Material in the clues has to be shifted about before answers come forth; this is the very important step in learning how to solve word problems.

Brain twisters should be presented to the class, puzzles that require students to employ various strategies to solve them. Too often problems presented in the primary grades are so fatuous that they require very little thinking. A student cannot become a good problem-solver unless he learns how to think. If the whole class works together on a puzzle, no one pupil will become frustrated or discouraged if the solution is not found immediately. In sharing techniques they will learn some of the skills of problem solving.

Problem-solving begins in the primary grades. Pupils must be taught to observe, analyze, and associate. They must learn how to read scientific material. Reading mathematical problems is not like reading a novel. You cannot speed read in mathematics. Teachers must encourage pupils to try, and give credit for each successful step and improvement. Problems at first must be simple so that everyone can solve them. Learning to look at pictures and writing stories about them develops in pupils the ability to draw a picture of a word problem when it is presented to them.

Many of the problem-solving methods that are stressed in the primary grades must be carried over to the middle grades. Students should be encouraged to read a problem and recount what details in the problem are not necessary. Then they should rewrite the problem with only the important details included. Next, they should draw a sketch or a picture of the problem, but should not be asked to solve the problem yet. W. W. Sawyer, an English mathematician, says, "If you can not draw a picture of the problem, you do not understand the problem."

Now ask the students to rewrite all word problems so that the question comes first. When the question is presented first, the students focus their attention on the solution and they discover as they read those parts of the story that help them answer the question. Teachers will be amazed to see how much it helps most students if the question is asked first.

The next step is to have students analyze ten word problems and pick out action words. Such words tell you to add, subtract, multiply, or divide. Let students make up their own lists rather than pass one out to them. Let them play a game of charades, acting out some of the action terms. For example, a team of six students might stand up and then exclude two students from the group. The rest of the students try to guess the action word, which here is "less than" or "not as many" or "take away." Or, the six might motion for several other students to join their group. In this case they are acting out the words "more than" or "increase." A more complicated game involves the group dividing into two sets of three and then expelling one student from the group. This action represented here is "multiply by 2, then subtract 1." Concentrate on the action words in a word problem that can be translated into mathematical symbols.

In other exercises students are given simple sentences to translate into mathematical sentences, or mathematical sentences to convert into word sentences. Practice of this type is essential before students actually try to solve word problems, for it is a prerequisite to solving problems. The teacher should always be available to help students who are having difficulty and to lend encouragement. This is a class activity.

Before students are required to solve mathematical sentences let them play the game called "Action and Opposite." The game begins by letting the letter n stand for the original number. The teacher writes $n + 4$ on the chalkboard and asks, "What is the action?" The students reply that the action is "add 4." Then the teacher writes $3n + 4$ and asks again "What is the action?" The students respond that the action now is "multiply by 3." To play "Opposite," she starts with $3n + 4$ and asks, "What is the opposite action to adding 4?" The students reply "subtract 4." She writes $3n + 4 - 4 = 3n$. She writes $3n$ on the board and asks students to tell her the opposite action of multiplying by 3. They reply, "dividing by 3." She writes $3n/3$ is equal to $1n$ or n. They are now back to the original number. Have the students write n on their papers, make up actions, then perform the opposite actions to get back to the original number. This activity is important, for often when students are confronted with the equation $3n + 4 = 10$ they do not know where the phrase $3n + 4$ comes from. When they realize that the first action was add 4 and that the second action was multiply by 3, they can perform the opposite action of subtracting 4 and then dividing by 3.

Before the students attempt to solve problems, re-emphasize the meaning of the equal sign. The symbol $=$ means "is the same as." Therefore, it is not correct to say that 50¢ is the same as ten nickels. If one side of the equation states an amount of money, the other side must also state an amount of money. If one side of an equation states number of coins, the other side must also state number of coins. This is a very important concept and requires clarification lest students start writing false equations.

There is always an unknown quantity involved in solving word problems. This unknown number is represented by a letter. Students should write what the variable (unknown number) stands for before they write the sentence. The letter $x =$ Joe's age is not true. The correct form is: The letter x represents the number of years in Joe's age. The letter always represents the *unknown;* it is not the number of the unknown. This may seem like nitpicking but if the variable is represented carelessly, the problem-solving is likely to be careless.

Students should practice solving mathematical sentences before they try to solve word problems. They must know how to solve equations and to recognize the action words and the opposite action words. They should write all equivalent equations, all equations that have the same solution. The first equations should be simple, requiring only one step. Then present more difficult two-step equations. Always require students to check their work by substituting the answer in the original equation.

Give students only a few word problems to solve at one time. All word problems should be solved in class where the teacher can give assistance as needed. Students must be required to draw a picture of the problem, then write a mathematical sentence. There are many different mathematical sentences that fit a word problem so the teacher should not insist that all pupils write the same mathematical sentence. Next, ask the students to solve the problem. And the last step is to check the solution by substituting the answer in the original sentence. Finally, students should study the answer to see if it makes sense in terms of the problem. All answers must be labeled to indicate what the number stands for. Four feet or 4 cards are more meaningful answers than simply 4.

The tape recorder is useful in helping students who have difficulty reading word problems. If they hear the problem as they are reading they will have a better chance of understanding it. For the slower students, the question in the problem should be posed first. When the question is asked first, students will know what they are looking for and will have a better chance of discovering the details in the problem. Slower students should be given simple problems, clearly stated, requiring only one step in the solution. Once they are successful with this type of problem they will have more confidence in their ability to tackle more difficult problems later.

Teach students to look for strategies in problem-solving. Devise problems that require students to think about ways of solving them. For example, problems such as the following require students to think of essential structure—in this case, place value. Students must find the

Send	Spend
+ More	− More
Money	Money

digits that can be substited for the letters. Take the following problem: An explorer walks 1 mile south, then walks 1 mile east, then turns and walks 1 mile due north and finds himself back where he started from. At what locations on the earth's surface is this possible? In this problem the startegy is to search for, or recall, what the learner knows about latitude and longitude and relate this information to direction and location. Then he discovers that the locations are at the North Pole and near the South Pole.

Students should be confronted with braintwisters and given the time to solve them. They should be encouraged to ask questions and to request help when they need it. They learn how to relate and devise strategies by doing problems that are not easy to solve. Too much of mathematics involves working problems that are the same as the problems pupils already have seen in their books or on chalkboards. Techniques of problem-solving are developed by trial and error. This is a slow process. Each teacher should work on the process at each grade level. Many students look at word problems and write down any answer because they feel that they must find an answer immediately. To avoid this tendency they should be given problems that require thought and strategy. They should be told that the problems are not easy and that they are not expected to find the results immediately.

SUMMARY

Learning how to solve problems can be one of the most satisfying though difficult experiences we can impart to our students. Teachers must change their attitude about problem-solving. They must learn to emphasize the method of solution rather than the solution. They must encourage students to experiment, to resort to trial-and-error methods, to estimate, follow their intuitions, and to guess in order to find a solution. They must teach pupils how to ask questions of themselves. They must emphasize flexibility and variety in solving problems rather than neatness and short-cuts. They must provide problems frequently so that students get adequate practice. Problem situations should be used as a basis for practice and as a substitute for drill exercises. Above all, if the teacher does nothing else, he should emphasize the method of solution rather than the answer. Once students learn the techniques of problem-solving they will discover new mathematical concepts, principles, and relationships of their own and in a sense become independent, creative mathematicians.

EXERCISES

1. Why is asking the question first in a word problem a sound approach?
2. How does playing "action and opposite" help students solve equations?
3. Why is drawing a picture of a word problem a good learning device?
4. Why is problem-solving not a skill?
5. Why are puzzle problems or braintwisters good practice for problem-solving?
6. Should students be taught to "guess" in mathematics? Why?

SELECTED READINGS

GROSSNICKLE, F. E., L. J. BRUECKNER, J. RECHZEH: *Teaching Elementary School Mathematics*, Chapter 17, Holt, Rinehart and Winston, Inc., New York, 1968.

SPENCER, P. L., and M. BRYDEGAARD: *Building Mathematical Competence in the Elementary School*, Holt, Rinehart and Winston, Inc., New York, 1966.

SPITZER, H. F.: *Teaching Elementary School Mathematics*, Chapter 8, Houghton, Mifflin Company, Boston, 1967.

Topics in Mathematics for Elementary School Teachers, Twenty-Ninth Yearbook of the National Council of Teachers of Mathematics: The Council, Unit 7, Washington, D.C., 1964.

Measurement

INTRODUCTION

There are two main types of measurements. One involves the use of discrete variables such as the cost of postage stamps, the size of cities, and the number of crayons in a box. Discrete data are usually expressed as integers. The second type involves the use of continuous variables such as heights, weights, time, and temperature. Continuous variables may be viewed as being represented on an uninterrupted scale. This chapter is concerned with continuous measurement.

Man has always been interested in measuring, and much of mathematics has developed because of this interest. Since the 1800's the names and types of units have changed from Perch, Ell-Flemish, and Logshead to today's Light Years, Parsecs, and Angstrom units, but the need for measurement continues to exist. A knowledge of the history of measurement is of great value to the elementary school teacher for it can provide approaches to teaching measurement.

In an attempt to measure such things as time, volume, area, temperature, energy, and the like, man has arrived at the following generalizations. These generalizations need to be considered when teaching children about measurement.

1. Measurements of continuous data are approximations, no matter how precise. In all measurement of continuous data there is some error.

2. Some things such as the height of a person, can be measured directly. Other things, such as distance to the sun, must be measured indirectly.

3. The units of measurement were developed over a long period of time and are of historical interest. Units of measure have been standardized for many countries.

4. Measurements are relative. For example, a 4000-foot mountain

might be considered by people in Kansas as "high" but by people in Colorado as "low."

LINEAR MEASURE

Before standard units of measurement are introduced pupils should be encouraged to use other units for measurement. Pieces of paper can be used to measure the length of a bookcase, pencils to measure the length of a desk, papers clips to measure the length of an eraser. After several pupils measure an object such as the length of a bookcase, using different sizes of papers, they will see that their measurements are different and cannot be compared because the unit of measurement varied. From this type of activity they will appreciate the need for standard units of measurement.

In the middle grades an historical study of the development of standard units of measurement might be undertaken. Ancient measures such as spans, hands, cubits, digits, and fathoms can be studied to see how they have led directly to present-day standard units of measurement.

The main point to be established in teaching linear measure is that a line segment is used to measure line segments. Also, it is important to emphasize that the measure of a line segment is the number of standard units and portions of the unit. Pupils in the primary grades should make their own rulers to measure line segments. This experience imparts meaning to the standard ruler and to measuring with a ruler.

Start with the number line to teach pupils how to use a ruler to measure line segments. A piece of tag board should be cut out in the shape of the letter T. The top should be 1 inch long. The other part of the T is simply a handle for the pupils to hold.

Now give the pupils a piece of construction paper which is 15 inches long. Draw a line segment across this paper with a dot near the left side labeled 0. Ask the pupils to lay the top of the T strip below the line with the left edge on dot 0. With a pencil make a mark on the

line to where the right edge of the T extends. Label this mark 1. Now place the T strip with the left edge on dot 1 and mark a dot on the line segment where the right edge touches it. Label this mark 2. Have the pupils continue until they have 12 segments marked off on the large line segment. Now with a pencil ask them to make a rectangle on the

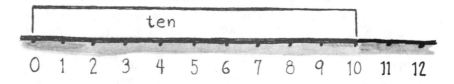

top of the line extending from 0 to 10. Label the interior of this rectangle *ten*. Now discuss with the pupils the meaning of the numeral 10, pointing out that it could mean 1 ten unit and no small units, or it could mean 10 of the small units. And the numeral 11 on the number line could mean one 10 unit and one small unit, or it could mean 11 of the small units. Similarly, the numeral 12 on the number line could mean one 10 unit and two small units, or it could mean 12 of the smaller units. After this review of place value and the meaning of a two-digit numeral, pupils can erase the rectangle above the line segment. Ask them to draw a new rectangle which extends from 0 to 12 on the top of the line segment. Inside the rectangle they write 1 foot. Explain that the small divisions on the line segment from 0 to 1, 1 to 2, and so on, are called 1-inch segments. Here, at this point, it is well to have a discussion about standard units of measurement and the units established by law. Explain that the number lines used in other units had line segments of different lengths without regard to 1-inch measurements because they were not being used for measurements at that time. Ask the pupils to tell the number of inches in 1 foot. Here the numeral 12 on the number line means 12 inches. The 12 inches is the same as the 1-foot measure. Point out to pupils that the 1-foot unit is similar to the unit 1 to ten—made up of ten small units. Since a certain number of small units are combined to form a larger unit, in this case combining 12 smaller units forms a larger unit of 12 inches or 1 foot.

The first ruler used in the primary grades should bear 1-inch markings only. As the first objective, ask the pupils to measure different line segments to the nearest inch. Insist that they take care in placing the left edge of the ruler at the left edge of the line segment they are

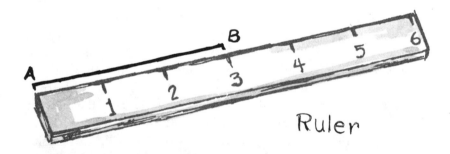

Ruler

measuring. Spend time helping pupils learn how to measure to the nearest inch before giving them rulers with 1/2-inch markings.

When the ruler with 1/2-inch markings is introduced, lead the discussion about the unit from 0 to 1 being divided into two congruent parts, each part being one half. Explain that it is the smaller marking on the ruler which indicates the one-half divisions. Help them learn to read $1\frac{1}{2}$ inches, $2\frac{1}{2}$ inches, and so on. Plan activities so that pupils can draw line segments to the nearest 1/2 inch and measure different line segments to the nearest 1/2 inch.

By the third grade, students can learn to use rulers with markings for 1/2- and 1/4-inch divisions. Many teachers find that using an overhead projector helps pupils learn about the ruler. Markings on the transparencies are clearer than drawings on the board and the pupils can compare them with their own ruler.

It is important to use the ruler frequently in class activities. If the instruction is not continuous, pupils will have to relearn the skill the following year. Plan to include the measurement of line segments in science, art, and social studies. Proficiency is acquired through frequent use of the skill. Let them measure the length of the classroom with a foot ruler. Then have them use a yard measure for the same classroom to illustrate that there are 3 feet in a yard but that the yard stick is a more efficient instrument for measuring long lengths. Plan other activities in which the pupils can decide which is the best standard unit to use in different situations. To measure the length of a book, a foot or a yard measure is not the best unit. To measure the length of the hallway in school, an inch measure is not the best unit. Choosing the best unit to use is one of the major difficulties pupils face here. Various activities should be designed to help them learn to make these decisions.

It is not necessary for students to memorize all the standard units of measurement for length. For example, 5,280 feet is the same as the standard mile. Pupils should know and memorize that there are 12 inches in 1 foot and 3 feet in 1 yard. Beyond this, they should learn to use tables of measurement and to know where to look for these tables.

The concept of time has always been difficult to teach to many pupils in the primary grades. Start your instruction with a discussion of the seasons and the calendar. These aspects of time are familiar to them and easy to grasp. It is, however, difficult for many to learn to tell time by a clock. Here again the number line is a useful tool with which to begin the unit. Draw a number line with divisions extending from

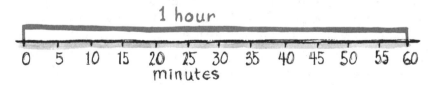

0 to 60 and let each small division stand for 1 minute. Now discuss with the pupils that there are 60 minutes in 1 hour. The midpoint of the segment from 0 to 60 is the dot marked 30. This means that 1/2 hour is

the same as 30 minutes. The segment from 0 to 60 can be divided into 4 congruent parts. The dot marked 15 is 1/4 of an hour, the dot marked 30 is 2/4 of an hour, and the dot marked 45 is 3/4 of an hour. To help them grasp this concept, illustrate with "less than" and "greater than" questions. Which is greater, 50 minutes or 1/2 of an hour? Which is less, 1/4 of an hour or 35 minutes?

Now show the pupils a clock with numerals for hours written inside the circle and numerals denoting minutes written outside the circle. Before placing the hands on the clock, lead a discussion about the numerals inside the clock. Pupils need to learn that there are 12 hours in one-half day. We measure time from 12 midnight to 12 noon, and from 12 noon to 12 midnight. Discuss the difference between 9 o'clock at night and 9 o'clock in the morning. At 9 o'clock in the morning pupils are in school; at 9 o'clock at night pupils are in bed. The clock is a circular number line. Instead of 0 marking the starting place, the numeral 12 is the starting point. Now attach the two hands to the clock with a paper fastener. The long hand, or minute hand, points to

12, the starting place, and the short hand, the hour hand, points to the hour. At four o'clock the long hand would be on 12 and the short hand on 4. Have the pupils take turns placing the hands on the clock to show various hours. Also, give them papers on which clock faces are drawn

so that they can draw the position of the hands at different hours. Show them other papers on which clocks have been drawn with the hands indicating various hours and ask them to tell the hour indicated by the hands. Explain now that there are two ways to write the hour indicated, either 4 o'clock or 4:00. Be sure that they learn 4:00, 3:00, and so on, because they will have to be familiar with this notation when minutes are introduced. Explain that the two zeros indicate there are no minutes beyond the hour. It tells them that the minute hand is on the starting point, 12.

After pupils can tell the hours and draw the positions of the hands for given hours, begin to explain minutes. Ask them to count by fives from 5, 10, 15 through 55 and point out that these are written on the outside of the clock. Where would 60 be written? On the circular number line, 60 was the same as what unit? When you reach 60 minutes it is equal to an hour and so the minute hand falls on 12, the starting point. Use a large clock to demonstrate. As the minute hand moves from 5 to 10, to 15, and beyond, the hour hand is moving slowly from one hour to the next. When the minute hand arrives back at 12, the hour hand is on the next hour. Help pupils see the relationship between the number line they studied in earlier grades and this circular number line. Each time the minute hand goes around the clock it is traveling the distance on the number line covering 60 minutes, which is the same as 1 hour. The hour hand keeps a record of the number of times the minute hand goes around the circular number line or clock face. Starting with both hands on 12 and moving the minute hand around the circle, the hour hand moves to 1. The next time the minute hand goes around the circle the hour hand moves to 2. This continues for 12 hours, then begins again. When pupils understand this point, they can then learn that when the minute hand lands on 6 (or 30 on the number line) it means 1/2 hour. They can also see that the hour hand is half-way between two numerals.

Now help them to tell time to the minute, explaining that 3:18 means 3 hours and 18 minutes. Eighteen minutes is beyond 3 hours so the hour hand has moved slightly toward the 4 and the minute hand has moved 18 minutes on its way to the next hour. The notation 6:52 means 6 hours and 52 minutes. Here the minute hand is almost completely around the circle and nearly back to the starting point. It is between 50 and 55. The hour hand has moved almost over to 7. Once pupils can interpret the notation 5:28 in terms of where the minute hand would be and where the hour hand would be, they are well on their way to understanding how to tell time.

Sometimes in teaching we think that starting with a simple idea is the only way to avoid confusion. This probably is not true in teaching pupils to tell time. Starting with the number line divided into 60 small units enables pupils to learn the rules of the game called telling time. They can see that the new unit called 1 hour is made up of the 60 small units because of what they learned about base and the use of the number line. Now applying this number line to the circular number line called the clock seems logical to them.

LIQUID MEASURE

In learning liquid measure, students must see and do. They must pour water or sand to learn that 2 pints is the same measure as 1 quart. In presenting the unit on liquid measure teachers should use the letter m above the equal sign. For example, 2 pints $\underset{=}{m}$ 1 quart means that 2 pints is the same measure as 1 quart. Children should realize that 2 pint containers are not the same as 1 quart container, but that the measurement is the same. Writing the letter m makes the mathematical sentence true and should be used consistently by the teacher. Again, a few of the measurements should be memorized, but the others can be found in tables. Call on your students' knowledge of fractions and point out to them that 1 pint is one half the measure of 1 quart, and that a cup is one fourth the measure of 1 quart.

TEMPERATURE

The unit on temperature can also be based on the number line. This time the number line is vertical, not horizontal. The markings on the number line progress in a sequence of twos. Children in the first grade learn to count by twos and they can use this knowledge in reading temperatures. The intrepid primary teacher will extend the number line to below zero and introduce negative numbers. Here 0 is the starting point. Thirty-two degrees above zero is the freezing point. All temperatures below 32 represent temperatures that are cold enough to freeze water.

WEIGHT

The number line is brought out again when pupils are taught the scale used for measuring weight. Each of the small units is now called an ounce. Sixteen of these units yield a new unit called a pound. Small items are measured in ounces and larger items, such as the weight of people, are measured in pounds. A very large unit of weight is the ton, which is made up of 2000 pounds. Various activities in science and mathematics can be utilized to help pupils learn how to use a scale and to measure various items in pounds and ounces.

SUMMARY

It is important not to accept measurements from pupils that are unlabeled. The measurement is a number, but pupils must also state what unit of measurement was used. It makes a great deal of difference if the answer is 6 inches or 6 feet. The numeral 6 alone does not convey enough exact information.

The measuring of space has been discussed in the chapter on geometry. Perimeter, area, and volume are very important topics of measurement which require great care in teaching. Perimeter is concerned with line segments and is measured in terms of units that are line segments. Area is concerned with the surface within a closed figure and is measured in terms of square units that can cover the surface. Volume is concerned with the interior of a solid figure and is measured by cubic units that can fill the interior.

Problems concerning measurement give pupils an opportunity to use the skills they have learned in computation. They can apply their knowledge and find some reason for having to learn multiplication and division. This is also the place where mathematics and science can become integrated. The practical problems of science involve measurement and to solve such problems mathematical skills are required.

EXERCISES

1. What is a standard unit of measurement?
2. What does precision in measurement mean?
3. In 6 inches, which is the measurement and which is the unit of measurement?
4. What is the one unifying concept that can be used in telling time, reading temperatures, and stating measurement in weights?
5. Why should the letter m be used in liquid measure?
6. Why is it incorrect to say, "Angle $CDE = 90$ degrees"?

SELECTED READINGS

PERRY, JOHN: *The Story of Standards,* Funk & Wagnalls Company, Inc., New York, 1955.

SPENCER, P. L., and M. BRYDEGAARD: *Building Mathematical Competence in the Elementary School,* Holt, Rinehart and Winston, Inc., New York, 1966.

SPITZER, H. F.: *Teaching Elementary School Mathematics,* Houghton, Mifflin Company, Boston, 1967, Chapter 13.

SWENSON, ESTHER: *Teaching Arithmetic to Children,* Macmillan, Inc., New York, 1973, Chapter 19.

The Metric System

INTRODUCTION

Few people realize that for over 100 years the legal system of measure in the United States has been the metric system. It was adopted by an act of Congress in 1866. However, the metric system has been mainly used in the field of science. Today all people are faced with the problem of learning the system because the Metric Conversion Bill (S-2483) was passed by the Senate in 1972 and is expected to pass the House in 1973. The conversion bill calls for a total change to be made in ten years.

"Instruction in metric measurement will need to begin when the child is first introduced to the concept of measuring an object and should continue to be taught, with growing levels of understanding and application in every succeeding grade. . . . Much practice will be needed in using metric standards and estimating in terms of metric units." These statements by the National Education Association in the U.S. Metric Study *Interim Report*, issued in July, 1971, are indicative of the philosophy that concepts of measurement should be stressed through the use of the metric system.

The most important idea is to teach the metric system by itself so that one learns to think in this language of measurement. The metric system should not be taught through conversion problems such as measuring in both inches and centimeters and then comparing the results. This mistake is made today in many textbooks, where a few pages are devoted to the metric system and all the problems are in conversion. The saying "Think Metric" is the real answer for the change that will develop in the next ten years.

WHAT IS THE METRIC SYSTEM?

Any logical system of measurement should be based upon one fundamental unit of length taken from some unchanging absolute standard in the physical world. This is true of the metric system, for the fundamental unit of length is the meter. The arbitrary length of the meter is shown by a platinum-iridium bar placed in the International Observatory at Sevres, near Paris, France. All primary units of the system are uniformly derived from the meter.

The units of length, area, weight, and volume should be directly related to each other. This is true in the metric system. The same six prefixes are used in naming all units of measurement in the system. These prefixes shall be explained.

A society that has a decimal numeration system should logically have a decimal system of measurement. Our numeration system is based on base ten. Charts will be shown to illustrate how each of the prefixes corresponds to the base ten system. This is far easier than having a system of measurement based on isolated facts, such as 12 inches is the same as 1 foot, 3 feet is the same as 1 yard, and 5,280 feet is the same as 1 mile.

The three principles just stated show why the metric system is the most simple and logically consistent system of weight and measurement. Now we shall examine this system in depth.

The working units of the metric system are easy to learn. The basic unit of length is the meter; the basic unit for weight is the gram; the basic unit for volume is the liter.

kilo means 1,000   milli means $\dfrac{1}{1,000}$

hecto means 100   centi means $\dfrac{1}{100}$

deka means 10   deci means $\dfrac{1}{10}$

These six prefixes, milli, centi, deci, deca, hecto, and kilo, are used in length, weight, and volume. The table below show how the prefixes

UNITS OF LENGTH

1 millimeter	(mm) =	0.001 of a meter
1 centimeter	(cm) =	0.01 of a meter
1 decimeter	(dm) =	0.1 of a meter
meter	(m) =	1 fundamental unit
1 decameter	(dkm) =	10 meters
1 hectometer	(hm) =	100 meters
1 kilometer	(km) =	1,000 meters

are used in length. All you need to do is substitute the word *gram* for *meter* in the table and you have the table of weight. If you substitute the word *liter* for *meter* you have the table for capacity or liquid. The three most important prefixes are milli, centi, and kilo. The other prefixes, such as deci, deca, and hecto, are used infrequently. For most practical purposes, the whole system of length, weight, and volume can be summarized as follows:

1,000 millimeters	=	1 meter
100 millimeters	=	1 centimeter
1,000 meters	=	1 kilometer
1,000 milligrams	=	1 gram
1,000 grams	=	1 kilogram
1,000 kilograms	=	1 meteric ton
1,000 milliliters	=	1 liter
1,000 liters	=	1 kiloliter

Machinists and garage mechanics will use millimeters all the time in their work. Tradesmen will measure in centimeters and meters. Clothing sizes will be stated in centimeters, and greater lengths will be measured in meters. Weights of canned goods, butter, meat, and other consumer goods will be measured in grams and kilograms; and the chemist will use milligrams. Large quantities in weight will be measured in kilograms and the metric ton. Liquids will be measured in milliliters and liters; for very large quantities, the cubic meter will be used in place of the kiloliter.

New models are needed in the minds of adults to replace old models that have been established in the other system of measurement. It is not unusual to speak of a man as being six feet tall, but in the metric system one needs to think of the man as two meters tall. A meter is about the height of a 5 year old child, or the arm stretch of a child in kindergarten. Children will grow up thinking in terms of meters and will not be as confused as the adults. The decimeter, which is one-tenth of a meter, is about the length of a new piece of chalk. A decimeter is also approximately the distance over the eyes across the face of a child. A centimeter, one-hundredth of a meter, is approximately the width of a finger. This is a good model to remind one of what a centimeter means in measurement. A millimeter, one-thousandth of a meter, is approximately the thickness of heavy tagboard. Millimeters are very small but small measurements will be used a great deal for precise measuring. A gram is approximately the weight of a paper clip. A sugar cube weighs about two grams, and a nickel weighs about five grams. Experience is the best teacher; activities with the metric system will bridge the gap to help us think metric.

ACTIVITIES FOR PRIMARY GRADES

Pupils need to learn the skills of measuring before they start to measure with any standard system of measurement. One of the skills is the skill of comparison. The terms "longer," "longest," "shorter," "shortest," "taller," "tallest," and "the same length" need to be taught or reviewed. The meaning of the terms of comparison is learned by working with objects and comparing them: Which is longer, the crayon or the pencil? Which is shorter, the eraser or the paper clip? Can you find any objects in the room that are approximately the same length? After comparing real objects and using the terms to describe the comparison, the pupils are ready for the semiconcrete stage. In this stage the pupils are ready to use straightedges to draw line segments that are longer, shorter, or the same length as a picture on a piece of paper.

The next skill of measurement is using unstandardized units of measure for linear measure. One activity could be where each pupil takes his pencil and measures the length of the table in front of the room: Why does Don need 14 pencils for his measurement if Sue needs only 11 pencils for her measurement? Another activity could be having the children use their own feet to measure the length of the room: Why does Chipper come out with 33 feet for his measurement if Mary comes out with 36 feet for her measurement? As pupils answer the questions of comparing their measurements they will start to discover that the longer the unit of measure, the fewer the number of units of measurement; and the shorter the unit of measure, the greater the number of units of measurement. These are important concepts in measurement and can only really be learned by actual experiences.

ACTIVITIES FOR PRIMARY GRADES

To use the metric system for linear measurement, pupils will first need to see the meter stick. Each class should have at least one meter stick for every four pupils. In this way a small group of pupils can look at the meter and see how long it is and start to use it to measure lengths in the room. One of the activities could be to measure the length of the room to the nearest meter. Another activity could be to measure the length of the chalkboard with the meter stick. Other activities could be finding objects in the room that are shorter than a meter and objects that are longer than a meter. Pupils need these activities to instill in their minds a model of the length of a meter because the meter is the basic unit of length for linear measure.

After using the meter for measuring, pupils should look at the markings on the meter. The markings go from 1 through 99. After 99 there is still a unit left on the edge, so the ruler is divided into 100 parts all the same size. The pupils have to be told that each of these 100 pieces of the meter is called a centimeter. Some of the pupils will know that the word "century" means 100 years. From this they will see the connection, that a unit called a centimeter is one-hundredth of a meter. Pupils have to be told the left edge of the meter is where the numeral 0 should be written and the right edge of the meter is where the numeral 100 should be written. Pupils should point to the marks that shows 20 centimeters, 50 centimeters, 35 centimeters, 65 centimeters, etc. After pupils are able to read the centimeter markings on the meter they should each be given a centimeter ruler that is 20 or 25 centimeters long. Using their ruler the pupils should go about the room measuring objects such as pencils, chalk, books, and erasers to the nearest centimeter. They should record their findings. The abbreviation of centimeter is cm, and pupils should be told this so they can use cm instead of writing centimeter.

Another type of activity is having pupils measure line segments drawn on paper for them. Also, the pupils should draw line segments according to stated measurements, such as 8 cm, 11 cm, 15 cm, etc. Maps can be made in which the pupils have to measure the lengths from one spot to another to the nearest centimeter. Also, pupils can make drawings of stickmen in which the arms are to be 6 cm, the legs are to be 13 cm, the body is to be 15 cm, and each of the fingers and toes are to be 2 cm.

A game that is called "How Long?" can be played. The teacher or a pupil holds up an object such as a pencil and asks, "How long to the nearest centimeter?" The other pupils call out their guesses. Then the object is measured; the winners are the ones that guess the length of the object. This will help pupils learn to estimate the length of an object to the nearest centimeter. To help with the estimation of a centimeter each pupil should measure the width of his middle finger at the second joint. In most cases the width will be very nearly 1 centimeter. Now the pupils will have a model of a centimeter that stays with them.

After the pupils have had many experiences measuring with centimeters they should go back to the meter stick and look at the markings 10, 20, 30, 40, 50, 60, 70, 80, and 90. The pupils can count how many sections of the meter are marked by ten centimeters. This section of the meter is called a decimeter. The meter is made up of 10 decimeters. The abbreviation for decimeter is dm; the letters dm can be used in place of the word decimeter. The word "deci" means ten. Comparison can be made to the decimal system, in which 10 dimes is the same as one dollar and 100 pennies is the same as one dollar. How many pennies is the same as one dollar? How many centimeters is the same as one meter? Four dimes is the same as how many pennies? Four decimeters is the same as how many centimeters? As pupils answer questions like these they will start to see the relationship between the metric system of measurement and the decimal system of numeration.

Pupils need activities of measuring with decimeters. The pupils can use centimeter rulers or meter sticks to measure objects to the nearest decimeter. Objects such as pencils, the length of a piece of paper, the length of a book, the length of the table, and many more can all be measured to the nearest decimeter. Guessing games also should be played: students should guess the length of objects in the room to the nearest decimeter; then measure the objects to see which students had the best answers. Estimation is important but it does take practice.

Activities in which the pupils use both decimeters and centimeters can be constructed on paper. Line segments can be measured and drawn to certain indicated lengths. Also, exercises can be created where pupils change from 5 dm 3 cm to 53 cm and from 72 cm to 7 dm 2 cm. Also, exercises can be made up where pupils indicate if 32 cm is greater than, less than, or equal to 4 dm. Working with decimeters, centimeters, and meters is a way of reinforcing the concept of ten that is used in our numeration system.

Many pupils in the primary grades enjoy a project called "All About Me." In this project the pupils measure all parts of their bodies and record the results. Many teachers put a strip of paper two meters high on the wall. It shows markings in decimeters and centimeters so the pupils can find their height to the nearest centimeter. If tape measures marked in metric units are not available, the pupils will need to use string to measure such things as the size of the head, the distance around the wrist, the waist measurement, etc. From this activity graphs can be made that show measurements such as the heights of the pupils in the class, the size of their heads, etc. Measuring yourself can really be a good ending to linear measurement.

In the primary grades the pupils should have the experience of weighing small objects with weights that are measured in grams. How much does a sugar cube weigh in grams? What is the weight of a nickel in grams? How much does your pencil weigh in grams? For larger objects the pupils should have kilogram weights. Does the hamster weigh a kilogram? What is the weight of the pet rabbit in kilograms? Recipes can be written in grams so that pupils have to measure out and weigh in grams.

Pupils can be asked to estimate volumes: look at the liter container and see if you can figure out the markings on its side. Do you think your milk carton is more or less than a half of a liter? How many liters will it take to fill the plastic pail? A recipe for "metric-ade" written in grams and liters can give the pupils experience in using both grams and liters. This will be only an introduction but will give some foundation for more work in the middle grades.

SUMMARY

The study of the metric system in the primary grades deals mostly with the linear measurement of centimeters, decimeters, and meters. The pupils need activities in which they learn to measure with these units. As they perform the activities they are creating models in their minds to help them understand the units. Pupils can understand 10 dimes is the same as a dollar, and 100 pennies is the same as a dollar. In the same manner they learn 10 decimeters is the same as a meter, and 100 centimeters is the same as a meter. The metric system will reinforce the decimal system that the pupils have learned in numeration units.

The use of grams and liters is only an introduction. Being exposed to the basic units of weight and volume will give some foundation for further study of the metric system in the middle grades.

ACTIVITIES IN THE MIDDLE GRADES

In the study of linear measurement in the middle grades there is a need for many meter sticks, a ruler that measures about 20 centimeters for each student, and some tape measures that are marked in metric units. The first activity is to be sure the students can read the

rulers. The meter is the basic unit and students have to see the meter
and get a good idea in their minds about the length of a meter. The
meter is divided into ten sections marked by the multiples of 10, and
each section is called a decimeter. Each decimeter is divided into ten
sections, and each section is called a centimeter. There are 100 centimeters in a meter. Each centimeter is divided into ten sections, and
each section is called a millimeter. There are 1,000 millimeters in a
meter. The abbreviations for the units should be taught so the students can write m for meter, dm for decimeter, cm for centimeter, and
mm for millimeter. Comparison can be made to decimals, which have
been taught in the numeration system. A decimeter is one-tenth of a
meter, a centimeter is one-hundredth of a meter, and a millimeter is
one-thousandth of a meter.

Activities are needed in which the students measure objects with
the rulers and the tape measures. Some middle grade teachers hand
out assignments that name objects in the room and indicate that the
length should be measured to the nearest given unit. For example, the
table can be measured to the nearest centimeter, the length of the
room can be measured to the nearest decimeter, and the length of a
pencil can be measured to the nearest millimeter.

Students should make a table showing the comparisons of the units
to one another in terms of millimeters, centimeters, decimeters, and
the meter. They need the comparisons for ratios to change from one

$$10 \text{ millimeters} = 1 \text{ centimeter}$$
$$100 \text{ millimeters} = 1 \text{ decimeter}$$
$$1000 \text{ millimeters} = 1 \text{ meter}$$
$$10 \text{ centimeters} = 1 \text{ decimeter}$$
$$100 \text{ centimeters} = 1 \text{ meter}$$
$$10 \text{ decimeters} = 1 \text{ meter}$$

unit to another. This type of problem is difficult because the process
involves two steps. The first step is to see if you are going from
smaller unit to larger unit or from larger unit to smaller unit. For
example, to go from 47 cm to _?_ m you are going from smaller unit to

larger unit and the answer will be smaller than the number indicated. This means you will use the operation of division. Next step is to find the ratio between the two units stated. The ratio of centimeters to meters is 100 to 1. Now you divide 47 by 100; the answer is 0.47 meters. To solve 7 m = ? mm you are going from a larger unit to a smaller unit, so the answer will be greater than the indicated number. This means you will multiply. The ratio of meters to millimeters is 1 to 1,000. You then will multiply 7 by 1,000; the answer is 7,000 mm. It is assumed that the students in the middle grades can multiply and divide by 10, 100, and 1,000 before they start the metric system. If students do not possess these skills they will not be successful in changing one unit to another.

Students should measure a length in the hall or out in the playground that is 10 meters long. This distance is called a decameter. Decameters are not used very often so not much attention is needed except to allow students to know there is a unit for 10 meters. On the playground the students can also measure a length 100 meters long. This unit is called a hectometer. On field day many students are involved in 100-meter, 200-meter, and 500-meter races. The students studying the metric system could do the measuring for these races. The large unit that is important is the kilometer, which is 1,000 meters. Students need to realize that this unit is used for long distances. Maps can be shown where the distances are stated in kilometers so the students can learn to read the distances.

All work on perimeter, area, and volume should be done with units of measure of the metric system. Students can construct the area of a square decameter and a square hectometer on the playground. Students can also construct a cubic centimeter and a cubic decimeter. The cubic centimeter is related to a gram and the cubic decimeter is related to a liter, so it is important that students have some idea of the models for each. Computing with units of length will be far easier than any other system. To change a square decimeter to square centimeters all that needs to be done is multiply by 10×10; the answer is 100 cubic centimeters. To add and subtract units you use the same method of operating that is used with whole numbers in base ten.

For example, to subtract 4 m 9 dm 5 cm from 6 m 7 dm 3 cm you

$$
\begin{array}{ccc}
\overset{5}{\cancel{6}}\text{m} & \overset{16}{\cancel{7}}\text{dm} & 13\text{ cm} \\
-4\text{ m} & 9\text{ dm} & 5\text{ cm} \\
\hline
1\text{ m} & 7\text{ dm} & 8\text{ cm}
\end{array}
$$

rename 1 dm as 10 cm and you rename 1 m as 10 dm. The algorithm involved is the same as subtracting whole numbers in base ten. Any teacher in the middle grades has to admit this is far easier than subtracting yards, feet, and inches.

The activities with grams, kilograms, liters, and milliliters are usually found in science activities in the middle grades. This is where students have experiences of measuring and weighing.

SUMMARY

The metric system should be used in perimeter, area, and volume problems that are taught in the middle grades. Students need to see the relationships among the units and be able to change one unit to the other. The activities in the class should allow the students to be involved in measuring objects inside and outside the classroom. Only as the metric system is used will students come to find models that are meaningful for them.

Teachers need to remember that the students they have today will use the metric system the rest of their lives and they need to learn the system from life situations.

EXERCISES

1. What are the basic units for length, weight, and volume in the metric system?
2. Name the three prefixes used most often in the metric system.

3. Change 16 centimeters to millimeters.
4. Change 72 centimeters to meters.
5. How many square centimeters is the same as one square meter?
6. How many cubic centimeters is the same as one cubic decimeter?

SELECTED READINGS

DONOVAN, F., *Prepare Now for a Metric Future*, Weybright and Talley, Inc., New York, 1970.

The Metric System of Weights and Measures, Twentieth Yearbook of the National Council of Teachers of Mathematics, Bureau of Publications, Teachers College, Columbia University, New York, 1948.

U.S. Metric Study Interim Report—Education, Washington, D.C., 1971.

Ratio, Proportion, and Percentage

A comparison of two numbers by division is a ratio. The two numbers involved are the number property of two sets. Statements such as "The ratio of automobiles to adults in the U.S.A. is 3 to 7" describe the comparison. It does not tell us how many automobiles or adults there are in the U.S.A., but it does tell us the comparison that exists between the two numbers. This comparison remains constant, 3 to 7, even if the number of automobiles and the number of adults change. Some mathematicians today use the term "rate" or "rate pairs" to indicate the comparison between two dissimilar sets, such as automobiles and adults. The traditional interpretation of ratio requires that only like things can be compared—for example, automobiles with automobiles and adults with adults.

Ratio is not presented as a number; a ratio is called a property belonging to two sets and the symbol used for ratio describes this property. Ratios do not perform in the same manner as members of the number system. Numbers in the number system may be added, subtracted, multiplied, and divided. Working with ratios involves working with one equivalence class at one time. Operations are not usually performed on ratios, although there are situations in which a problem requires the combining of two ratios. For example, Mary bought 3 suckers for 10¢ and 2 suckers for 5¢. What was the total number of suckers and the total cost? The addition $3/10 + 2/5 = 3/10 + 4/10 = 7/10$ would yield an incorrect result. Actually, the addition would involve adding numerators to numerators and denominators to denominators: $3/10 + 2/5 = 5/15$, or 5 suckers for 15¢. In this situation it is best to handle the problem in two steps: (1) find the total suckers; (2) find the total cost without writing in fractional form.

In problem-solving, ratio is used most often to find equivalent ratios or proportion. A proportion is two equal ratios. An infinite set of equivalent ratios can be generated in the same way that equivalent fractions are generated. The concept of ratio also is a useful way to view percentages. Its various uses make the study of ratio worthwhile in the elementary grades. Recent informal studies have shown that pupils in the primary grades can use ratio effectively to solve verbal problems involving small quantities. A foundation for understanding ratio can thus be laid and then thoroughly developed in the middle grades.

TEACHING RATIO AND PROPORTION IN THE PRIMARY GRADES

To begin the study of ratio, two sets of objects can be placed on a flannel board, such as is shown here.

The suckers and pennies should be divided into three subsets that contain the same number of suckers and pennies. Pupils should compare each sucker to 3 pennies; this is the ratio of 1 to 3. Then two subsets can be considered, 2 suckers to 6 pennies, or the ratio of 2 to 6. Last, compare all the suckers to the pennies. The ratio then becomes 3 to 9. Many situations such as this should be planned by the teacher to afford pupils practice in setting up sets of objects and expressing their number property in a ratio.

If sets of objects are drawn on paper and given to each child, all pupils can become involved in dividing the sets into the same number of subsets. Then the pupils can write the ratio represented below the pictures. Another type of activity involves matching. Pupils can draw a line from a picture of sets to a ratio that expresses the comparison of the number property of the sets.

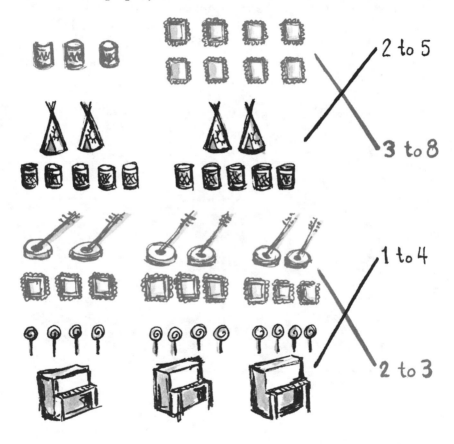

A good way to prepare pupils for equivalent ratios is to give them a drawing of two sets of objects and ask them to write down as many ratios as they can find in the drawing. The following drawing shows three subsets of boys and balloons. Below the drawing pupils should write the ratios 1 to 4, 2 to 8, and 3 to 12.

As the teacher goes about helping pupils, she can point out that they should work first with one subset, then with two subsets, and finally with three subsets.

A more advanced exercise involves getting pupils to record the results of finding ratios in a table. The pupils look at the drawing that

				Squares	2	4		8
				Triangles	3		9	

accompanies the table and then fill in the empty places with the numbers that make up the ratios. After the table is filled in, the teacher can explain that all the ratios are the same, they stand for the same comparison, and are called equivalent ratios. Pupils should recall that equivalent sets are sets that have the same number property, equivalent fractions are fractions that name the same number, and now equivalent ratios name the same comparison.

It is unfortunate that often in mathematics the same symbol is used to stand for different meanings. Thus, + is the symbol for the operation of addition and also the symbol for positive numbers. Ratio can be expressed in fraction form but in the primary grades the fraction shows a fractional number represented by a geometric figure and this is different from comparing the number property of two sets. Therefore, in the primary grades most textbooks do not use the fraction as a symbol. The two forms used are 2 to 3 or 2 : 3. Most teachers prefer the form with the word "to" instead of the colon.

Another type of activity that is needed is to state a ratio as 2 to 5 and have pupils make drawings that express that ratio. A point should be made that 2 to 5 is different from 5 to 2. In the first you show a set of two units first then a set of five, and in second you show a set of five first then a set of two.

In classes where the number line has been used for addition and subtraction, pupils can use the number line to show ratios. For example, the number line can be used to show that 2 candy bars cost 15 cents.

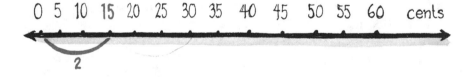

Then pupils can draw arcs on the number line to show that 4 candy bars cost 30 cents, 6 candy bars cost 45 cents, and so on. The data obtained from the number line can be recorded in a table so that pupils

Candy bars	2	4		8	
Cents	15		45		75

see the equivalent ratios. As they fill in the empty places, they will be recording the equivalent ratios.

All these activities in the primary grades will help prepare pupils for more advanced work in the middle grades. Readiness must be developed in the primary grades. All pupils must be readied and prepared for new concepts so that all will be successful with them.

RATIO, PROPORTION AND PERCENTAGE IN THE MIDDLE GRADES

Early work with ratio should involve activities similar to the ones described for the primary grades. Sets of objects should be displayed and the students should indicate the ratio being represented. Many ratios can be stated for one drawing by having pupils divide the sets into equivalent subsets. In the following drawing, comparing the squares to the circles, the ratios represented are 4 to 3, 8 to 6, and 12 to 9.

Now direct them to write the ratios comparing the circles to the squares. The ratios will be reversed. It is important that students understand that the ratio always is stated according to the way the comparison is stated. After sets, use the number line for some ratio exercises and have the students record the ratios in a table. In this way they see that the ratios all express the same comparison and are therefore equivalent.

Students need to be shown the four ways of expressing ratios. Using the word "to" is the most familiar to them because it was used mostly in the primary grades. The other methods employ the colon, fraction form, and the ordered pair. Therefore 2 to 3, 2 : 3, 2/3, and (2,3) all express the ratio 2 to 3. Students should practice writing ratios in all four forms.

Usually the work with ratios follows the work with fractional numbers. In studying fractional numbers students have learned how to simplify a fraction, to rewrite a fraction so that the only common factor of the numerator and denominator is 1. The same understanding is involved in learning how to simplify a ratio. A ratio is rewritten so that 1 is the only common factor of the two numbers in the ratio. The ratio 6 to 9 or 6/9 has a common factor besides 1, which is 3. Both numbers in the ratio are divided by 3 and the ratio 2 to 3 or 2/3 is the result. This means that 6 to 9 and 2 to 3 are equivalent ratios and that 2 to 3 is the ratio in simplest form. Here students review simplifying fractional numbers by dividing both numerator and denominator by the largest common factor and then use the same technique to simplify ratios. Also review the generating of equivalent fractional numbers by multiplying both numerator and denominator by the same number. This same technique is used in generating equivalent ratios. You multiply both numbers in a ratio by the same number to get other ratios that are equivalent.

One type of activity that gives students practice in finding ratios in simplest form is to state one problem and then have them answer a number of questions about the problem. An example follows.

In a recent election Dick received 21 out of a total of 35 votes cast, and Jane received 14 out of the 35 votes cast.

1. What is the ratio of the number of votes Dick received to the total number of votes cast? _____ What is the simplest form of this ratio? _____

2. What is the ratio of the number of votes Jane received to the total number of votes cast? _____ What is the simplest form of this ratio? _____

3. What is the ratio between the number of Jane's votes and the number of Dick's votes? _____ What is the simplest form of this ratio? _____

4. For every two votes Jane received, how many votes did Dick receive? _____

In learning the order of fractional numbers most students were taught a method called cross-multiplication. For example, if they are to determine which fraction is greater, 7/8 or 8/9, they would multiply to find the product of 7×9 and then the product of 8×8. The first prod-

$$7 \times 9 \overset{?}{=} 8 \times 8$$

$$63 < 64$$

$$\frac{7}{8} < \frac{8}{9}$$

uct is less than the second product so the fraction to the left is less than the fraction to the right. If the products are equal, then the fractions are equal. If the product to the left is greater than the product to the right, the fraction to the left is greater than the fraction to the right. This same technique is used in finding equal and unequal ratios. If the ratios are equal, then the relationship is called a proportion. A proportion is two equal ratios. Students need to practice using cross-multi-

$$\frac{3}{4} \overset{?}{=} \frac{15}{20} \qquad\qquad \frac{2}{3} \overset{?}{=} \frac{10}{14}$$

$$3 \times 20 \overset{?}{=} 4 \times 15 \qquad\qquad 2 \times 14 \overset{?}{=} 3 \times 10$$

$$60 = 60 \qquad\qquad 28 \neq 30$$

$$\frac{3}{4} = \frac{15}{20} \qquad\qquad \frac{2}{3} \neq \frac{10}{14}$$

plication to test whether the ratios are equal, thus determining whether or not the relationship is a proportion.

One type of activity, devised to practice that tests whether or not ratios form a proportion involves having students write $=$ or $\neq$ between two stated ratios. They determine equal or not equal by using cross-multiplication.

1. $\dfrac{3}{4} \not\equiv \dfrac{6}{9}$ 2. $\dfrac{2}{5} \not\equiv \dfrac{3}{11}$ 3. $\dfrac{15}{12} \equiv \dfrac{5}{4}$

The concept of proportion is used most often to find an unknown part of a ratio. For example, 2 is to 3 as what number is to 15? Students write this problem in a proportion, using the letter n to stand for the unknown number.

$$\frac{2}{3} = \frac{n}{15}$$

$$2 \times 15 = 3 \times n$$

$$30 = 3 \times n$$

$$\frac{30}{3} = \frac{3}{3} \times n$$

$$10 = 1 \times n$$

$$\text{Therefore, } \frac{2}{3} = \frac{10}{15}$$

In the first step you multiply 2×15, which equals $3 \times n$ because this is a proportion. In the second step 2×15 is multiplied to yield the product 30, which also equals $3 \times n$. Now you must solve the equation for n. You undo multiplication by division. The unknown n is being multiplied by 3, so you undo this multiplication by dividing both sides of the equation by 3. This operation is shown in the third step, where 30 and $3 \times n$ are divided by 3. The last step shows that 30 divided by 3 is 10 and that 3 divided by 3 is 1. So 10 equal $1 \times n$ or n. The unknown number in the proportion is 10. Thus, 2 is to 3 as 10 is to 15. The unknown number can appear in any of the four positions of a proportion and the solution will be the same. Another example is 3 is to what as 5 is to 8? Students first write the proportion. Then they cross-multiply.

$$\frac{3}{n} = \frac{5}{8}$$

$$3 \times 8 = n \times 5$$

$$24 = n \times 5$$

$$\frac{24}{5} = n \times \frac{5}{5}$$

$$4\frac{4}{5} = n \times 1$$

After establishing that 24 equals $n \times 5$, the students must decide how to get the unknown n by itself. They undo the multiplication by dividing both sides of the equation by 5. This time the unknown number is a fraction, which can be rewritten as $4\frac{4}{5}$. Students will need help in solving the number sentences, but help can be administered in group work where the teacher can assist the students as needed.

Many word problems can be solved using proportions, especially ones involving percentages. But practice should precede the actual solution of word problems dealing with proportions, so that pupils will feel confident as they approach the problems.

PERCENT

Percent is a special ratio in which one set has a number property of 100. The word "percent" means per hundred. Students should understand clearly and immediately why they should learn the concept. To get this point across, give them some data such as the following: Here are the scores Bob received on some spelling tests—8 correct out of 13, 7 correct out of 11, and 9 correct out of 15. Which was the highest score? It is difficult to answer the question from the data supplied. Most people do not know if 8/13 is larger or smaller than 7/11. But if the three scores are given in percentages, they can be compared immediately. The fraction 8/13 is the same as 62%, 7/11 is the same as 63%, and 9/15 is the same as 60%. Thus, 7/11 was the best score. Another type of data that boys understand are baseball averages. These can be used to illustrate the importance of percentages.

First, have the students change percentages to fraction and decimal form. Some students will require a brief review of tenths and hundredths. Students must know how to convert percentages to fraction or decimal form, because they can not operate with percentages.

The trouble spots in beginning the study of percentage are usually the same in any class—changing a percent that is less than 1 to a decimal and writing percents greater than 100% as a whole number or in mixed form. Students usually tend to say that 50% is 0.50 and 1/2 is 0.50. They must go from 1%, which is 0.01, to 1/2%. If they write 0.05 for 1/2%, then they must confront the question whether 0.01 is greater or less than 0.05 and if 1% is greater or less than 1/2%. Finally, many will see that 0.005 is one half of 0.01 and then that 1/2% is the same as 0.005. In dealing with percentages greater than 100, students need to be reminded that they are dividing by 100 when they change from a percentage to a decimal. The unseen decimal point is to the right of the last digit. In 345%, the decimal point is after the 5. When you divide by 100, the digits move two places to the left; hence, 3.45 is the same as 345%. Students who have difficulty operating with decimals will have difficulty operating with percentages. They need more practice with decimals before they tackle work on percentages.

SUMMARY

In the middle grades only a few word problems are presented that require the use of percentages. Most of the work with percentage is confined to the seventh and eighth grades. The middle grades should be devoted to readying pupils, so that in the higher grades they will understand clearly the meaning of percent. They should practice changing percentages to fractions and decimals so that they will be ready to use this skill in solving work problems when the day comes.

Pupils in the middle grades use percentages in reading graphs in mathematics and social studies. Their science experiments sometimes involve percentages. The concept should be used in the curriculum, because percent is a handy way of comparing many situations.

EXERCISES

1. Explain the meaning of 3 to 7 using the words "sets," "relations," and "comparison."
2. Why can we say that percent is a special ratio?
3. What is a proportion?
4. How can you generate equivalent ratios?
5. What method can be used to verify if two ratios form a proportion?
6. Why do we use percentages more than other ratios in our daily life?

7. Why must students learn to convert percentages to decimals or fractions?

8. Is a ratio a number? Explain your answer.

SELECTED READINGS

FEHR, H. F., and T. J. HILL: *Contemporary Mathematics for Elementary Teachers*, Chapter 16, D. C. Heath and Company, Boston, 1966.

MUELLER, F. J.: *Arithmetic—Its Structure and Concepts*, Chapter 23 and 24, Prentice-Hall, Inc., Englewood Cliffs, N. J., 1964.

SCHAAF, W. L. *Basic Concepts of Elementary Mathematics*, Chapter 11, John Wiley and Sons, New York, 1965.

VAN ENGEN, HENRY: "Rate Pairs, Fractions and Rational Numbers," *The Arithmetic Teacher*, Vol. 7, No. 8 (December 1960), pp. 389–399.

Glossary

ADDEND An addend is any number which when added to another number gives you a sum. In $5 + 3 = 8$, the 5 and the 3 are addends.

ADDITION The operation of addition combines two numbers, called addends, to give you a third number, called a sum.

ANGLE An angle is a geometric figure formed by two rays, not in the same line, which have the same endpoint. The endpoint is called the vertex.

ASSOCIATIVE PROPERTY FOR ADDITION The way in which three addends are grouped does not affect the sum. Example: $(3 + 5) + 4 = 3 + (5 + 4)$.

ASSOCIATIVE PROPERTY FOR MULTIPLICATION The way in which three factors are grouped does not affect the product. Example: $8 \times (5 \times 7) = (8 \times 5) \times 7$.

BINARY OPERATION A binary operation involves only two numbers. All the basic operations are binary. When more than two numbers are to be added or multiplied, they must be grouped.

CARDINAL NUMBER A cardinal number is the number of a set. A cardinal number answers the question, "How many?"

COMMUTATIVE PROPERTY FOR ADDITION The order of adding two numbers does not affect the sum, as $3 + 5 = 5 + 3$.

COMMUTATIVE PROPERTY FOR MULTIPLICATION The order of multiplying two factors does not affect the product, such as $5 \times 7 = 7 \times 5$.

COMPOSITE NUMBER A composite number has other whole number factors besides itself and 1. For example, 8 is a composite number because it has the factors 2 and 4 besides 8 and 1.

CONGRUENT Two geometric figures are congruent when they have the same size and shape.

DECIMAL A decimal is a fractional number in which the denominator is not written because it is indicated by the position of the decimal point. Every denominator in a decimal number is a power of 10.

DENOMINATOR In the fractional numeral the numeral written below the bar is the denominator. The denominator of a fraction answers the question, "How many what?"

DIGIT A digit is any one of the 10 symbols used in the decimal system of numeration. The digits are: 0, 1, 2, 3, 4, 5, 6, 7, 8, and 9.

DISJOINT SETS Two sets are disjoint when they have no common members.

DISTRIBUTIVE PROPERTY This property states that if an indicated sum is multiplied by a number, each addend must be multiplied by that number and these products added. Thus $4 \times (3 + 7) = (4 \times 3) + (4 \times 7)$.

DIVISIBLE One number is divisible by another number if the first number is a factor of the second number. Thus 12 is divisible by 2, 3, 4, and 6 because each number is a factor of 12.

EMPTY SET The empty set contains no elements. The designation for the empty set is { } or $\emptyset$.

EQUAL SETS Equal sets have the same elements or members. For example, $\{1, 2, 3\}$ and $\{3, 2, 1\}$ are equal sets.

EQUATION An equation is a mathematical statement indicating that two expressions name the same number. Equations can be either true or false.

EQUILATERAL TRIANGLE A triangle is equilateral if its sides are congruent.

EQUIVALENT SETS Two sets are equivalent if their members can be brought into one-to-one correspondence.

EXPANDED NOTATION The expanded notation of a number is the notation that indicates the total value of each of its digits. The expanded notation of 357 is $300 + 50 + 7$.

EXPONENT The exponent tells how many times the base should be used as a factor. In 5^3 the numeral 3 is the exponent and the numeral 5 is the base. The expression 5^3 means $5 \times 5 \times 5$.

FACE VALUE   The face value of a digit in a numeral answers the question, "How many?" It is the cardinal value of the digit. The face value of digit 7 in 72 is seven.

FACTOR   If two or more numbers are multiplied, each number is a factor of the product. In the expression $7 \times 8 = 56$ the numerals 7 and 8 represent factors.

FINITE SET   A finite set has a specific number of members. The set {1, 2, 3, 4, 5} contains five members; hence it is a finite set.

FRACTIONAL NUMBER   A fractional number is a number expressed as $\frac{a}{b}$ in which a can be any whole number and b can be any counting number.

IDENTITY ELEMENT FOR ADDITION   The identity element for addition is 0. Zero added to any number is that number.

IDENTITY ELEMENT FOR MULTIPLICATION   The identity element for multiplication is 1. Any number multiplied by 1 is that number.

INEQUALITY   An inequality is a number sentence showing that two expressions are the names for different numbers. The symbols for inequality are $\neq$, $<$, and $>$. These mean not equal, less than, and greater than.

INFINITE SET   A set with an unlimited number of members is an infinite set. The set {0, 1, 2, 3, . . .} is an infinite set. The three dots indicate that the set is infinite.

INTERSECTION OF TWO SETS   The intersection of two sets is a new set composed of the members included in both sets. The symbol for intersection is $\cap$ and is called *cap*.

INVERSE OPERATION   Addition and subtraction are inverse operations, as are multiplication and division. An inverse operation or opposite operation undoes the operation of which it is the opposite.

LEAST COMMON DENOMINATOR   The least common denominator is the smallest number that is divisible by all denominators in the set of denominators.

LINE SEGMENT   A line segment is the set of points on the shortest path connecting two points in a plane.

LOWEST COMMON MULTIPLE   The lowest or least common multiple of a set of whole numbers is the smallest number divisible by all the numbers in the set.

MEASUREMENT   Measurement is the process of finding the number of standard units in an object or thing. The measure of a line segment can be 6 inches. The six is the measure and inches is the standard unit.

METRIC SYSTEM   The metric system of measures is based upon the decimal system of numeration.

MULTIPLE   A multiple of a number is the product of any whole number and that number. For example, a multiple of 3 is 12 because 3×4 is 12.

MULTIPLICATIVE INVERSE   When two numbers are multiplied and their product is 1, each is the multiplicative inverse of the other. This is sometimes called the reciprocal.

NUMBER LINE   A number line is a line having numbers corresponding to points on the line.

NUMBER SYSTEM   A number system is a set of numbers and one or more operations.

NUMERAL   A numeral is a symbol or expression used to represent a number.

NUMERATOR   In a fractional numeral, the numeral written above the bar is called the numerator. The numerator answers the question, "How many?"

OBTUSE ANGLE   An obtuse angle is an angle that measures between 90 and 180 degrees.

ORDERED PAIR   An ordered pair (a,b) means that a is the first member and b is the second member. The only time the ordered pair (a,b) equals the ordered pair (b,a) is when $a = b$.

PLACE VALUE   Place value is the property of our numeration system that gives a digit a different value depending upon the digit's position in a numeral.

POLYGON   A polygon is a plane closed figure that is simple, which means it has only one interior. The simple closed figure is made up of more than two line segments.

PRIME FACTORIZATION   Prime factorization or complete factorization consists of finding all the prime factors of a number. The prime factorization of 18 is $2 \times 3 \times 3$.

PRIME NUMBER   A prime number has no whole-number factors except itself and 1. The first prime number is 2.

PRODUCT   The product is the answer obtained when the operation of multiplication is performed on a pair of numbers. In $6 \times 7 = 42$, the number 42 is the product and the numbers 6 and 7 are factors.

QUADRILATERAL   A quadrilateral is a four-sided polygon.

QUOTIENT   The quotient is the answer in a division problem.

RAY   A ray is a set of points extending indefinitely in one direction from a point called an endpoint.

RECIPROCAL   When two numbers are multiplied and the product is 1, each number is the reciprocal of the other.

RENAME   To rename a number is to express the number with different numerals. For example, 42 can be renamed as $30 + 12$.

RIGHT ANGLE   A right angle is an angle that measures 90 degrees.

SET   A set is a collection of objects, things, or numbers. The word *set* is generally accepted as an undefined term in mathematics.

SUBSET   Each element or combination of elements in a set forms a set called a subset of the given set. The empty set is a subset of every set.

TOTAL VALUE   The total value of a digit in a numeral is the product of the digit's face value and its place value. The total value of digit 6 in 769 is 60 because $6 \times 10 = 60$.

UNION OF TWO SETS   The union of two sets is a new set composed of all the members that are in either the first set or the second set or both. The symbol for union of sets is $\cup$ and is called *cup*.

VARIABLE   A variable is a symbol used to represent a number.

Answers to Exercises

CHAPTER 1

1. You need materials written in units. The units should have pre- and posttests so you can evaluate the progress of the student.
2. The scope and sequence chart is used as a road map. Teachers can take detours if there are no prerequisites for the detours.
3. Not to evaluate the progress of the student on some standards of the marketplace but to use the evaluation to help prescribe the next step in the learning process.
4. Using paper tests; but a teacher also needs to use his eyes and ears in diagnosing the abilities of a student.
5. The words "show me" should be used in place of the words "you're wrong."

CHAPTER 2

1. A and D have the same number property, 2.
   B and C have the same number property, 3.
2. Members of a set can be listed in any order.
   a. $A \cup C = \{c, a, t\}$
   b. $C \cap E = \{c, a, t\}$
   c. $B \cap E = 0$ or $\{\ \}$
   d. $B \cup E = \{c, o, a, t, 4, 6\}$
   e. $B \cup D = \{a, 4, 6, 0, 1\}$
3. $N(A) = 2$ $N(B) = 3$ $N(C) = 3$ $N(D) = 2$ $N(E) = 4$

337

4. (a)   A   E   (b)   B   D   (c)   B   C

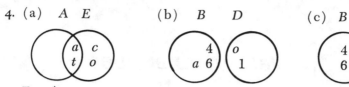

5. $E \cup \emptyset = E$
6. $F \cap \emptyset = \emptyset$
7. B and D do not have any members in common.
8. (a) set N is finite   (b) set W is infinite
9. Zero is in the set of whole numbers but not a member of the set of counting numbers
10. The empty set is a subset of every set.

CHAPTER 3

1. Zero is a number and we have place value.
2. (a) fa, do; re, re, do; mi, re; do, do, do, do, do; re, do, do, do; do, fi; etc.
   (b) fa, fa, re; mi, re, mi, re; re, re, re, re, re; mi, mi, mi, do; etc.
3. (a) $342 = (3 \times 25) + (4 \times 5) + (2 \times 1)$
         five
             $= 75 + 20 + 2$
             $= 97$
   (b) $26 = (2 \times 7) + (6 \times 1)$
         seven
             $= 14 + 6$
             $= 20$
   (c) $1011 = (1 \times 8) + (0 \times 4) + (2 \times 1) + (1 \times 1)$
         two
             $= 8 + 2 + 1$
             $= 11$
4. (a) $54 = 50 + 4$
   (b) $679 = 600 + 70 + 9$
5. $10 = 12$
     twelve

6. Digit 3 has face value 3, place value 1000, total value 3,000.
   Digit 7 has face value 7, place value 100, total value 700.
   Digit 8 has face value 8, place value 10, total value 80.
   Digit 9 has face value 9, place value 1, total value 9.
7. In base six the digits are 0, 1, 2, 3, 4, 5.
8. 131 base five
9. 11110 base two
10. 81 base ten

CHAPTER 4

1. (a) sum   (b) sum   (c) addend   (d) addend   (e) addend
   (f) addend
2. (a) 40   (b) 156   (c) 38   (d) 45   (e) 28   (f) 31
3. (a) commutative
   (b) associative
   (c) zero is identity element
4. $47 = 3$ tens 17 ones
5. (a) > (b) < (c) = (d) < (e) = (f) =
6. Unseen number must be added to the seen number.
7. Use "take away" only with objects.
8. Because 1 ten renamed as 10 ones is the only renaming performed.
9. Whole minus part equals part.

CHAPTER 5

1. x x x x x x
   x x x x x x
   x x x x x x
   $3 \times 7 = 21$
2. $5 \times 8 = 8 + 8 + 8 + 8 + 8$
3. The distributive property of multiplication over addition.

4. $3 \times 8 = 24$
$$3 \times 8 = 24$$
$$\overline{6 \times 8 = 48}$$

5.   748
     $\times\, 96$
     $\overline{71{,}808}$

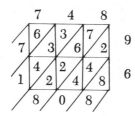

6. Property of zero.
7. Identity element.
8. commutative, associative
9. $(40 + 7) \times 6 = (40 \times 6) + (7 \times 6)$
$$= 240 + 42$$
$$= 282$$

10. Addition is prequisite for multiplication.

CHAPTER 6

1. (a) Multiplication facts
   (b) Multiplication multiples of 10, 100, 1000
   (c) Subtraction
   (d) Place value
2. Subtracting equal addends.
3. What is largest whole number times 5 less than or equal to 17?
4. $7 \times n = 56$
$$56 \div 7 = n$$
5. Can practice algorithm with one-digit division easier than with two- or three-digit divisor.
6. $100 + 30 + 2$
     $3\overline{)300 + 90 + 6}$
7. Division where remainder is zero.
8. Estimating the answer.

CHAPTER 7

1. $\{0, 8, 16, 24, 32, 40, 48\}$
2. $\{13, 17, 19, 23, 29\}$
3. $108 = 2 \times 2 \times 3 \times 3 \times 3$
4.
$$16 = 2 \times 2 \times 2 \times 2$$
$$24 = 3 \times 2 \times 2 \times 2$$
   L.C.M. $= 2 \times 2 \times 2 \times 2 \times 3$ or 48
5.
$$18 = 3 \times 3 \times 2$$
$$54 = 3 \times 3 \times 3 \times 2$$
   G.C.F. $= 3 \times 3 \times 2$ or 18
6. Eleven is prime, factor of 77 is 11, then L.C.M. is 77.
7. Odd number because the sum of an odd number of odd numbers is odd.
8. One of the factors of both numbers are even numbers.
9. 0 and 1
10. 1, 2, 3, 4, 6, 12

CHAPTER 8

1. $\dfrac{3 \times 2}{4 \times 2} = \dfrac{6}{8}$ $\dfrac{3 \times 3}{4 \times 3} = \dfrac{9}{12}$ $\dfrac{3 \times 4}{4 \times 4} = \dfrac{12}{16}$ $\dfrac{3 \times 5}{4 \times 5} = \dfrac{15}{20}$ $\dfrac{3 \times 6}{4 \times 6} = \dfrac{18}{24}$
   and many others.
2. Geometric regions, sets of objects, and the number line.
3. Any number divided by itself, except zero, is 1.
4. Multiply by a fraction whose numerator and denominator are the same as multiplying by 1. Multiplying by 1 does not change the original fraction.
5. $\dfrac{5}{9}$ $\dfrac{7}{11}$
   $55 < 63$
   $\dfrac{5}{9} < \dfrac{7}{11}$
6. $\dfrac{3}{7}$

7. $\dfrac{8 \div 4}{28 \div 4} = \dfrac{2}{7}$

8. $\dfrac{3}{4} = \dfrac{7+7+7}{7+7+7+7} = \dfrac{3 \times 7}{4 \times 7} = \dfrac{21}{28}$

9. $\dfrac{7}{9} \overset{?}{=} \dfrac{8}{11}$

$77 > 72$

not proportional

10. No, $(3, 4)$ is $\dfrac{3}{4}$ and $(4, 3)$ is $\dfrac{4}{3}$

CHAPTER 9

1. Seven is prime and 8 is composite, and 7 is not a factor of 8. There-fore, L.C.D. is 7×8 or 56

2. $8 = 2 \times 2 \times 2$

   $36 = 2 \times 3 \times 2 \times 3$

   L.C.D. $= 2 \times 2 \times 2 \times 3 \times 3$ or 72

3. $6 = 5 + \dfrac{5}{5}$. Student must be able to rename 1 as a fraction whose numerator and denominator are the same.

4. To help students to add or subtract whole numbers and also to add or subtract fractional numbers.

5. Most students know that 1/2 equals 2/4. They need a harder prob-lem to learn how to find L.C.D.

6. $\dfrac{4}{7} = \dfrac{4+4+4}{7+7+7} = \dfrac{3 \times 4}{3 \times 7} = \dfrac{12}{21}$

7. The denominator and the place value of a digit both ask the ques-tion, "How many what?"

CHAPTER 10

1.

5/6

x	x	x	x	x	
x	x	x	x	x	
x	x	x	x	x	

3/4

15/24 or 5/8

2. Property of one.
3. The reciprocal.
4. The answer or product is less than either factor.
5. $.3\overline{)\,.06}$ Multiply both divisor and dividend by ten.

$$\frac{.06 \times 10}{.3 \times 10} = \frac{.6}{3} \text{ or } .2$$

6. To simplify the work: $\dfrac{8}{\underset{3}{\cancel{15}}} \times \dfrac{\overset{2}{\cancel{10}}}{3} = \dfrac{16}{9}$

CHAPTER 11

1. A polygon is a simple closed curve made up of more than two line segments.
2. (a) Line segment by end points.
   (b) Line by two points on the line.
   (c) Ray by endpoint and one point on ray.
3. Pyramids have triangular regions for faces; prisms have rectangular regions for faces.
4. Both are infinite, go on forever.
5. Multiply length of one side by 6.
6. Sides are all equal but square has angles that are 90 degrees; angles of rhombus are not 90 degree.
7. Geometric shapes do not include interior regions.

CHAPTER 12

1. Gets students to concentrate on what is being asked.
2. Shows students where equation comes from.
3. Gives students a model for the problem.
4. It is not a way to work all problems; it involves logic and reasoning.
5. They make pupils realize that you do not always find an answer immediately. Sometimes, information must be adjusted.
6. Yes, guessing is a way of solving difficult problems. Use results or guesses to show next approach to problem.

CHAPTER 13

1. Measurement that is uniform—decided by others as a unit of measurement.
2. The smaller the unit of measurement, the more precise is the measurement.
3. The number 6 is the measurement; inch is the unit of measurement.
4. Number line.
5. The symbol m means measure, 2 pts. is the same measure as 1 qt.
$$2 \text{ pts.} \overset{m}{=} 1 \text{ qt.}$$
6. Angle CDE is a geometric figure; 90 degrees is a measure. Angle $CDE \overset{m}{=} 90°$ is correct.

CHAPTER 14

1. Three and 7 are number properties of sets. The sets are compared by relating 3 to 7.
2. Percent means per hundred.

   $\dfrac{n}{100}$ is a ratio, and percent is a ratio where the denominator is always 100.
3. Two equal ratios.
4. Multiply by the property of one.
5. Cross multiplication
$$\frac{3}{4} = \frac{15}{20} \qquad \begin{array}{c} 3 \times 20 = 4 \times 15 \\ 60 = 60 \end{array}$$
6. To compare ratios such as 7 out of 11, 8 out of 13, and 9 out of 17 is difficult. But if the ratios are changed to percents, such as 62%, 64%, and 71%, they can be compared with ease. Percents make comparisons easier.
7. Cannot use percent for operating; need to use either decimal or fractional number.
8. No comparison made up of two numbers.

CHAPTER 15

1. The basic unit for length is the meter, for weight the gram, for volume the liter.
2. Milli, centi, and kilo are the three most important prefixes.
3. 160 millimeters
4. 0.72 meters
5. There are 10,000 square centimeters in a square meter.
6. 1,000 cubic centimeters

Index